FOLLIES IN AMERICA

FOLLIES IN AMERICA

A HISTORY OF GARDEN
AND PARK ARCHITECTURE

KERRY DEAN CARSO

CORNELL UNIVERSITY PRESS
Ithaca and London

Publication of this book was made possible, in part, by a
grant from Furthermore: a program of the J. M. Kaplan
Fund.

First published 2021 by Cornell University Press
Printed in the United States of America

Library of Congress Cataloging-in-Publication Data

Names: Carso, Kerry Dean, author.
Title: Follies in America : a history of garden and park
    architecture / Kerry Dean Carso.
Description: Ithaca [New York] : Cornell University Press,
    2021. | Includes bibliographical references and index.
Identifiers: LCCN 2020042662 (print) | LCCN 2020042663
    (ebook) | ISBN 9781501755934 (paperback) |
    ISBN 9781501755941 (adobe pdf) |
    ISBN 9781501755958 (epub)
Subjects: LCSH: Follies (Architecture)—United States—
    History—18th century. | Follies (Architecture)—
    United States—History—19th century. | Garden
    structures—United States—History—18th century. |
    Garden structures—United States—History—19th century.
Classification: LCC NA8460 .C29 2021 (print) |
    LCC NA8460 (ebook) | DDC 712.0973—dc23
LC record available at https://lccn.loc.gov/2020042662
LC ebook record available at https://lccn.loc.gov
    /2020042663

To Brian, Owen, and Nathaniel
and to the memory of
Teddy Dean Carso

CONTENTS

ILLUSTRATIONS

Acknowledgments

Two follies bookend my commute from northeastern Pennsylvania to SUNY New Paltz: the High Point Monument in High Point State Park in New Jersey and Sky Top Tower at Mohonk Mountain House. The High Point Monument is a hollow obelisk that overlooks my home from a mountaintop in the same way Sky Top Tower watches over the SUNY New Paltz campus. These two follies have been my thought-provoking companions between home and classroom. It was a different folly that first brought me to this project: Kingfisher Tower in Cooperstown, New York. Kingfisher is so obviously a folly in the English garden tradition that it made me wonder if there were others out there in the American landscape. No one had addressed these follies in a scholarly way, and, fascinated, I set out to document these wonderful and eccentric buildings to see what they might tell us about American history and culture.

I first want to thank the mentors and professors who introduced me to landscape architecture and design. At Harvard University, I took an architectural history class with Neil Levine, who inspired me to pursue my interest in architectural history in graduate school. At Boston University, Keith Morgan and Naomi Miller mentored me in architectural history and landscape design studies. I owe a great debt to the late David Schuyler, who supported my work after I first met him in Cooperstown in 2000. Through the years, I turned to David for his expertise, and I always appreciated his generosity in sharing his knowledge. David introduced me to Michael McGandy at Cornell University Press, and for that too, I am very grateful. David passed away just as this book went into production, and I will miss him greatly.

It has been a pleasure working with Michael McGandy, and everyone else at Cornell University Press, including Clare Jones, Ellen Murphy, Jennifer Savran Kelly, and Brock Schnoke. Thank you also to Mary Gendron, Rebecca Faith, and Enid Zafran. The two peer reviewers helped me to sharpen my ideas. I am thankful for a publication grant (Research and Creative Projects Award) from SUNY New Paltz in 2018. A SUNY New Paltz sabbatical in 2013–14 gave me time to research and write.

In the course of my research for this book, I had fellowships at a number of libraries, including Winterthur, the Huntington Library, the Library Company and Historical Society of Pennsylvania, and the International Center for Jefferson Studies at Monticello. I was the recipient of the Geoffrey Beard Scholarship from the Attingham Summer School, which allowed me to study the English country house tradition with wonderful colleagues in the summer of 2004. In 2006, with a Research and Creative Projects Award from SUNY New Paltz, I returned to England to study more gardens firsthand.

Numerous scholars, librarians, archivists, and other individuals have assisted me in my research or responded to my work, including Tom Allen, Jhennifer Amundson, Anna Vemer Andrzejewski, Bill Beiswanger, J. Jeremiah Breen, Gretchen Buggeln, Amy T. Collins, Wendy Cooper, Ted Dewsnap, Linda Eaton, Harvey Flad, Joel Fry, Ritchie Garrison, Jonathan Gross, Robyn Gullickson, Barbara J. Heath, James N. Green, Brock Jobe, Joan LaChance, Maggie Lidz, Anthony Light, Ann Lundberg, Ann Smart Martin, Paula Mohr, Barbara Burlison Mooney, John Rhodehamel, Vanessa Bezemer Sellers, Carol Soltis, Anne Verplanck, Richard Guy Wilson, and Aaron Wunsch. At the start of this project, I submitted a query to the Society of Architectural Historians Listserv asking for suggestions of follies to study. I was delighted to receive numerous emails from scholars eager to share information with me. I cannot thank them enough for this tremendous support early on in my research. Another research query to the Charles Brockden Brown Society (facilitated by Michelle Sizemore) led to another question answered (thank you to Philip Barnard).

Jane Clark gave me permission to visit her property on Otsego Lake to view Kingfisher Tower up close and to photograph the building. My SUNY New Paltz colleague Bill Rhoads invited me to present my research on the summerhouses of Mohonk Mountain House at the Ulster County Historical Society in 2008. I have presented my research at numerous venues throughout the years, and I am grateful for the responses and suggestions I received from audience members. In particular, I found the "Art of Revolutions" conference at the American Philosophical Society in 2017 to be a brilliant gathering of scholars with many ideas to share with me. Parts of this book previously appeared in *The Hudson River Valley Review, Aeternum: A Journal of Contemporary Gothic Studies*, and *The Art of Revolutions*, published by the American Philosophical Society.

I am fortunate to have a lively and supportive group of art history colleagues at SUNY New Paltz: Elizabeth Brotherton, Keely Heuer, Jaclynne Kerner, Ellen Konowitz, William Rhoads, Laura Silvernail, Susan DeMaio Smutny, Beth Wilson, Jaimee Uhlenbrock, and Reva Wolf. I want to thank Susan for assisting me with images for this book. I am so lucky to have wonderful friends whose support encourages me, including Rachel Dressler, Theresa Flanigan, and Andrea Varga.

I dedicate this book to my husband Brian and our boys, Owen and Nathaniel, and to the memory of Teddy Dean Carso. Owen and Nat have undoubtedly learned more about follies than any other kids their age. My mother and late father have always supported me in everything that I do, as have my father-in-law and late mother-in-law. Since my mother moved to Pennsylvania, she has accompanied me on a number of site visits, always curious about what we might see. I want to thank Frank, Megan, Jackson, and Madeline for their continued support and love.

FOLLIES IN AMERICA

Introduction

In Jane Austen's parody *Northanger Abbey* (1818), the delightfully obtuse Catherine Morland, the "heroine" of the novel, becomes enthralled with the notion of visiting Blaize (Blaise) Castle in Bristol, England, with her friends. On hearing the words "Blaize *Castle*," Catherine cries, "What, is it really a castle, an old castle? . . . is it like what one reads of? . . . are there towers and long galleries? . . . Then I should like to see it. . . . but may we go all over it? May we go up every staircase, and into every suite of rooms . . ."[1] What Catherine has in mind, of course, is the venerable Castle of Udolpho, that gloomy, authentically medieval pile featured in Ann Radcliffe's paradigmatic Gothic novel, *The Mysteries of Udolpho* (1794), the very novel that Austen spoofs in Northanger Abbey. What Catherine does not realize is that Blaize Castle is anything but an old castle. It was a recent addition to the English countryside at the time of Northanger Abbey's late eighteenth-century setting, having been constructed in 1766. Blaize Castle is, in fact, a folly, a summerhouse built by Thomas Farr. That Catherine is fooled into thinking the castle is an authentic medieval structure shows her own folly. This episode from Austen's *Northanger Abbey* provides a humorous entrée into the subject of this book, a cultural and architectural history of follies and ruins, not in England, where they seem to abound, but in the United States, a place not necessarily known for its follies. In fact, these playful, whimsical structures can tell us much about early American culture.

Writers have spilled a great deal of ink defining follies. These buildings are curious, to say the least, and hence those with a penchant for the slightly absurd are naturally attracted to them. Indeed, there is a group in England called The Folly Fellowship, dedicated to the study of useless buildings, which leads its members on tours and catalogs the many publications about these diminutive structures. But how does one define a folly? As Gwyn Headley, one of the leaders of the fellowship, states, "It is easier to define what a folly is not, rather than what it is." Headley goes on to note "the reluctance of establishment architectural historians to involve themselves too closely with the type, for it is a minefield for the ambitious academic. The properly trained architectural historian needs to verify the context and category of buildings, to know where they stand in the order of things. Follies, however, are riotous and undisciplined, seductive and irrational. They are going to cause problems."[2]

In *The Penguin Dictionary of Architecture and Landscape Architecture*, the authors define the term *folly* as "a costly but useless structure built to satisfy the whim of some eccentric and thought to show his folly; usually a tower or classical ruin in a landscaped park intended to enhance the view or picturesque effect."[3] In addition to garden structures, I have found many American buildings that are follies outside of gardens but that can trace their origins to the garden folly. No serious studies of this building type in the United States exist at this time, perhaps because of the "frivolous" nature of follies. Despite popular denigration of follies, architectural historians need to take a more serious look at these buildings. We need to look beyond the lightheartedness of follies and try to determine their social and cultural context. My approach is interdisciplinary, and I am especially interested in the literary context and/or storytelling possibilities of these buildings. Since most follies have, in the words of the *Oxford Companion to Gardens*, "a certain excess in terms of eccentricity," these buildings often contribute to a narrative either unto themselves or in relation to the garden as a whole.[4]

In England, follies and ruins are most often located in landscape gardens. They serve to ornament the landscape, provide shelter from the elements, and, in the particular case of towers, provide spectacular views of both the surrounding gardens and the English countryside. These structures often express literary or nationalistic narratives. Architectural historian Spiro Kostof declares, "The [English landscape] garden was composed to be read as a narrative, like a pastoral romance or poem. Mock temples, pyramids, grottoes, rustic cottages, real or sham ruins, baths, hermitages were carefully planted to be viewed as storied pictures."[5] Henry Hoare, the owner of Stourhead Gardens in Wiltshire, England, based his landscape design on both Claude's seventeenth-century painting *Coast View of Delos with Aeneas* (1672) and the original literary source, *The Aeneid* by

Virgil, as scholars have shown.[6] But while art and literature inspired the design of Stourhead, politically charged follies dominate the landscape at Stowe Gardens in Buckinghamshire, England, designed in the first half of the eighteenth century. A bastion of Whig secessionism in opposition to the prime minister, Robert Walpole, Stowe's landscape features the "Elysian Fields," where The Temple of Ancient Virtue, an Ionic temple, celebrates antique luminaries, while near it once stood the Temple of Modern Virtue, a ruin surrounding a headless figure thought to represent Walpole. Stowe contains numerous follies with particular messages. One of the most famous follies at Stowe is the Temple of Liberty, designed by James Gibbs in 1741. The sandstone Gothic temple features a triangular plan with an iconographical program proclaiming nationalistic pride in Saxon history.[7] Themes of nationalism are common among English follies, and the same is often true of American garden buildings.

Early American artists, authors, and critics often commented on the absence of associational architecture of bygone eras in the American landscape. Buildings introduce "memory" into a landscape. Americans wistfully dreamed of European landscapes and the architectural remnants of the glory days of nationhood they contained. American writers and artists struggled to create literature and art that would distinguish the new nation from its European sources. Their desire to emulate the Old World in order to achieve greatness while simultaneously striving for originality suggests the contradictions of the period. The landscape painter Thomas Cole addressed this very topic in his "Essay on American Scenery" (1836), in which he noted that some had deplored the American landscape's "want of associations" (created by aged buildings and ruins with their attendant history and legends), while he proclaimed that the wild aspects of American scenery had much to offer the viewer.[8] Even so, the pull of European scenes was great on many American artists, and especially on Cole. The painter often invoked Archibald Alison's theory of associationism, which became influential in the early nineteenth century.[9] Associationism encouraged viewers to allow their imaginations to fill old buildings and landscapes with figures from the past or from literature associated with the locale. This kind of Romantic reverie encouraged fancy, which is the impetus for many of Cole's paintings. The artist implicitly acknowledged the theory of associationism when, in "Essay on American Scenery," he wrote, "He who stands on Mont Albano and looks down on ancient Rome, has his mind peopled with the gigantic associations of the storied past. . . ." Cole acknowledged that a viewer may experience the Sublime in a landscape of the American West, but "it is the sublimity of a shoreless ocean unislanded by the recorded deeds of man."[10] In sum, Cole admitted that the American landscape lacked the instances of associations sparked by old architecture.

One way to satiate the universal desire for contemplating the passage of time was for architects to design historicized garden and park buildings, such as temples, towers, summerhouses, and ruins, for the American landscape.

This book does not include metal prospect towers because they do not introduce memory into the landscape. Instead, these towers presage the future. An image from Fairmount Park in Philadelphia in 1866 highlights the difference between ornamental historicism in landscape architecture and early modernism (figure I.1). The prospect tower at Georges Hill is more akin to the skyscrapers

FIGURE I.1.   James Cremer, *Views of Fairmount Park Philadelphia* (album), Observatory, Georges Hill, Fairmount Park, 1866, p. 11. The Library Company of Philadelphia.

sprouting up in late nineteenth-century American cities with their embrace of the new materials of the machine age than to traditional follies. While the pavilion in front of the tower may also be constructed of metal, it is more highly ornamented with nods to the architectural past in its exoticized round arches. The pavilion is associational architecture, while the tower, with its lack of ornamental architectural vocabulary, is an example of early modernism. The conclusion to this book will examine this metal tower, along with Kingfisher Tower in Cooperstown, New York, in the context of the nation's one hundredth birthday.[11]

The inspiration for this book is the desire to discover American examples of the building types one finds in an eighteenth-century English landscape garden, such as Stourhead or Stowe. These gardens contain small-scale buildings that direct the viewer through the landscape while providing a narrative of instruction and delight. In the United States, these buildings can be found in settings that include private gardens, rural cemeteries, public parks, and sites of natural beauty such as Niagara Falls. The building types found in English landscape gardens are the starting point for the investigation, but the book will stray from the garden and examine how associationist buildings appear in other settings, including cities and sites of natural beauty.[12] This book is neither a catalog nor a finding aid to the locations of extant follies. Rather, it is an examination of what these overlooked buildings mean in the cultural and social context of an era.

Follies were part of a larger discourse on the benefits of sylvan retreat, and as such they represented a response to increasing anxieties about urbanization and industrialization in the nineteenth-century United States. The ideological meanings of individual follies depended on such considerations as style and site. The rustic style summerhouse was antithetical to the city, because the materials were gathered from nature. Summerhouses in the pleasure grounds of insane asylums and hospitals presented an antidote to the disease within the institutions, as access to nature and gardens was deemed necessary for healthy recreation. Follies provide a window into major themes in nineteenth-century American culture. The little buildings point to tensions between Jeffersonian agrarianism and urban life while embodying the Romantic fascination with nature. Follies represent the taming of the American wilderness through the construction of lookout towers and summerhouses at sites of natural wonder. Prospect towers suggest the ascendancy of middle-class tourism and highlight issues of power inherent in the elevated gaze. Lastly, the "improvement" of rural and suburban houses and grounds reflect the themes of gentility and social class aspirations.

FIGURE I.2.   Louis Linscott, *Middlesex Canal*, Woburn, MA, n.d. Middlesex Canal Association.

Two examples show the variety of folly building in the young United States. Figure I.2 illustrates a scene along the Middlesex Canal in Woburn, Massachusetts, in the mid-nineteenth century, as imagined by a twentieth-century artist, Louis Linscott (1876–1966). In the foreground, we see a canal boat, laden with cargo, plying the man-made waterway. Opened in 1803, the 27-mile long Middlesex Canal initiated the industrialization of the Merrimack Valley. That same year, the canal's chief engineer Loammi Baldwin enlarged the family residence (originally built in 1661) to the three-story house visible in the background of this painting by local artist Linscott. Between the house and canal, Linscott depicts a tidy garden, celebrated in Baldwin's time, with trees, bushes, formal flower beds, beehives, and two gardeners, one male and one female, tending to the flowers. Near the center of Linscott's composition, we spy a little latticed summerhouse with a Gothic pointed arch. A pleasant scene, to be sure. But clearly the garden functions as a buffer of nature between the engineer's house and the commerce occurring close at hand. While the canal represented Baldwin's livelihood and his professional success, industrialization writ large brought growth and transformations to the towns along the canal's path. The garden mediates between the private domesticity of home and the public life of work. Make no mistake: Linscott meant for Baldwin's garden—and the little summerhouse at its center—to also be a showcase of wealth and gentility visible to those traveling along the canal in this twentieth-century imagining of a nineteenth-century garden.

This summerhouse also suggests the ephemeral quality of these little structures. Baldwin's garden no longer exists; the house was moved to a different location to make way for a shopping plaza.[13] Today Baldwin House is a Chinese restaurant called Sichuan Garden. Similar fates befell many nineteenth-century landscapes and little summerhouses that do not survive intact to the present day or are rebuilt over the years. Despite their ephemerality, some have managed to survive. A summerhouse similar to the one in the Linscott image endures at Winterthur Garden, the estate of Henry Francis du Pont (1880–1969) in Delaware. Moved from the nearby property Latimeria to the grounds at Winterthur in 1929 and rebuilt as needed over the years, the summerhouse is a survivor from the genteel gardens of the past.

Another canal folly illustrates the narrative function of such buildings. John Hartwell Cocke built Temperance Spring at Bremo in Virginia in 1845 (figure I.3). Cocke was a temperance advocate and director of the Kanawha Canal, constructed in the 1830s to connect the Atlantic Ocean and the Ohio River. Late in life, he began contemplating building a temple along the canal, which passed through his property. Dedicated to the Sons of Temperance (a fraternal

FIGURE I.3.   Alexander Jackson Davis, Temperance Spring, Bremo, State Route 656 vicinity, Bremo Bluff, Fluvanna County, VA, 1845. Library of Congress, Prints and Photographs Division, HABS VA, 33-FORKU.V, 1–20.

temperance society founded in the South), and, in Cocke's words, "the Great Moral reform of the nineteenth century," the temple was meant to remind passing boatmen of the evils of liquor. Cocke worked with architect Alexander Jackson Davis on the design, a Doric temple with steps leading to a "pulpitum," from which Cocke may have planned to lecture to boatmen and passengers on the waterway. Davis's role in the design was to lend historical accuracy to the project, and in a letter to Cocke, after a lengthy discussion of proper Greek design, he acknowledged his own "pedantry."[14]

On September 19, 1849, Cocke held a family picnic to celebrate both his sixty-ninth birthday and the completion of the temple. Someone read a temperance "Declaration of Independence," possibly from the pulpitum, along with an address. Cocke contemplated decorating the temple with pictures from Cruikshank's "The Bottle," and its sequel, "The Drunkard's Children" (published in England in 1847 and 1848), popular pictorial narratives of the downfall of a family through alcohol abuse. A better example of a didactic and narrative temple can scarcely be imagined. Whether Cocke's temple succeeded in dissuading people from drinking alcohol is a mystery. Cocke included in the design access to a natural spring from which visitors were encouraged to drink the pure water; ironically, rumors circulated that the boatmen used the liquid to enhance their mint juleps.[15]

The story of Temperance Spring suggests that follies did not always successfully transmit the message their owners intended. But this fact did not stop people from trying to encode messages, stories, and even myths in the American landscape. Often, follies embodied both personal and national aspirations. During the period between the founding and the American centennial celebration in 1876, Americans shaped the land while shaping the nation. Designed landscapes played an important role in buttressing American nationhood.[16]

Thomas Jefferson bridged the worlds of politics and aesthetics and helped to establish the picturesque style in the United States in its early years.[17] As the author of the Declaration of Independence and the designer of one of America's first landscape gardens in the English style, Jefferson is a key figure in this study. Integral to the early history of the picturesque in America are Jefferson's tour of English gardens with John Adams in 1786 and his unexecuted projects for his plantation landscape at Monticello near Charlottesville, Virginia (c. 1776), begun around the time Jefferson wrote the Declaration of Independence. From the nation's founding to its centennial, follies told stories of national identity. In 1876, the year of the American centennial celebration and the end date for this book, nationalism continued to play an important role in architectural design. In a period of increasing nationalism, historicized garden buildings, such as temples, towers, summerhouses, and ruins, brought European architectural styles to America, legitimizing the American landscape. By imprinting the land with symbols of European culture, landscape gardeners brought their idea of civilization to the American wilderness and helped define gentility in the young nation.

CHAPTER 1

The English Landscape Garden in America

In 1786, Thomas Jefferson and John Adams went
to England on a diplomatic mission and, with time to spare, took the occasion
to examine some of the most well-known English landscape gardens of the
time, including highlights such as Painshill, Stowe, the Leasowes, Hagley, and
Blenheim (Jefferson began his tour two days early and visited Chiswick, Twickenham, Hampton Court, and Woburn Farm).[1] The two Americans were eager
to see these gardens firsthand; Jefferson had studied English landscape gardens
in book publications and had already started making landscape plans in the English style at his home Monticello in Virginia. In the eighteenth century in
England, naturalistic, irregular gardens replaced the rigid, geometric French-style
garden of the seventeenth century. Winding paths leading to pleasantly surprising vistas became popular at aristocratic English country houses, in opposition
to the controlled, authoritarian landscape of, for instance, Louis XIV's Versailles
designed by André Le Nôtre. Follies played a crucial role in one's experience of
an English landscape garden. In bringing follies to the young United States,
Americans were making explicit connections between the old country and the
new. In a nation that in the nineteenth century was still finding appropriate
ways to express its architectural aspirations, follies represented genteel ambi-
tions, and in larger estates, functioned as explicit indicators of wealth.

In an English landscape garden, the designer revealed these buildings not
all at once, but incrementally, training the plants and molding the landscape

to maximize the delight in discovering the previously hidden treasure of a little temple ensconced in nature. These eye-catchers led the viewer through the landscape and provided respite, shade, and covering in case of rain. Viewers may have felt they were exploring with autonomy, but follies helped define the path through the landscape. While appearing natural, English landscapes were man-made, with trees pruned to maximize views and streams dammed to create artificial ponds. The technological advance of the ha-ha made the English landscape garden's naturalism possible; the ha-ha is a sunken fence that divides a landscape without material obstructions. The unusual name of this garden feature derives from the expression of surprise when one perceives, in the words of Horace Walpole, "a sudden and unperceived check to one's walk."[2] Only visible from one side, the ha-ha hides the evidence of man's hand in the landscape. The purpose of the ha-ha is to keep grazing animals away from the country house while maintaining the appearance of an uninterrupted, sloping lawn. In his "Essay on Modern Gardens," Horace Walpole (1717–1797) made the distinction between French gardens, which were formal, and their English counterparts, which were natural looking. Walpole credits the architect William Kent, who "leaped the fence, and saw that all nature was a garden."[3] The formal French traditions of parterres and topiary gave way to naturalistic gardens featuring serpentine paths and ha-has. In early America, the ha-ha was uncommon, perhaps because of the relative rarity of elaborate country houses, the expense of building stone walls, the separation between agricultural and garden pursuits, and that the ha-ha did not deter deer, which, like Kent, can leap fences.[4] However, Thomas Jefferson and George Washington built ha-has at Monticello and Mount Vernon, respectively.[5] Jefferson had seen an English ha-ha firsthand at Stowe in Buckinghamshire and later built one at Monticello.[6]

While visiting the gardens, Jefferson carried with him a copy of Thomas Whately's *Observations on Modern Gardening* (1770) as a guide the way tourists in the following century would carry Sir Walter Scott's novels as they toured ruins.[7] Jefferson was explicit about the importance of Whately as a tour guide, as he begins his notes by stating that he went to the gardens "described by Whateley [sic] in his book on gardening." He calls Whately's descriptions "models of perfect elegance and classical correctness," which are "remarkable for their exactness."[8] Jefferson examined the particular spots Whately recommended, noting that each location was recognizable because of Whately's precise descriptions. About follies, Whately tells us that buildings were probably introduced into gardens to "afford refuge from a sudden shower, and shelter against the wind; or, at the most, to be seats for a party, or for retirement," but he notes that they have since become landscape ornaments.[9]

Jefferson recorded his reactions to the gardens with an aim to document "practical things as might enable me to estimate the expence [*sic*] of making and maintaining a garden in that style."[10] Jefferson had a designer's eye; he noted specific garden features and decided whether they were effective or not. For instance, at Lord Burlington's house Chiswick, Jefferson decided that the garden was overly contrived; he was especially disapproving of the obelisk placed in the middle of a small pond, calling it "useless."[11] The obelisk appears in front of a small, round temple in the Ionic order in the garden at Chiswick. Jefferson must have been interested in seeing this little temple, as he had used it as the basis for his own drawing of a garden temple intended for the Monticello landscape years earlier around 1778 (figure 1.1). For his source at the time of his drawing, he used William Kent's *Designs of Inigo Jones* (1727), which illustrates the Chiswick garden pavilion (of course, the Chiswick pavilion strongly resembles the Roman Pantheon, a popular source for round garden temples in the eighteenth century).[12] The garden tour was, then, an opportunity for Jefferson to see and evaluate the buildings he had previously only studied in books. On the verso of the drawing, Jefferson provided his specifications for the temple, deciding ultimately that he should build it "on the point of land between the meadow and intended fish pond in the park."[13] However, Jefferson never built the temple, as all but one of his folly designs at Monticello remained on paper.

Before Adams joined him on the tour, Jefferson visited Alexander Pope's garden at Twickenham outside of London. Translator of Homer's *The Iliad* (1715–1720) and *The Odyssey* (1725–1726) and author of satirical verse, including *The Rape of the Lock* (1712, 1714), Pope also wrote about gardens, including his essay "Of Gardens" (1713) in which he satirizes topiary, the artificial trimming of bushes into ornamental shapes. In his essay "An Epistle to The Right Honourable Richard Earl of Burlington" (1731), Pope instructs the landscape designer to "Consult the Genius of the Place in all;" in other words, respect the natural topography.[14] In 1719, Pope began designing a garden at his country house along the Thames River. Using statuary to create a classical garden iconography, Pope "was the English Homer and Virgil who would restore classical literature and return England to strict Roman virtues."[15] The highlight of the garden was Pope's grotto, consisting of three chambers, including an elaborate tunnel carved out beneath the road separating Pope's house and garden; the tunnel connected the basement of his house and his garden.[16]

Jefferson does not give a detailed description of Pope's garden in his notes, so it is useful to consult another visitor to understand the full effect of Pope's achievement. Thirty-eight years before Jefferson's visit, an anonymous visitor

FIGURE 1.1.   Monticello: Ionic portico and dome. Coolidge Collection of Thomas Jefferson Manuscripts, recto, probably 1778, by Thomas Jefferson. Special Collections Jefferson N91; K62 20.1 × 16 cm (7 15/16 × 6 5/16 in.). Collection of the Massachusetts Historical Society. http://www.masshist.org/thomasjeffersonpapers/doc?id=arch_N91

from Newcastle penned a description of the garden in 1748, three years after Pope's death. The Newcastle visitor described the situation of the house and the "subterraneous Passage, or Cavern" in which Pope had "found a Spring of the clearest Water" which created a "perpetual Rill" echoing throughout the space at all times. In the grotto, he discovered "many Openings and Cells" with columns with no set orders, "but aptly favouring the particular Designs of the Place," and "roughly hew'd out of Rocks and Beds of mineral Strata."

Pope affixed "Plates of Looking glass" on the roof and sides of the grotto, in order to reflect the objects in the cavern. The Newcastle visitor wrote: "Cast your Eyes upward, and you half shudder to see Cataracts of Water precipitating over your Head, from impending Stones and Rocks," creating a "Mixture of Realities and Imagery." Once out of the grotto, which was inscribed with a quotation from Horace, and into the Wilderness, the Newcastle visitor encountered a temple decorated with shells.[17] When Jefferson visited years later, the garden was altered greatly, but the grotto had survived (it still does today, although the house and garden are gone). Jefferson noted the situation of the grotto below the road and also mentioned Pope's obelisk (a monument to his mother), a mound with a spiral walk, and a rookery.

Once again, Jefferson must have been quite intrigued by what he saw of Pope's garden, as years earlier he had planned a grotto for Monticello. In 1771, Jefferson recorded his plan for a water feature at Monticello in his pocket memorandum book. To the north of his house by a spring, he intended to place "a sleeping figure reclined on a plain marble slab, surrounded with turf;" on the slab would appear a common pseudoclassical inscription in Latin. Above the cistern, Jefferson at first considered a two-story structure with a concealed Aeolian harp below. The roof of the structure, Jefferson thought, may be "Chinese, Graecian, or in the taste of the Lanthern of Demosthenes at Athens." But in the next paragraph of his memorandum book, he quickly abandoned his fairly elaborate first idea with the words "This would be better." His new plan was "to dig into the hill and form a cave or grotto," with its sides and arch made of moss-covered clay. He would "Spangle it with translucent pebbles . . . and beautiful shells" over a pebbled floor. The figure lying on a "couch of moss" would be better situated in this fully realized grotto than in his earlier plan. And the inscription, taken from Alexander Pope and inscribed in the grotto at Stourhead Garden in Wiltshire, would be in English rather than Latin:

> Nymph of the grot, these sacred springs I keep.
> And to the murmur of these waters sleep:
> Ah! spare my slumbers! gently tread the cave!
> And drink in silence, or in silence lave![18]

Jefferson knew Pope's English version of the Latin inscription from an edition of Pope's works in Jefferson's own library and recommended the volume to a friend in 1771. In addition to Pope, Jefferson likely consulted other books in his library including Whately's *Observations on Modern Gardening* and William Shenstone's essay "Unconnected Thoughts on Gardening" published with R. Dodsley's "A Description of The Leasowes." Jefferson expert William Beiswanger notes that these early ideas "are significant as some of the first expressions of mature ideas on landscape gardening recorded in America—ideas which were inspired by literary associations and probably influenced by several important works on the theory of landscape gardening."[19] Jefferson's grotto never came to fruition at Monticello, but no doubt as he explored Pope's grotto at Twickenham, he had in mind all the possibilities at his own plantation house in Virginia.

Jefferson also visited Woburn Farm, near Chertsey. In *Observations on Modern Gardening*, Whatcly emphasizes the follies in this passage: "On the top of the hill is a large octagon structure; and not far from it, the ruin of a chapel. To one of the lawns the ruin appears . . . from the other is seen the octagon. . . . This lawn is further embellished by a neat Gothic building . . ."[20] Landscape historian Rudy J. Favretti notes that while Jefferson disapproved of some elements at Woburn Farm, "he highly approved of the concept."[21] Indeed, the description of Woburn has many elements, including temples and Gothic buildings, which Jefferson includes in his own designs. Woburn was a *ferme ornée*, an ornamented farm, combining pleasure grounds and agricultural pursuits. According to Andrea Wulf, Woburn's combination of "beautiful groves with tidy farmland" coincided with Jefferson's "vision of America as a continent of both sublime beauty and vast lands that would feed the nation."[22] Although the idea of the *ferme ornée* was appealing to Jefferson, the execution was all important. Visiting the Leasowes, William Shenstone's celebrated *ferme ornée* in Shropshire, Jefferson complained, "This is not even an ornamented farm. It is only a grazing farm with a path round it."[23] He also lamented that Woburn was "merely a highly-ornamented walk through and round the divisions of the farm and kitchen garden."[24]

Despite some of his objections to particular features in the gardens he visited, Jefferson observed that overall "the gardening in that country [England] is the article in which it surpasses all the earth. I mean their pleasure gardening. This indeed went far beyond my ideas."[25] Even with his Francophilia and general disdain for English culture, Jefferson clearly admired the English garden tradition. During their tour, he and Adams noted that many of the plants featured in English gardens were native to America. Wulf writes that Jefferson "could wholeheartedly embrace [English gardens] without feeling unpatriotic because they were populated with American plants and shaped by ideas of liberty."[26] As for his native country, Jefferson foresaw a nation of gardens, bolstered by the natural beauty of America. In his "Hints to Americans Travelling in Europe" (1788), Jefferson listed "Objects of Attention for an American." "Gardens" occupy the fourth position on his list. He writes that gardens are "Peculiarly worth the attention of an American, because it is the country of all others where the noblest gardens may be made without expence [*sic*].

We have only to cut out the superabundant plants."[27] Here Jefferson acknowledges what he perceived to be the superiority of the American natural landscape. But he looks to England for "models" in the art of gardening: "Their sunless climate has permitted them to adopt what is certainly a beauty of the very first order in landscape."[28]

In his notes, Jefferson's lingers on Stowe, the country house and garden of Richard Temple (1675–1749), first Viscount of Cobham, who engaged some of the most celebrated garden designers of the time, including Charles Bridgeman, William Kent, and Lancelot "Capability" Brown. "A favorite stop for eighteenth-century tourists" and exerting influence "almost comparable to that of Versailles," Stowe was a must-see garden for our American travelers.[29] Designed by William Kent in 1735, the Elysian Fields at Stowe are a folly-rich and politically charged space where the visitor once encountered the Temple of Ancient Virtue (a round temple based on the Temple of Vesta at Tivoli, still extant) juxtaposed with the Temple of Modern Virtue, a ruin (no longer extant) enclosing the headless figure of Robert Walpole, Lord Cobham's political enemy.

An image from B. Seeley's *Stowe: A Description of the House and Gardens* illustrates the range of follies at Stowe (figure 1.2): the gateway designed by Kent; the Doric Arch; the Temple of Modern Virtue in ruins next to the pristine Temple of Ancient Virtue; and the shell bridge. Jefferson owned a copy of Seeley's 1783 edition of *Stowe: A Description of the House and Gardens*, and the richly illustrated volume provided visual fodder for his interest in folly design.[30] Near the two temples across a stream named the River Styx, stood Kent's Temple of British Worthies, a semicircular exedra with niches featuring busts of such luminaries as Shakespeare and Queen Elizabeth. Jefferson did not comment on these follies but saved his highest praise at Stowe for the Temple of Friendship and the Temple of Venus, the siting of which he found had "a good effect."[31] Adams, meanwhile, was not as interested in design principles, but more in interpretative meaning. He found the temples to Bacchus and Venus "quite unnecessary" as people need no "artificial Incitements" to these amusements. He declared that other temples—including the Temple of Ancient Virtue and the Temple of British Worthies—"are in a higher taste."[32] The allegorical message of Lord Cobham's politically charged Stowe—aligning "the venality and debauchery of England with an inevitable collapse of the entire country"—would have appealed to Jefferson and Adams, who fretted that immorality could lead to the fall of their new nation.[33] While at Stowe, Adams notes that he climbed Lord Cobham's Pillar, a monument built by Lady Cobham and completed by Capability Brown after a James Gibbs design in 1747–1749. The tallest structure at Stowe, the tower features

The Gate-way by Kent.

The Doric Arch.

A Ruin.

The Temple of Antient Virtue.

The Shell Bridge.

B. Seeley delin.

G. L. Smith sculp.

Plate V.

FIGURE 1.2. *Stowe: A Description of the House and Gardens*, Buckingham: B. Seeley, 1788, preceding p. 17. RB345898. The Huntington Library, San Marino, CA.

a large statue of Lord Cobham at the top. By means of an interior spiral stair-case, Adams (and presumably Jefferson, although he makes no mention of it) ascended the tower to take in the view of the English countryside.[34] The purpose of the tower was for Lord Cobham to "survey the landscape achievements of a lifetime."[35] Jefferson had contemplated towers at Monticello as well (to be discussed in chapter 4).

Jefferson was one of the first Americans to dream of an English-style landscape garden in America. Many others followed. By the mid-nineteenth century, country houses were quite fashionable for the elites, and gardens were indicators of gentility. Examples of gardens replete with follies serve to illustrate the phenomenon. Armsmear, the estate of Samuel and Elizabeth Colt in Hartford, Connecticut, was lavish and symbolic of the vast wealth attained through industrial innovation, in this case, the manufacture of Colt guns. Constructed between 1855–1857, Armsmear was an eclectic architectural concoction. The house was Italianate in overall form with a tall campanile combining flourishes of Orientalism with references to Colt's personal history of encounters with the Czar of Russia and Sultan Abdul Mejid I of the Ottoman Empire. Based on London's Crystal Palace and New York's Crystal Palace, where he exhibited his revolving pistols, the house's conservatory was a domed iron and glass construction.[36] Colt hired Copeland and Cleveland, a landscape architecture firm in Boston, to design the extensive gardens. The labor required to create and maintain this wonderland was enormous; indeed, the head gardener supervised thirty men to "trim Nature to perfection."[37] Picturesque and English in inspiration, the garden was visible from Elizabeth's morning room, which, "surrounded by a veranda, commands one of the most lovely, serene, and English of views—a view which has been compared to that of Richmond Hill so celebrated by Walpole and Pope—a long, green, perfect lawn, a fountain, and an artificial lake . . . in which stands two water-nymphs and a bronze colt."[38] The garden featured two artificial lakes, one of which is visible in figure 1.3. Here we see exotic peacocks roaming the grounds and two gazebos on the lake. The one on the left was known as "Elizabeth's Bower," a Gothic Revival trellised summerhouse situated on the water—"The point of most perfect vision," according to a contemporary account—to maximize views of the garden and the grounds beyond it.[39] The main purpose of the summerhouse was not for "effect," but as a "resting-place . . . from which to enjoy the view."[40] Colt scattered sculpture around the grounds, much of it classical in inspiration, but one sculpture was self-referential. In the artificial lake illustrated in figure 1.3 stood a bronze rampant colt, a copy of the one originally gracing the dome of Colt's Armory until its destruction by fire in 1864.[41]

FIGURE 1.3.   Armsmear. Plate following page 48 from *Armsmear: The Home, The Arm and the Armory of Samuel Colt: A Memorial*. *AM1866 Barn 3144.Q (Colt). The Library Company of Philadelphia.

From his campanile, Colt enjoyed a view of his armory, visible in the distance in figure 1.3, with its unique onion dome. Here we see a clear juxtaposition between the Edenic garden and the behemoth industrial complex that made it possible. Once an area became overdeveloped and industrialized, men like Colt inserted genteel greenery to offset the loss of contact with nature. Clearly, the Armsmear garden functioned as an antidote to industrialization but only for Colt and his invited guests, because outsiders could only sneak a peek from adjacent streets and from the factory village where the workers lived. According to Elizabeth's father who resided in the house after Samuel's death, a watchman with a revolver guarded the house.[42]

Other gardens were open to the public. A devoted Anglophile originally from Sheffield, England, Henry Shaw (1800–1889) modeled his gardening pursuits after a man he admired, William Spencer Cavendish, the sixth Duke of Devonshire, whose estate Chatsworth in Derbyshire, England, was an inspiration to Shaw.[43] Shaw became a successful businessman in imported manufactured goods and settled in St. Louis, Missouri. In 1849, the architect George I. Barnett designed both a town house and villa, Tower Grove House, for Shaw. For the house, Barnett employed the popular Italianate style, asymmetrical with a tall square tower. An enthusiastic gardener deeply interested in horticulture and botany, Shaw immediately began planting a garden at Tower Grove, with labor provided by slaves and immigrants.[44]

By the nineteenth century, botany had become a popular science, and a way "to promote gentility—refinement, respectability, and politeness—characteristics necessary for a cultivated life."[45] Shaw saw botany as essential to the advancement of the nation and its people.[46] After visiting Chatsworth's arboretum and conservatories in 1851, Shaw decided to create a botanical garden at Tower Grove, accessible to the public, as was Chatsworth. Shaw's Garden, now known as the Missouri Botanical Garden, opened in 1859.[47] Shaw's garden was not picturesque but, following the precepts of the British botanist and landscape designer John Claudius Loudon, it was "gardenesque." The gardenesque was not a style, but "a method of planting and display," which "dictated that plants, shrubs, and trees be treated individually, as specimens."[48]

Clearly, plants were the main attraction in Shaw's botanical garden, but the gardenesque did not preclude the inclusion of follies. Shaw sprinkled decorative summerhouses with exotic bulbous domes and a vaguely Eastern flavor around his botanical garden, many of them two stories in height.[49] Shaw then began plans for a public park, Tower Grove Park, which opened in 1872. In 1871–1873, Shaw's team of gardeners and builders constructed twelve polychromatic pavilions, or "summerhouses" as Shaw called them, including an elaborate folly at the center of a Hemlock labyrinth. But the ultimate folly in terms of shear whimsy was the ruin, constructed out of the remnants of the Lindell Hotel blaze in St. Louis in 1867 (figure 1.4). Touted as the largest hotel in the world, the Lindell Hotel was reduced to rubble in the fire, and Henry Shaw moved a number of the ashlar stones, some of them pleasingly rusticated, to Tower Grove Park, creating a mock ruin by a sailboat pond.[50] At the center, the ruin features a post-and-lintel door frame, a kind of threshold between the pond and the park that lay beyond. The repurposing of the hotel ruin into an artificial arrangement suggests a certain optimism in the future (the hotel was rebuilt). This optimism suggested that even though such a large building could be reduced to rubble, the stones could live on in a pleasant garden setting.

English landscape gardens and the literature surrounding them were the main source of inspiration for Americans designing picturesque gardens. However, the French tradition of the *jardin anglais* or *jardin anglo-chinois* was also influential. Irregular and naturalistic, the *jardin anglo-chinois* emerged out of the rococo *chinoiserie* tradition and developed parallel to English landscape gardens. The "anglo-chinois" moniker both acknowledges the similarity to English designs while also implying that the English borrowed from Chinese traditions.[51] The English architect William Chambers published *Design of Chinese Buildings* in English and French in 1757, and his interpretation of architecture in gardens is especially noteworthy. Chambers wrote that he saw

FIGURE 1.4.   Ruins, looking northeast, from Tower Grove Park, Sailboat Pond, 4255 Arsenal Street, Saint Louis, Independent City, MO. Library of Congress, Prints and Photographs Division, HABS MO,96-SALU,46H—6.

Chinese garden buildings as "toys in architecture" and that their "oddity, prettiness, or neatness of workmanship" admits them into "cabinets of the curious."[52] Many French gardeners took this idea to heart and embraced follies, or *fabriques* as they are called in France, and the little buildings then appeared across the European continent. Associational to a high degree, *fabriques* allowed the garden wanderer to make connections between the fanciful architecture of the garden and historical concepts and exotic places. As Monique Moser explains: "The garden becomes an encyclopaedia [*sic*]; a walk round it is like turning over the pages of the book of the world . . . The garden was no longer merely a succession of pictures; it became at once a cabinet of curiosities and an open-air library, for literary quotations abounded."[53]

Often, French picturesque gardens were on a smaller scale, and buildings took on more prominence than in England.[54] Sometimes *fabriques* were of dazzling size. At François Racine de Monville's aristocratic estate Le Désert de Retz in Chambourcy (1774–1789), the house doubled as a *fabrique* that took the form of a ruined classical column (the *Colonne Détruite* or Broken Column), vastly overscaled, "beyond the bounds of science fiction." Had the column been complete, it would have risen 384 feet in the air.[55] Of course, the Broken Column was the opposite of most *fabriques* in that miniaturization was more common.[56] The jagged roofline and fissured walls of the Broken Column contributed to its regard "as the most extraordinary folly in Europe."[57] Thomas Jefferson visited Désert de Retz with Maria Cosway in 1786 and later mentioned the ruined column in one of his famous "Head and Heart" letters to Cosway. With passion, he exclaimed "How grand the idea excited by the remains of such a column!"[58]

Although Jefferson makes no mention of visiting the Jardin de Monceau, the garden is important for its profusion of *fabriques*. Louis Carrogis, known as Carmontelle (1717–1806), designed the Jardin de Monceau for Louis-Philippe-Joseph d'Orléans, the duc of Chartres (1747–1793), on the outskirts of Paris in 1773. Carmontelle wrote of his desire to design a garden "based on fantasy, . . . the extraordinary, and the amusing, and not on the desire to imitate Nature."[59] The Jardin de Monceau was a precursor to theme parks, "built as an elaborate entertainment facility, a magical place evoking other lands and other periods in history."[60] Carmontelle wanted to create a festive atmosphere in opposition to the theme of melancholic morality more commonly found in English gardens. The painting *Carmontelle Handing the Keys for the Pleasure Grounds at Monceau to the Duc de Chartres* (c. 1775), attributed to Carmontelle, shows us a wonderland of *fabriques* in which artifice crowds out nature (figure 1.5). The garden appears to be a jumbled assortment of fantastic buildings; however, scholars have argued that the buildings refer to Freemasonry, as the duc de Chartres was the Grand Master of the Grand Orient de France, and those "who possess[ed] a key in advance" were able to understand the meaning in the clutter.[61] In this interpretation, the garden ornaments "evoked the great theological empires of world history: Egyptian (e.g., the pyramidal monuments in the Wood of Tombs), Roman (e.g., the Circus or Naumachia and the Temple of Mars), Chinese (e.g., the Chinese Merry-Go-Round), Islamic (the Minaret, the Turkish and Tartar Tents), and Feudal-Christian, that is the age of Clovis and Charlemagne (e.g., the Ruined Castle)."[62]

Although replete with follies, Carmontelle made it clear that Monceau was not an English garden, writing "It was hardly an English garden that one was hoping to create at Monceau, but . . . the uniting in one garden of all times and places. It is a simple fantasy, the desire to have an extraordinary garden, a pure amusement . . . we should bring the changing scenes of opera into our gardens . . ." The theatrical potential for *fabriques* culminated in this enormous stage set, designed by a man who had previously been responsible for the duke's theatrical entertainments.[63]

FIGURE 1.5.   Carmontelle (Louis Carrogis), *Carmontelle (1717–1806) Giving the Keys of the Parc Monceau in Paris to the Duke of Chartres (1747–93)*, oil on canvas. Musée de la Ville de Paris, Musée Carnavalet, Paris, France.

No American garden came close to the hedonistic and folly-crazed Jardin de Monceau. However, the ideas expressed in the *jardin anglo-chinois* held some interest in the nineteenth-century United States, especially in two gardens associated with the French tradition: Le Petit Versailles in Louisiana and Point Breeze in New Jersey. Le Petit Versailles was the plantation and garden estate of Valcour Aime (1798–1860), a wealthy Creole planter in St. James Parish, Louisiana. Built between 1842 and 1853, Le Petit Versailles takes the form of a *jardin anglo-chinois*.[64] Aime remodeled an existing house on the site in the imposing Greek Revival style in 1836 and began transforming the bayou around the house into a landscape garden to "solidify his reputation as a man of exotic tastes."[65] In his journal on September 3, 1841, he noted that he had "prepared the ground for an 'English Park.'"[66] It might seem unusual to name one's irregular "English Park" after Louis XIV's famous formal French garden, but of course contained within the Versailles estate was the Petit Trianon, Marie Antoinette's *jardin anglo-chinois*, a picturesque assemblage of *fabriques*. The name "Le Petit Versailles" acknowledges Aime's French heritage and embraces the French tradition of asymmetry in the *jardin anglo-chinois*.[67] In referencing the French King and Queen's estate, Aime was claiming an aristocratic status; even though Aime acknowledged his garden was *petit*, it was still *Versailles*.

While most English-style gardens followed the topography of the natural landscape, Aime's garden was topographically man-made due to the swampy conditions of the site. In another departure from English precedent, Aime enclosed Le Petit Versailles with garden walls, making it a hybrid of English and French traditions.[68] Given the lack of natural beauty at the site, Aime's undertaking was enormous. On September 15, 1843, he noted that more than 100 people worked on one day on his garden construction, which included building an artificial lake filled with water from the adjacent Mississippi River.[69] Enslaved people contributed greatly to Aime's garden. An entry from his journal on April 27, 1844, provides insight into the Herculean effort required:

> Had the negresses begin to fill in the garden on the 24th, had the pond filled with river water on the 27th. The task of cleaning the ponds requires 18 negroes, one with the pump, the rest with buckets. I filled in for 13 days and I have not finished.[70]

The result of this labor was an elaborate garden, abounding with follies and primed for the extravagant parties of Aime.[71] A visitor, Eliza Ripley (1832–1912), described Le Petit Versailles in 1847, noting the exoticism of the garden and stating that Monsieur Valcour, in a nod to the purported Chinese origin of irregular garden design, could have "received his inspiration in landscape gardening from the queer little Eastern people." She goes on to describe "summer houses draped with strange, foreign-looking vines . . . and a pagoda on a mound." A flight of steps led to this octagonal pagoda which featured stained-glass windows, and "struck [Ripley's] inexperienced eye as a very wonderful and surprising bit of architecture."[72] In addition to the pagoda, the garden featured a stone fort on an island accessible by means of a stone bridge. Named St. Hélène after the island where Napoleon was exiled after Waterloo, the fort even had a cannon. Built into the mound on which the pagoda stood, a cave or ornamental grotto doubled as an icehouse. Aime concocted sham ruins of artificial tree trunks decorated with oyster shells to complete his garden's effect.[73]

Point Breeze, known in the nineteenth century as Bonaparte's Park, was the estate of Joseph Napoleon Bonaparte (1768–1844), former King of Spain and Naples and Napoleon I's older brother. Bonaparte came to the United States after the Battle of Waterloo. Near Bordentown, New Jersey, Bonaparte constructed a picturesque landscape garden inspired by the French gardens of Ermenonville and Mortefontaine.[74] Laid out by the Marquis René-Louis de Girardin in 1763, Ermenonville was a celebrated French garden inspired by the *ferme ornée* tradition. Less like the Jardin de Monceau with its libertine character and theatrical scenery, Ermenonville was more "moral and sentimental."

The tomb of writer Jean-Jacques Rousseau (1712–1778) was located on an island at Ermenonville and became a pilgrimage site for Romantic admirers even after Rousseau was reinterred in the Panthéon in Paris in 1794 at the suggestion of Joseph Bonaparte.[75] Ermenonville also featured *fabriques* such as the ruined Temple of Philosophy. Bonaparte and the Marquis were friends, and Bonaparte admired Rousseau, so it is not surprising that Ermenonville would influence Bonaparte's nearby garden at Mortefontaine, which had already been romanticized by a previous owner when Bonaparte purchased the estate in 1798. At Mortefontaine, Bonaparte added ornamental features including a triumphal arch.[76] Bonaparte lived in exile in Switzerland for a year at Château de Prangins where he also made improvements, until his relocation to the United States in 1815.

At his New Jersey estate, Bonaparte built on a grand scale, creating an artificial lake and numerous garden embellishments.[77] Calling himself the "Count of Survilliers" to remain incognito after his flight from Europe, Bonaparte, like Aime in Louisiana, used Point Breeze as a setting for luxurious parties. One visitor in 1825 described nine courses of delicious food served on solid silver with six waiters at the ready. The visitor took note of European swans gracing the artificial lake and "statues and busts of Parian marble" ornamenting the alcoves in the garden. As one exuberant visitor noted, lining the walls of Bonaparte's impressive house were paintings by "Coregeo [sic]! Titian! Rubens! Vandyke! Vernet! Tenniers [sic] and Paul Potter."[78] In 1824, the Marquis de Lafayette made a visit to the United States and to Point Breeze where Bonaparte "lavishly entertained" him.[79]

An 1847 map of Point Breeze drawn after Bonaparte's death shows the picturesque quality of the grounds with their meandering paths (figure 1.6). At #6, the map indicates the location of a "Belvedere" with site lines from the mansion (#1) to the landscape beyond the garden. Also visible is the range of landscape features: the artificial pond, a sweeping lawn, arable lands, a pine forest, a four-acre garden, and an orchard. The irregular paths take advantage of views of water.[80] According to one nineteenth-century account, "Rustic cots or rain shelters, bowers and seats, sheltered springs and solitary retreats were interspersed [throughout the park]."[81] After Bonaparte's house burned in 1820, leaving only the house's observatory, a visitor recounted the sight of the ruined structure, seemingly intentional as an eye-catcher in the landscape:

> I cannot give you any idea of the romantic beauty of the grounds or even of the tasteful manner in which they were laid out . . . We visited the site of his former château, but every trace of the conflagration had been removed. The only portion of the building left is the observatory,

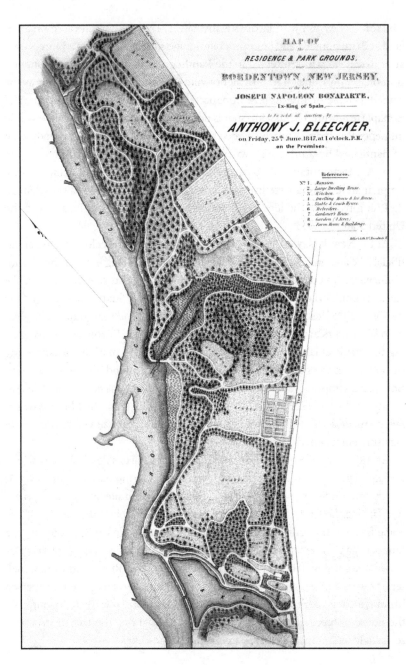

FIGURE 1.6. Map of the residence and park grounds, near Bordentown, New Jersey, of the late Joseph Napoleon Bonaparte, ex-king of Spain. New York: Miller's Lith., 1847. Library of Congress Geography and Map Division, Washington, DC.

which is surrounded by a stone enclosure and looked like a miniature ruin left purposely in this dilapidated state to add to the picturesqueness of the scene. A narrow stream winds itself gracefully through one part of the grounds, over which several rustic bridges are erected. Equally rustic seats are scattered beneath the shade of the tall trees on its banks, and upon its clear surface a block of snow-white swans were floating about.[82]

That the visitor imagined the ruined part of Bonaparte's house as a picturesque garden ornament suggests the ease with which even nonintentional ruins could enter the garden as scenery. It also reminds us of Shaw's later incorporation of fire ruins in Tower Grove Park; in both cases, Bonaparte and Shaw bestow a sense of antiquity by incorporating architectural fragments that have survived the cataclysm of fire as points of melancholy interest, inviting poetic reverie about the vicissitudes of time.

Continental European influences were not confined to Louisiana and New Jersey. In Cincinnati, Adolph Strauch (1822–1883) worked as a landscape designer whose most celebrated accomplishment was Spring Grove Cemetery in Cincinnati.[83] Strauch was born in Prussia, trained in Vienna and Paris, and familiarized himself with gardens in Germany, the Netherlands, Belgium, and England. In his native province of Silesia in Prussia, near the modern-day border between Germany and Poland, Strauch worked for Prince Hermann von Pückler-Muskau (1785–1871), whose picturesque estate, Muskau, encompassed 1,350 acres and featured garden pavilions.[84] Later, at the Botanic Gardens exhibition at the Crystal Palace in London in 1851, Strauch met a Cincinnati businessman named Robert A. Bowler. On a visit to the United States in 1851–1852, Strauch became stranded in Cincinnati when his steamer was late; remembering Bowler, he visited the Cincinnatian and stayed on as Bowler's landscape gardener, improving the grounds at Bowler's estate Mount Storm between 1852 and 1854.[85] Bowler's estate is now Mount Storm Park, and the Temple of Love, possibly designed by Strauch, still stands from the nineteenth century. The design of this circular temple derives from ancient sources—the Greek tholos building type, the Choragic Monument to Lysicrates in Athens, and Temple of Vesta at Tivoli in Italy—as well as a more recent interpretation of these ancient structures: Marie Antoinette's Temple of Love in the Petit Trianon garden at Versailles.[86]

Whether English, French, or German in inspiration, follies fit into a larger context of national ambition in early America and how European taste factored into genteel aspirations. William Hamilton (1745–1813) was a loyalist during the American Revolution and an unabashed Anglophile. Hamilton was arrested in 1778 for the first time, tried for treason and acquitted. He later served jail time after a second arrest.[87] While in London after the Revolution, Hamilton befriended the Adamses, angling for reentry into American society (John Adams was eager to reintegrate Tories into American society).[88] While in England from 1784–1786, Hamilton likely toured English landscape gardens with Whately's book as his guide (he did not record the names of specific gardens, but he visited English counties such as Buckinghamshire, Wiltshire, Oxfordshire, Hertfordshire, and others known for their gardens).[89] He wrote to a friend that "the verdure of England is its greatest Beauty & my endeavors shall not be wanting to give the Woodlands [his American house] some resemblance to it."[90]

Hamilton could not afford to live on a grand scale in England, so, in historian Catherine E. Kelly's words, he "set about creating an Anglicized country estate in the belly of the republican beast [Philadelphia]."[91] There Hamilton transformed an existing structure (c. 1770) into an up-to-date neoclassical house (1786–1789) with a prominent temple front, creating one of the most fashionable high-style residences in Philadelphia.[92] The landscape around the house was integral to the impressive quality of the ensemble: located on a rise above a bend in the Schuylkill River, The Woodlands was visible to all who traversed the river by boat or ferry. At his country seat, Hamilton created a landscape circuit for guests. Led from the portico into the garden, one visitor described a "large verdant lawn surrounded by a belt of a walk."[93] With shrewd pruning of vegetation, Hamilton opened up prospects and created arbors of shade and respite. Statues, busts, urns, and seats adorned the landscape. Along a natural walk by the river, by "a charming spring," Hamilton planned a grotto lined with shells. His greenhouse terminated the walk.[94] Hamilton's use of a ha-ha ensured that vistas connecting the house, garden, and larger river landscape would remain unbroken.[95]

While Jefferson's garden existed to an extent in his mind's eye and on paper, Hamilton brought to realization "America's first large-scale garden in the English style," a feat that "testified both to the pervasive Anglo-American investment of gardens as badges of gentility."[96] On his return to Philadelphia, Hamilton used his estate as an entrée into genteel society, above the fray of politics. He deferentially corresponded with Washington and Jefferson and liberally sent them seeds from his greenhouse.[97] Jefferson asked Hamilton for advice for his landscape garden at Monticello. Acknowledging the predominance of The Woodlands, Jefferson wrote that "The Woodlands [was] the only rival which I have known in America to what may be seen in England." According to Jefferson, it was to The Woodlands that Americans "are to go for models in this art."[98]

Meanwhile, The Woodlands became symbolic of what the young United States could achieve in the cultural arena of art and architecture. William Birch included a print of The Woodlands in his book *Country Seats of the United States* (1808–1809), solidifying the house's place in American visual culture. About the tradition of country houses, Birch praised such estates as forming "the National character favourable to the civilization of this young country, and establish[ing] that respectability which will add to its strength."[99] But, Kelly argues, Hamilton created a distinctly *English* estate, a "rebuke" to those patriots who had threatened him and his family during the Revolution. Paradoxically, observers such as Birch and Jefferson saw The Woodlands as "an *American* triumph, as a product of American independence."[100] This "deeply contradictory" state of affairs allowed an English importation (the country house and picturesque landscape garden represented by The Woodlands) to proliferate in print form during the early republic as a symbol of American elites' nationalist aspirations.[101]

Not everyone was so eager to adopt the English tradition of landscape gardens. In his comments on the tour of English gardens, Adams commented more on the overall idea of landscape gardens rather than the specific design features that so captivated Jefferson. Adams hoped that the gardens would not become popular in his native country:

> It will be long, I hope, before ridings, parks, pleasure grounds, gardens, and ornamented farms, grow so much in fashion in America; but nature has done greater things and furnished nobler materials there; the oceans, islands, rivers, mountains, valley, are all laid out upon a larger scale.[102]

Adams appreciated the natural beauty of the United States, and he did not embrace the artificiality and ostentation of English gardens. Adams's response is prophetic of the nineteenth-century celebration of American landscape as exceptional. While American gardens did not rival their English counterparts in scale or grandiosity, Americans did aspire to European standards, and the building of temples, towers, summerhouses, and ruins were important in the shaping of American cultural identity.[103] And, as this book will show, it was not just elites who craved the legitimacy a garden could bring. In the nineteenth century, everyone from middle-class farmers to urban workers participated in the folly experience, which was not merely recreational and amusing, but also didactic and enlightening.

CHAPTER 2

Temples
Neoclassicism and the Nation

As legend had it, Thomas Jefferson read the Declaration of Independence on July 8, 1776, to a small group of enthralled listeners at the temple summerhouse of the Edwards-Womrath estate (Dr. Enoch Edwards's house in Frankford near Philadelphia). Early twentieth-century newspapers tell us that members of the Continental Congress occasionally visited the Edwards-Womrath estate, although there was no hard historical evidence that these visits actually occurred.[1] In the nineteenth century, photographer Robert Newell had perpetuated this Fourth of July myth in his collection *Old Landmarks and Relics of Philadelphia*. Newell included a photograph of the summerhouse (c. 1870) in a compilation of photographs likely distributed during the Philadelphia Centennial celebration in 1876, complete with a caption detailing the Jefferson connection (figure 2.1).[2] Hence, this small building took on important cultural meaning, as the potential location of the first Independence Day celebration.[3] Awkward as it may be with its ridiculously oversized balustrade and roof, the little building's architecture reminds us of Jefferson's home Monticello near Charlottesville, Virginia, with its gleaming neoclassicism and white columns. Even the railing at the summerhouse echoes the *chinoiserie* decoration at Monticello. With these patriotic associations, a seemingly insignificant building becomes central to the nation's birth. The commemorative buildings of the early United States that most immediately

FIGURE 2.1.   Womrath Pavilion. Robert Newell. *Philadelphia Photographs* (album). "House and grounds where the 1st '4th of July' was celebrated.'" Enoch Edwards' property, c. 1870. P9062.53b. The Library Company of Philadelphia.

come to mind are on a much larger scale: for instance, the Washington Monument in Washington, DC (designed by Robert Mills, 1836; completed by Thomas L. Casey, 1885). However, smaller buildings also contain significant cultural information. Through their style and details, these garden structures highlight the iconography of the new nation and sometimes even relate fictional stories, contributing to the mythmaking of the United States.

Temples took their place in the garden alongside a variety of other garden structures in different styles and building types, including at Thomas Jefferson's Monticello. According to playwright William Dunlap, a visitor to Monticello, Jefferson professed in dinner conversation a partiality for English gardens over the formal French style.[4] Temples appeared in the landscape plan Jefferson designed circa 1776 but never executed at Monticello. For instance, Jefferson designed a Tuscan monopteros or round temple around 1804 (unexecuted).[5] Also significant is James Madison's temple covering an icehouse at Montpelier (figure 2.2). Inspired by the monopteros building type, Jefferson may have had some influence in the Montpelier design.[6] Although the ultimate source is

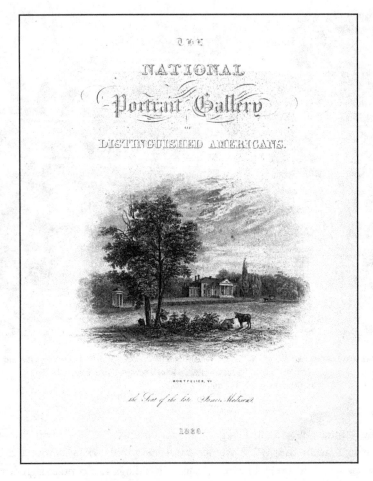

FIGURE 2.2.   "Montpelier, VA: Seat of the Late James Madison." James Herring, *The National Portrait Gallery of Distinguished Americans*, vol. III, 1836. James B. Longacre and James Herring. Frontispiece, RBR E176.N27. Courtesy of the Winterthur Library's Printed Book and Periodical Collection.

ancient, antiquity is filtered through eighteenth-century picturesque thought, evidenced by the fact that James Madison's icehouse resembles the rotunda in the Elysian fields at Stowe, an important eighteenth-century English landscape garden.

To understand the symbolism of American neoclassicism, it is useful to examine a later example, the "Temple of Confederation," an ink and watercolor drawing by nineteenth-century architect Alexander Jackson Davis (1803–1892), of a classicized gazebo erected on Newark Common on the Fourth of July in 1826 (figure 2.3). This temple was erected on the fiftieth anniversary of the

FIGURE 2.3.   Alexander Jackson Davis, *Temple of Confederation*, ink and watercolor drawing, 1826. Collection 114 71×8. Courtesy of the Winterthur Library's Joseph Downs Collection of Manuscripts and Printed Ephemera.

Declaration of Independence, coincidentally the day of Jefferson's death. In a pamphlet describing the Jubilee, the meaning of the temple was explained:

> The following is the allegory intended by the temple. The centre standard, which is first erected, represents the standard of Liberty, around which our Countrymen rallied in the early part of the revolution: The *fleur-de-lis*, the declaration of Independence: The thirteen columns and arches, the original states; and the names inscribed upon the columns, their representatives at the time our Independence was declared. Each

arch represents a state; and the raising of the temple by the patriots of '76, the act of confederation: The transparent letters forming the word Confederation, the effect of their confederation: The whole temple, the confederacy: The vane, that fame which was consequent on the declaration of Independence and the Confederation: The plane upon which it is built, that equality upon which the government was originally based; and the evergreens with which the temple is adorned, the perpetuity of that government.[7]

The temple has thirteen columns, representing the original thirteen colonies, and the names of signers of the Declaration of Independence and Revolutionary War heroes are inscribed on the structure.[8] Clearly, patriotic Americans embedded a great deal of cultural significance into this plaything of a structure.

This use of patriotic iconography began well before the Jubilee. For the Fourth of July in 1790, the celebration at Gray's Garden near Philadelphia included a "Federal Temple" ornamented with a vault of twelve stones, "representing the Federal Union—the keystone now completed by the accession of Rhode Island." Thirteen shepherdesses and thirteen shepherds proceeded to the temple, which became the dramatic backdrop for "an ode to Liberty."[9] At a New York pleasure garden, "Vauxhall," garden structures again became a vehicle for patriotic expression when "The 16 summer houses being the names of the sixteen United States, each were decorated with the Emblematical Colours belonging to each State, and ornamented with Flowers and Garlands" for a Fourth of July celebration in 1799.[10]

The house and garden of early American orator and lawyer William Paca (1740–1799) in Annapolis, Maryland (1763–1765), also makes an iconographical statement.[11] Fortunately for posterity, the painter Charles Willson Peale captured Paca's garden in a full-length portrait of Paca in 1772 (figure 2.4). The portrait's visual evidence and archeological excavations at the site led Historic Annapolis researchers to reconstruct the garden and its summerhouse and Chinese bridge in the 1970s.[12] As art historian Joseph Manca has argued, the Paca portrait presents iconography that positions Paca between competing passions in the life of a prominent figure in eighteenth-century American life, that of civic engagement and its contrast, genteel retreat. According to Manca, the bust of Cicero to the left of Paca in the portrait represents the "tumult of politics" and the Roman civic duty of participation in public life, while the garden signifies the "private satisfaction" of removing oneself from the public sphere and indulging in the pleasures of the garden.[13] Atop the summerhouse Peale painted a statue of Mercury, although Manca concludes that

FIGURE 2.4. *William Paca* (1740–1799). Charles Willson Peale (1741–1827). Oil on canvas, 1772. MSA SC 4680-10-0083. Collection of the Maryland State Archives.

neither the Cicero bust nor the Mercury statue likely existed in Paca's garden, only in the painted world Peale creates with his brushes and palette. Peale inserted the ancient references to Cicero and Mercury for iconographical reasons.[14] Mercury was a symbol of both commerce and more significantly in this instance, eloquence; the latter connotation links the summerhouse to the foreground of the painting where the bust of Cicero gazes in the direction of the painting's patron who commandingly glances in another direction. Mercury's inclusion and the Roman god's association with eloquence highlights both Cicero's fame as "a well-spoken defender of rights and political liberty" and Paca's own reputation and life's work as an orator.[15] Another statue of Mercury graced an altogether different temple in the garden of the Fairmount Waterworks in Philadelphia (figure 2.5). Constructed in the aftermath of the deadly yellow fever epidemic of the 1790s in Philadelphia, the Waterworks (1812–1815), designed by Frederick Graff (1775–1847), was a must-see tourist destination in the nineteenth century for anyone interested in technological wonderment. The engine house resembled a Federal-style country house, but instead of halls and parlors inside, visitors encountered the machinery of the Waterworks.[16] Like a country house, the Waterworks featured gardens from which visitors observed views of Philadelphia's actual villas on the Schuylkill River. Machines and gardens coexisted comfortably at the site, and those interested in promenading and leisurely recreation enjoyed the South Garden and Cliffside Walk. In 1825, a visitor named John P. Sheldon wrote to this wife that he discovered in the vicinity of the waterworks, "Delightful seats, surrounded by various kinds of trees and shrubbery, with gardens containing summer houses, vistas, embowered walks, etc."[17] Graff's little neoclassical temples provided visitors with respite and a view.[18] In figure 2.5, we see a temple with the

FIGURE 2.5.   J. T. Bowen [A View of the Fairmount Water-Works with Schuylkill in the Distance. Taken from the Mount.]. Philadelphia: [J. T. Bowen], 1838. 3.04a. **W8 [p. 2004]. The Library Company of Philadelphia.

figure of Mercury crowning its summit in the foreground, and another temple with an eagle atop, closer to the river.

The Philadelphia sculptor William Rush (1756–1833) carved Mercury in 1829, and Rush's son John carved the eagle in 1835. The sculptors infused these architectural ornaments with nationalistic iconography appropriate to a site that showed off the technological innovations of the new nation. These sculptures were part of a larger program of allegorical figures in the neoclassical style throughout the Waterworks. Why Mercury? Art historian Arthur S. Marks argues that the allegorical sculptures that appeared above the doorways to the millhouse relate to the Prometheus myth.[19] In that story, Mercury chained the Titan Prometheus to the mountain for his daily punishment by the eagle. But Mercury had other reasons for appearing at the Waterworks. According to Marks:

> He was, for example, a god of commerce and merchants; hence the purse or documents he holds. As the winged messenger to the gods, he was linked with travel and traffic of the sort seen daily before him. Resonating with Prometheus' role as the bestower of civilization and the restorer of arts, Mercury was also said to be the 'inventor' of medicine, letters, music, and 'several other Arts' . . . . And, finally, if the extended scene spread before him was one of tempered Arcadian harmony and serenity . . . that prevailing mood, too, was Mercury's responsibility . . . through the inclusion of Mercury Rush was able to bring still greater fullness to the Fairmount sculptural program.[20]

Rush presents Mercury fully clothed and in a walking stance, like the ship figureheads Rush had carved earlier in his career.[21] John Rush's carved eagle served as both a symbol of the nation and a reinforcement of the Prometheus theme, according to Marks.[22]

That the Waterworks became emblematic of the progress of the young United States is obvious when reading an account by an Englishman who wrote about his visit to Philadelphia in *Men and Manners in America* (1833). Thomas Hamilton complained that Philadelphians asked him "a dozen times a day" whether he had been to the Waterworks. When he said no, people told him he "positively must visit them; that they were unrivalled in the world; that no people but the Americans could have executed such works, and by implication, that no one but an Englishman, meanly jealous of American superiority, would omit an opportunity of admiring their unrivalled mechanism."[23] Annoyed by this attitude, Hamilton resolved to omit the Waterworks from his travel plans. The statue of Mercury and the eagle encouraged the prideful opinions of Philadelphia's citizens. Although the little temples were minor structures in the larger scheme of the Waterworks complex, they played an important role in the neoclassical iconography of the site while providing an overview of both the spectacular scenery and feats of engineering. The temples enhanced visitors' experiences and directed their view to points of interest.

In addition to their iconographical purposes, temples often functioned as retreats from the world. Jefferson designed more than twenty garden structures for the Monticello landscape, only one of which—a neo-Palladian summerhouse—was actually constructed (and has been recreated).[24] The solitary occupation of reading was Jefferson's chief pastime while inhabiting this summerhouse.[25] Jefferson's friend Charles Willson Peale built a Chinese summerhouse, of which no images survive, at Belfield, the *ferme ornée* he created in Germantown, Pennsylvania, when he retired to farm life at age 69 in 1810.[26] Peale dedicated this structure to meditation and inscribed within it instructions for meditating "on the Creation of worlds," and the variety, number, diversity, beauty, and delicacy of earth's animals. He continued, "then let me ask myself, why am I here? am I blessed with more profound reason than other Animals, if so, Lett [*sic*] me be thankful: let me meditate on the past, on the present and on the future."[27] At Nazareth Hall Garden in Nazareth, Pennsylvania, a watercolor in the Winterthur collection shows the pleasure grounds of this Moravian boys school, complete with a summerhouse which proclaims in large lettering "Sacred to MEDITATION." Despite the serious purpose of the summerhouse, the school's pupils subverted its intended design. James Henry, the author of *Sketches of Moravian Life and Character* (1859), states that in the early nineteenth century, this summerhouse "was always occupied by some congenial conclave, discoursing on themes that most interested the youthful imagination, in the full play of boyish fancy and frivolity."[28] In contrast, there is little doubt that Jefferson and Peale took their summerhouse meditation more seriously. What did Jefferson read in his neo-Palladian temple? Whatever it was, it was probably morally instructive. In 1771, Jefferson wrote "The entertainments of fiction are useful as well as pleasant. That they are pleasant when well written every person feels who reads. But wherein is its utility, asks the reverend sage? I answer, everything is useful which contributes to fix in the principles and practices of virtue."[29]

Indeed, teaching virtue becomes one of the primary uses of architectural follies in the didactic landscapes of the early republic. At Belfield, Peale engaged in agricultural pursuits and landscape design (figure 2.6). Jefferson and Peale corresponded about their shared enthusiasm for gardening; in 1812, Peale wrote to Jefferson, "Your garden must be a museum to you."[30] In 1784, Peale had opened an art museum featuring his portraits of Revolutionary War era figures in his Philadelphia home; the museum expanded to include

FIGURE 2.6.   Charles Willson Peale, *Belfield Garden*, 1816. Oil on canvas, 28 × 26 ¼ in. (71.1 × 66.7 cm). Philadelphia Museum of Art, promised gift of the McNeil Americana Collection, x-8282.

natural history exhibits and moved to the American Philosophical Society in Philadelphia in 1794 and to the second floor of Independence Hall in 1802. According to Peale, the museum's purpose was "to instruct the mind and sow the seeds of Virtue."[31]

Belfield, like Peale's Museum, was didactic. Peale was explicit on this point: "I am . . . occupied . . . sometimes to the beautifying of my Garden with ornimental [sic] Objects to give moral instruction."[32] On the obelisk that he created "to terminate a Walk in the Garden," he inscribed mottoes such as "Never return an injury, It is a noble Triumph to overcome Evil by Good," and "Neglect no Duty."[33] These inducements to virtue are common among garden ornaments in nineteenth-century America, providing a narrative of morality. In the garden, Peale also placed a pedestal at the termination of another walk, and on it, he inscribed "ninety memorable events of North America with their dates, beginning [sic] with the first discoveries of North America and ending with the battle of New Orleans."[34] On July 31, 1819, he wrote in a letter that his pedestal was nearly finished, but that he had reserved space for a line "to commemorate that America sent the first Ship across the Ocean by Means of Steam." This is a reference to the first steam-powered transatlantic passage in 1819 by the ship *Savannah*.[35] Hence, Peale celebrated the mechanical prowess of the new nation—a clear example of American nationalism, not in the arts, but in the engineering sciences.

Is there a nationalistic impulse in the choice of neoclassicism in the early republic? Certainly, the round temple is a popular form for landscape structures in the early republic, as we saw at Monticello and James Madison's Montpelier. Peale described his Belfield temple in a letter in 1813 as "an Elligant Summer House on that commanding spot. . . . It is a hexicon [*sic*] base with 6 well turned pillars supporting a circular Top & dome on which is placed a bust of Genl. Washington."[36] Peale then noted that thirteen pillars would have been more appropriate. There are obvious connections here between the symbolism of the classical temple form with its links to the ideals of democratic republicanism and nationalist zeal as represented by the bust of Washington. The bust reflects the larger cult of Washington that flourished after his death in 1799. Art historian Julia Sienkewicz suggests that a visitor standing inside the temple "would occupy a position inside this nation, and in direct lineage with Washington." Situated at the highest point in the garden, the temple provided the spectator with a panorama of the landscape and offered "a miniaturized crystallization of the nation beyond."[37]

To understand the iconography of Peale's Belfield temple, it is useful to examine his earlier artistic use of the round temple form in the 1780s. By 1781, Peale had established himself as the leading Philadelphia painter; Peale knew well the power of images as ideological tools to influence viewers, and he contributed to the political spectacles of the Revolutionary War era.[38] In 1781, Peale celebrated the arrival of General George Washington in Philadelphia by festooning his house with backlit transparencies, "pieces of paper or canvas" decorated with forms drawn with "ink or thin paints" with a wax and turpentine coating.[39] The purpose of these transparencies was to encourage Congress to provide salaries for the army. An in-depth description of Peale's efforts appeared in the *Pennsylvania Packet* on December 4, 1781. In front of one of the home's windows, Peale displayed a transparency of the "Temple of Independence," a two-dimensional structure with clear iconographical meaning. Peale inscribed words onto his temple, including the "first cause" of American outrage at British control ("STAMP-ACT, DUTIES ON TEA, & BOSTON PORT-BILL"). For the foundation of the temple, Peale included a list of battles, and on the first story Peale wrote "BY THE VOICE OF THE PEOPLE." The Ionic temple showcased thirteen columns, representing the states. The frieze celebrated "ILLUSTRIOUS SENATORS" while the temple's pediment featured the words "BRAVE SOLDIERY." Statues of Justice, Hope, and Industry, complete with their attributes, ornamented the pediment. The Corinthian second story contained "statues in niches," with the words "HEROES FALLEN IN BATTLE," while the attic story exhibited statues of Agriculture, the Arts, Sculpture, Architecture, and Commerce. The building's dome featured a statue of Fame. The spectacle of this transparency and the others decorating Peale's house foreshadows Peale's future as founder of his Philadelphia Museum and his showman's instincts for display.[40]

Peale's transparent temple becomes the prototype for a three-dimensional temple constructed for Philadelphia's Grand Federal Procession on the Fourth of July in 1788.[41] This parade celebrated the ratification of the US Constitution and was saturated with iconographical significance. For the event, Peale designed a round temple known as the "Grand Federal Edifice" or "New Roof" (the latter title referring to an anti-Federalist satire by the organizer of the parade, Francis Hopkinson, who had published the essay in the *Pennsylvania Packet* on December 29, 1787). Placed "on a carriage drawn by ten white horses," Peale's Corinthian temple—ten feet in diameter, eleven feet high— was the last and most complex float in the parade. Peale decorated the temple's frieze with thirteen stars but completed only ten of the columns, leaving three unfinished to represent the states that had yet to ratify the Constitution.[42] The words "In union the fabric stands firm" decorated the pedestal. Inside the temple, ten men representing "the citizens at large" sat in chairs; at the end of the parade, these men "gave up their seats to the representatives of the states . . . who entered the temple and hung their flags on the Corinthian columns to which they respectively belonged." This last theatrical flourish brought the abstract concept of representative government into full display for the spectators.[43]

The parade ended at Bush Hill, the country estate established by Andrew Hamilton (1676–1741) and expanded by his son James in the eighteenth century.[44] Named "Union Green" for the day, the lawn in front of Bush Hill hosted an estimated seventeen thousand people for speeches and a dinner. Planted on the Union Green for the Republican celebration, Peale's Grand Federal Edifice must have resembled a temple folly, if only for an afternoon. The temple gave the spectators something to look at, but also provided a view, "a wide field of vision," to use art historian Elizabeth Milroy's phrase. This field of vision encompassed the whole of the country as well as the specific view available from Bush Hill of other estates owned by prominent Philadelphians.[45] Milroy writes "At Union Green, the Bush Hill lawn symbolized the larger national territory."[46] At the end of the festivities, the temple returned "in great triumph" to the statehouse on Chestnut Street.[47]

A building type invented by the Romans, revived during the Italian Renaissance, and repurposed by Americans in the age of Palladianism, the domed round temple had specific ideological significance in eighteenth-century and early nineteenth-century America. Peale used the round temple form as a vehicle to express the iconography of the emerging nation. By building a temple dedicated to George Washington in his didactic garden at Belfield, Peale was emphasizing the links between architecture and nationalism. As Sienkewicz has argued, Peale's garden and his museum served the same purpose in Peale's mind. Like his museum, Peale opened Belfield to the public, and the garden's "overt iconography" combined "national history" and individual "moral and philosophical integrity."[48] Peale hoped that his garden would "build a new breed of rationally-thinking, civic-minded citizens."[49]

Neoclassical garden temples did not signify rational Enlightenment thinking in all cultural productions of the period, however. The battle between Enlightenment rationality and Gothic superstition finds a full explication in Charles Brockden Brown's early American novel *Wieland* (1798), which features a neoclassical temple folly at the center of the story.[50] The narrator Clara begins with her father Wieland's emigration to America from the Old World with a missionary desire to convert Native Americans. Although his attempts at this are unsuccessful, his civilizing impulse also extends to the landscape. The elder Wieland builds a summerhouse shaped like a classical temple on his estate Mettingen on the Schuylkill River outside of Philadelphia.[51] Clara calls this "the temple of his Deity," to which he retired alone twice daily for his devotions.[52] She describes the temple thus:

> At the distance of three hundred yards from his house, on the top of a rock whose sides were steep, rugged, and encumbered with dwarf cedars and stony asperities, he built what to a common eye would have seemed a summerhouse. The eastern verge of this precipice was sixty feet above the river which flowed at its foot. The view before it consisted of a transparent current, fluctuating and rippling in a rocky channel, and bounded by a rising scene of cornfields and orchards. The edifice was slight and airy. It was not more than a circular area, twelve feet in diameter, whose flooring was the rock, cleared of moss and shrubs, and exactly levelled, edged by twelve Tuscan columns, and covered by an undulating dome.[53]

Wieland furnished his temple with no objects, "without seat, table, or ornament of any kind."[54] Wieland's temple then is unlike most follies in that it was not a place of recreation or leisure but a solitary devotional site. We learn that the temple was within view from at least two windows in the main house at Mettingen, as Wieland's wife and her brother are able to view the temple from their chamber windows, and so its siting was standard for summerhouse design. The temple combined three aesthetic categories: the pastoral, represented by meadow between the house and the temple; the picturesque, represented by the approach up a flight of irregular stairs; and the sublime, represented by the precipice sixty feet above the river.[55]

Scholars have suggested the visual sources for this temple were engravings of the paintings of the seventeenth-century French landscape painter Claude Lorrain. Brown was familiar with Claude's work and even composed a poem "Devotion" (1794) that is a literary translation of a Claudian landscape.[56] Prints of Claude's preparatory drawings were available to Brown in the United States in *Liber Veritatis*, Richard Earlom's collection of engravings. Larry Kutchen suggests that Claude presents a mixture of styles, including the pastoral and the picturesque, the latter "tending toward the sublime." Kutchen illustrates Claude's painting *Imaginary View from Tivoli* (1642) as a potential source for Brown; the painting features an uneven landscape with a bridge leading to the foot of a rocky hill crowned with a round temple based on ancient Roman precedent.[57] Clara's description of Wieland's temple resembles Claude's vision in the placement of the round temple on a stony promontory overlooking a river.

Mediating between the picturesque and the sublime in Brown's novel is the classical temple itself. Rational and proportional, neoclassical temples usually signaled stability; however, Wieland's temple turned out to be anything but orderly. After building the temple, Wieland becomes increasingly agitated about his own impending doom, and one evening at dusk he hurriedly makes his way to "the Rock," as it is often called in the novel. Concerned about her husband's disordered state of mind, Wieland's wife tries in vain to see the temple from her bedroom window in the dusky atmosphere. Here Brown employs the Burkean sublime quality of obscurity to layer mystery upon the unfolding scene. She sees a light illuminating the edifice accompanied by the sound of an explosion. The elder Wieland dies from injuries sustained in the blast, seemingly an act of spontaneous combustion. Inexplicably, the temple remains unharmed despite the "fiery cloud" and its construction of "combustible materials."[58] The neoclassical temple had become a site of gothic horror.[59]

When Wieland's children Theodore and Clara become adults, they return to Mettingen and reclaim the temple as a true summerhouse, decorating it with a bust of Cicero (particularly venerated by Theodore Wieland) and enlivened by a harpsichord. "This was the place of resort in the evenings of summer. Here we sung, and talked, and read, and occasionally banqueted," Clara tells us.[60] The temple becomes the site of the Wieland children's education. With this repossession, the formerly awesome and mysterious temple becomes

a source of didacticism and Enlightenment culture, in line with its neoclassical style, a "rationalist's paradise," in Jane Tompkins's words.[61] Despite this
whitewash of the gothicized temple, the structure still reminds the younger
Wieland of his father's demise.[62]

Unfortunately, Theodore and Clara Wieland are unable to tame the little
temple with their genteel activities, and soon enough, Theodore hears a voice
he believes to be his wife's, telling him to stop as he approaches the temple.
This, the reader later learns, is a performance of ventriloquism, that madden-
ing act of disorientation perpetrated by the intruder at Mettingen, Francis Carwin. Carwin's ventriloquism often takes place in and around the temple folly.
The Wielands begin to question their own sensory perception, ultimately leading to Theodore Wieland's awful murder of his family at the end of the novel.
The neoclassical temple fails then to tame the wilderness of both the landscape and the demented mind of the patriarch, despite Theodore's classical
training and love of Cicero.

Wieland warns the reader that the civilizing impulse of embedding seemingly rational, neoclassical structures in an otherwise wild and sublime North
American landscape can lead to catastrophe. As Jennifer Harris argues,
"Brown's construction of a potentially hostile and haunted landscape, rather
than a triumphant site of Revolutionary struggle and nationhood or the terrain of an idealized agrarian farmer-subject, resonates with gothic elements."[63]
Thus Brown's novel reminds us that contemporaries did not always view neoclassical temples in the same way Peale did, with his hyperrational temple dedicated to George Washington in his didactic garden. In the nineteenth century,
a favorite theme for landscape painters were scenes of ruined classical temples,
another way in which solid classical edifices succumb to Romanticism's world
of imaginative possibility.

Still, to be sure, temple summerhouses played a role in national mythmaking; a case in point is the summerhouse at George Washington's home Mount
Vernon. Prominently situated on the Potomac River with views of both the
water and the colonnade of the house, this summerhouse became the locus
for fictional stories relating to General Washington (figure 2.7). The word
"fictional" is appropriate to use because the building was not in existence in
Washington's day, even though, as we shall see, nineteenth-century writers
and artists depicted the General at the summerhouse. It was actually built
above an icehouse by Washington's nephew Bushrod Washington in the nineteenth century. In his book *Mary and Martha: The Mother and the Wife of George
Washington* (1886), historian Benson Lossing presumably fabricated a letter
from Martha Washington, describing her husband's dream in which Washington imagined that an angel appeared in the Mount Vernon summerhouse.

FIGURE 2.7.   Summerhouse at Mount Vernon. Benson J. Lossing, *Mary and Martha, the Mother and the Wife of George Washington*, New York: Harper & Bros., 1886. RB 473413. The Huntington Library, San Marino, CA.

The angel whispered in Mrs. Washington's ear, and Martha slowly vanished from his sight. According to Lossing, Washington interpreted this dream as a premonition of his own impending death.[64] That this supernatural event takes place not in Mount Vernon itself but in the summerhouse highlights the importance of the structure in stories about the General circulating in nineteenth-century America. Like many sites associated with the founders, this summerhouse became a commemorative space with legends attached.

Lossing was not the only Washington acolyte drawn to the summerhouse. Indeed, this summerhouse at Mount Vernon received a fair amount of attention in the nineteenth century. We see the little building in the distance at Mount Vernon in a painting entitled *Washington and Lafayette at Mount Vernon, 1784 (The Home of Washington after the War)* painted by the American artists Thomas Rossiter (who was responsible for the figures) and Louis Rémy Mignot (who was responsible for the landscape) in 1859. In the foreground of this genre painting, under the famous Mount Vernon piazza, we see Washington and Lafayette among members of the household enjoying the calm of late afternoon. Rossiter made the point that Mignot studied the landscape closely and asked questions of older folks still in residence at Mount Vernon to ensure accuracy. According to Rossiter, Mignot's purpose was to make sure "that the topographical features are delineated as far as possible to accord with the date of the picture, and the house restored to the condition which it must have possessed."[65] Rossiter's assertion is, of course, anachronistic since the summerhouse did not exist in Washington's day. Rossiter continued his myth-making with his later painting *Palmy Days at Mount Vernon* (1866) (figure 2.8). Rossiter had made a visit to Mount Vernon and wrote about his experience in his book *Description of the Picture of the Home of Washington After the War Painted by T. P. Rossiter and L. R. Mignot* (1859).[66] In this painting, we see Washington, Patrick Henry, Alexander Hamilton, James Madison, and Washington family members including Martha Washington. Truly, the summerhouse functions as an outdoor parlor, complete with parlor activities, and an attentive slave in the margin.[67] The vines around the neoclassical column of the summerhouse remind us that the little building, although replete with the comforts of the parlor, is still part of nature. This scene could never have actually taken place in this location because it was built after Washington's death. Like Lossing, Rossiter overlaps his own constructed narrative onto the Mount Vernon landscape.

In the 1850s, visitors to John Bartram's Garden in Philadelphia encountered similar stories about Washington. John Bartram (1699–1777) had established a botanic garden on the site circa 1728; after his death, his sons took over the

FIGURE 2.8. Thomas Prichard Rossiter, *Palmy Days at Mount Vernon*, 1866. [M-4970]. Courtesy of the Mount Vernon Ladies' Association.

business. A number of important historical figures visited Bartram's Garden, including members of the Constitutional Convention in 1787. George Washington and Thomas Jefferson made visits in 1787 and 1783, respectively.[68] Later, one of Bartram's descendants, William Middleton Bartram (1838–1916), drew a plan of the garden as he remembered it from his childhood (the plan dates to c. 1890–1900 but reflects the garden's layout between 1840 and 1850). Bartram noted the location along the garden's southern edge of three summerhouses, clearly marked on the plan.[69] A visitor to the garden in 1852 described the "walks, and seats and arbors, which everywhere abound."[70] One particular arbor attracted attention as the supposed resort of George Washington. In 1850, a writer in *The Horticulturist* related an anecdote, passed down by Bartram descendants, that Washington, "a frequent visitor at the garden," would often sit in a "sort of arbor" with his friends as a respite from the cares of war or governmental debates in Philadelphia. The author romantically imagines that perhaps "many a secret march and sudden surprise was determined upon amid these sylvan shades." In full narrative mode, the author then asserts that both Franklin and Jefferson met with Washington under this very arbor at Bartram's Garden to "discuss the affairs of the infant republic."[71] By 1853, the garden spot (perhaps the same one or another shady arbor, either man-made or natural) had become known as "Washington Arbor," where not only Washington and Franklin met, but also "William Bartram [John Bartram's son] breathed his last" in 1823.[72] Clearly, tourists visiting sites relating to the era of the nation's founding hallowed the spots with Romanticized notions of nationalism.

These garden structures functioned as associationist architecture, raising their importance from architectural follies to sacred meeting spaces of the founding fathers, in much the same way the Womrath summerhouse came to embody Independence Day. By the time of the nation's centennial celebration in 1876, the Womrath summerhouse had taken on a commemorative role, albeit fictional, in the history of the United States.[73] Likewise, the round temples that appeared in private gardens and on display in public Fourth of July celebrations contributed to the emerging iconography of the new nation, legitimizing the young United States with classical allusions. Although temples generally embodied order and stability, Charles Brockden Brown subverted the usual interpretation of neoclassical architecture. In Brown's novel, the events at Wieland's temple suggest the Gothic anxieties of the new nation, presenting an alternative narrative to Jefferson and Peale's. Although overlooked in scholarship to date, these little temples reveal the complexity of classical iconography in the early republic.

CHAPTER 3

Summerhouses
Nature Meets Culture

In 1774, Thomas Jefferson purchased a scenic site in the Shenandoah Valley, the "Natural Bridge," a place the Reverend Andrew Burnaby described in 1759 as "a natural arch or bridge, joining two high mountains, with a considerable river running underneath."[1] Jefferson wrote in 1786 that he was considering building for himself a "hermitage" at Natural Bridge but never actually did.[2] He also considered calling Monticello "Hermitage," a name that emphasizes the house's purpose as a rural retreat. According to Edward S. Harwood, style did not define the hermitage building type, which could range from "a ruined gothic castle to a cave, and from a primitive hut to a rustic Pantheon." Use of any structure as a rural escape from the cares of the world was the defining characteristic of the hermitage. Harwood uses Jefferson's homes Monticello and Poplar Forest, as well as Andrew Jackson's Hermitage near Nashville, Tennessee, as examples of buildings defined as hermitages by their use as retreats rather than by their styles, which are all neoclassical.[3] However, in nineteenth-century garden design, rather than country house design, most so-called hermitages in the United States were in the rustic style. Although Jefferson never planned any rustic summerhouses at Monticello, he did appreciate the style. In 1788, Jefferson paid a visit to Wilhelmsbad, Hanau, Germany, where he admired a rustic garden ornament, "a centry box . . . covered in bark so as to look exactly like the trunk of an old tree," which he calls a "good idea . . . of much avail in a garden." In the same garden, Jefferson also appreciated the theatrical installation of a hermit. He wrote "There is a hermitage in which is a good figure of a hermit in plaister [*sic*], coloured to the life, with a table and book before him, in the attitude of reading and contemplation."[4] Such hermitages were prevalent in English landscape gardens; the most famous perhaps is William Kent's design in the 1730s for both a hermitage and a building known as Merlin's Cave in Queen Caroline's garden at Richmond, England. The Queen hired a hermit, the poet Stephen Duck, to inhabit Merlin's Cave to complete the stagecraft of a recluse in nature.[5]

The popularity of hermits and hermitages carried into the nineteenth century in the United States. For instance, the "tea house" on Tea Island in Lake George provided an escape for vacationers. In a print (figure 3.1), the little rustic structure appears organically nestled in the trees, an outpost of civilization in an otherwise natural spot. Tea Island was a popular destination for tourists escaping the hectic pace of life in the real world. Harriet Martineau described an outing to the island in her book *Retrospect of Western Travel* (1838). Martineau's portrayal of a lazy afternoon enjoying the rusticity of Tea Island is telling. Tea Island, she began, was

Figure 3.1.   C. Cousen. *Caldwell (Lake George)*, 1838. George Virtue, Publisher. W. H. Bartlett; hand colored lithograph.

. . . just big enough for a very lazy hermit to live in. There is a teahouse
to look out from, and, far better, a few little reposing places on the margin; recesses of rock and dry roots of trees, made to hide one's self in
for thought or dreaming. We dispersed; and one of us might have been
seen, by any one who rowed round the island, perched in every nook.[6]

Martineau's comments recall the popularity of hermits in this period. Francis
Abbot, the "Hermit of the Falls," built a hut at Niagara Falls and entertained
visitors before his death in 1831. His existence inspired numerous works of
literature, celebrating the lifestyle of rustic retreat.[7] The rustic style, defined
as expressing "a manner of building in imitation of simple or coarse nature,
rather than according to the rules of art," was often the style of the garden
hermitage in the United States, and, more broadly, a popular style for summerhouse construction.[8] As architectural historian W. Barksdale Maynard has argued, summerhouses "though small, loomed large in the world of architectural
thought, as they were seen to embody cherished ideas; they were places affording poetic solitude and opportunities for nature worship."[9]

The most important proponent of summerhouse construction in the
nineteenth-century United States was Andrew Jackson Downing (1815–1852),
who advocated rural and suburban life for middle-class strivers through his journal *The Horticulturist* and his pattern books.[10] Downing explained why his "countrymen should have good houses." A good house, according to Downing,

is a powerful means of civilization. A nation, whose rural population is
content to live in mean huts and miserable hovels, is certain to be behind
its neighbors in education, the arts, and all that makes up the external
signs of progress. With the perception of proportion, symmetry, order
and beauty, awakens the desire for possession, and with them comes that
refinement of manners which distinguishes a civilized from a coarse and
brutal people. So long as men are forced to dwell in log huts and follow
a hunter's life, we must not be surprised at lynch law and the use of the
bowie knife. But, when smiling lawns and tasteful cottages begin to em-
bellish a country, we know that order and culture are established.[11]

Downing recommended "open and covered seats," including summerhouses,
as embellishments to both the country house and the "ferme ornée."[12] To
beautify one's grounds with summerhouses, then, was to partake in civilizing
the continent. Historian David Schuyler explains the national importance of
Downing's precepts, when he writes that Downing "insisted that an appreciation of the beautiful in nature and the improvement of domestic architecture

in the United States were keys to the nation's cultural development and accurate measures of 'the progress of its civilization.'"[13]

A summerhouse appears in John F. Kensett's painting *View from Cozzens' Hotel Near West Point* (1863), a scenic landscape of the charming, picturesque irregularities of the Hudson Valley (figure 3.2). Barely noticeable in the view is a little summerhouse, perched on the edge of the cliff, with a view toward the river. Such a building provides tourists in the painting with a shady retreat for convivial conversation. The summerhouse is not the subject of the painting, but the structure itself would have allowed the guests of Cozzens to enjoy that subject—the view—more effectively. Miniscule in comparison to the vast extent of landscape before it, the summerhouse building type may appear inconsequential because of its size and purely recreational use; however, these little garden and park structures tell us a great deal about nineteenth-century American culture. As a landscape painting, this image is not a literal transcription of the view from Cozzens' Hotel; nevertheless, Kensett's inclusion of the summerhouse is important, because it expresses the ideological significance of the building type among the middle class of the northeastern United States. Despite their diminutive size and (often) ephemeral nature, summerhouses are part of a larger discourse on the benefits of sylvan retreat, a response to urbanization and industrialization. Indeed, the summerhouse as a

FIGURE 3.2.   John Frederick Kensett, *View from Cozzen's Hotel Near West Point, NY*. 1863. Oil on canvas. Overall 20 × 34 in. (50.8 × 86.4 cm): The Robert L. Stuart Collection, the gift of his widow Mrs. Mary Stuart, New-York Historical Society, S-189. Digital image created by Oppenheimer Editions.

building type is inherently linked to Jefferson's agrarianism, his belief in the primacy of the individual farmer (who, in much of nineteenth-century prescriptive literature, is the target audience for summerhouse designs) and his suspicious stance toward cities. In some ways, the summerhouse—constructed purely of natural materials—was antithetical to the artificial city.

Summerhouses are innately paradoxical. While they are not necessary for the sustenance of life in the way that a dwelling is (and therefore could be considered frivolous), practical farmers' periodicals encouraged their readers to construct summerhouses. In the idle days of winter, farmers were instructed to build rustic summerhouses to keep busy. A summerhouse on one's farm, then, indicated industry, even while its purpose was merely recreational. Summerhouses also functioned as signifiers of gentility.[14] Pattern books and periodicals taught their middle-class readers how to create the appearance of leisure and taste without much expense of time or money (hence, materials were either inexpensive or available on one's property). Ideal summerhouse designs and descriptions of uses were available to readers of prescriptive literature, such as pattern books, as well as other forms of illustrated popular literature. Summerhouse designs appear early in the nineteenth century in builder's guides (such as Asher Benjamin's The American Builder's Companion [1806]) and continue to appear late into the nineteenth century in books such as A. J. Bicknell & Company's Detail, Cottage and Constructive Architecture (1873) and William T. Comstock's Modern Architectural Designs and Details (1881).

Architectural historian Elizabeth Cromley has provided us with a succinct definition of the summerhouse in her essay "A Room with a View" in Resorts of the Catskills (1979):

> The gazebo or summer house is an offspring of the verandah—like a little segment of a front porch freestanding in nature. It has all the qualities of a civilized outpost, a place to rest and watch the natural and social spectacle. As a creation of culture placed in nature, it also suggests protection against the raw and the untamed.[15]

A summerhouse then was a place where nature met culture. In the nineteenth century, summerhouses were popular for many different settings, from gardens and parks to pleasure grounds and resorts.

American authors often borrowed ideas and designs from English and French sources. In 1860, The Gardener's Monthly illustrated "rustic pavilions and belvideres [sic]" furnished by their Paris correspondent.[16] Figure 3.3 shows a page from English landscape architect Shirley Hibberd's book Rustic Adornments for Homes of Taste (first published in 1856).[17] Hibberd defines the function

FIGURE 3.3.   "Rockery and Wilderness." Shirley Hibberd, *Rustic Adornments for Homes of Taste*, London, 1856. After p. 277 RBR SB453 H62a. Courtesy of the Winterthur Library's Printed Book and Periodical Collection.

of a summerhouse, which could be useful, ornamental or, ideally, both. The uses include "rest, shelter, meditation, conversation, reading, observation, and perhaps conviviality."[18] But, as Hibberd writes, summerhouses could also be used as work spaces; his "out-door sanctum" had been the scene, weather permitting, of all of his "literary work." But clearly, relaxation was the most prominent occupation of a summerhouse user; according to Hibberd, "there is no better vindication of a summer-house than the opportunity it affords for the quiet enjoyment of a book or an afternoon nap." Hibberd laments that in the days of rail travel, people do not read at leisure in a beautiful place; indeed, writes Hibberd, not one book has been written "professedly" for the summerhouse.[19] Obviously, Hibberd was a proponent of the idea of retreat, a genteel aim of both the English and the Americans and one often propagated by "villa books," as W. Barksdale Maynard has shown in his essay on Thoreau's house at Walden.[20]

Hibberd was not alone in using his summerhouse as a work space. Washington Irving, along with his brother William and the writer James Kirke Paulding, used a summerhouse in New Jersey to write for their satirical periodical *Salmagundi* (1807–1808). Situated along the Passaic River and surrounded by trees, the breezy little summerhouse was on the grounds of Old Gouverneur

Place, or Mount Pleasant, a country house Irving dubbed "Cockloft Hall." Illustrated in an 1869 edition of *Salmagundi*, this neoclassical summerhouse (figure 3.4) became so associated with Irving that after his death, the Metropolitan Fair in New York City featured a replica in 1864. The replica, a "temple" to Irving, displayed a landscape painting of the view from the original building, which by 1859 had fallen into ruin. *The New York Times* noted that the replica was a "venerable building of simple unattractive architecture, moss-covered and apparently in decay."[21] Outside of the summerhouse, a woman dressed as Irving's character Katrina Van Tassel from Irving's story "The Legend of Sleepy Hollow" greeted fairgoers who paid ten cents to enter the summerhouse, which was filled with both Irving memorabilia and other relics from American history. The popularity of the "Salmagundi summerhouse" is a testament to the celebrity culture of the nineteenth century and the cult of the author phenomenon. What began as a summerhouse work space

FIGURE 3.4. Summer House, Cockloft Hall. Frontispiece. William Irving, James Kirke Paulding, and Washington Irving, *Salmagundi, or, the Whimwhams and Opinions of Launcelot Langstaff, Esq., and Others*, New York: G. P. Putnam and Son, 1869.

FIGURE 3.5.   Mark Twain's study in Elmira, New York. October 20, 1937. New York State Archives. New York (State). Education Dept. Division of Archives and History. Photographs of historic sites and structures, 1936–1963. Series A0245-77. Chemung County.

becomes a tourist attraction in which Irving's admirers could feel both close to a favorite author and proud of their nation's standing in the world of literature and beyond.

Like Irving, Mark Twain (1835–1910) retreated to a summerhouse to write, working on some of his best-known books, including *The Adventures of Tom Sawyer* and *Adventures of Huckleberry Finn*, within its walls (figure 3.5). The summerhouse was located at the country residence of his in-laws at Quarry Farm in Elmira, New York.[22] Twain described Quarry Farm's location, evoking the hermit tradition: "We have no neighbors. It is the quietest of all quiet places, and we are hermits that eschew caves and live in the sun."[23] The summerhouse was a gift from Twain's sister-in-law Susan Crane in 1874. Octagonal in form, the little building was located in Twain's time about 100 yards from the main house. A steep walk of uneven steps led to the elevation on which the summerhouse sat, a real rural retreat, surrounded by and covered in plant life. Twain wrote:

> It is the loveliest study you ever saw, it is octagonal with a peaked roof, each face filled with a spacious window, and it sits perched in complete isolation on the top of an elevation that commands leagues of valley and city and retreating ranges of distant blue hills. It is a cozy nest and just

room in it for a sofa, table, and three or four chairs, and when the storms
sweep down the remote valley and the lightning flashes behind the hill
beyond and the rain beats upon the roof over my head, imagine the
luxury of it.[24]

Twain's description highlights what makes summerhouses appealing: it is iso-
lated in nature and provides an extensive view; it has enough room for several
pieces of furniture, should welcome conviviality disrupt the solitude and convert the summerhouse into a parlor in nature; and it protects Twain from the
weather outside. The popular press likened the form of Twain's summerhouse
to a pilothouse on a riverboat, harkening back to Twain's youth as a riverboat
pilot on the Mississippi River.[25] Edwin Wildman writes: "From the great height
of Quarry Farm, sitting in his Pilot House, Twain could look out across a wide
valley for miles and miles, and, perhaps, imagine himself again at the steering
wheel, high on the hurricane-deck of a Mississippi steamer."[26] The summerhouse is just one of many landscape ornaments at Quarry Farm, including an
arbor and a playhouse, inspired by the writings of Downing. The family considered building a prospect tower, a dream that never came to fruition.[27]

In addition to providing space for the production of narrative, summerhouses also found their way into nineteenth-century narratives, including
Nathaniel Hawthorne's novel *The House of the Seven Gables* (1851). At the heart
of the novel is the House of the Seven Gables itself, but another bit of architecture takes center stage in the enclosed garden behind the old Pyncheon
house. Hawthorne describes the summerhouse there as a "ruinous little structure, which showed just enough of its original design to indicate that it had
once been a summer-house." [28] Hawthorne also calls it a "ruinous arbor."[29]
Repaired by Clifford Pyncheon and Holgrave, the Pyncheons' daguerreotypist
boarder, the summerhouse becomes the scene of tête-à-têtes between
Phoebe Pyncheon and her cousin Clifford, and between Phoebe and Holgrave,
as well as larger gatherings on Sundays. The meetings between Phoebe and
Holgrave are romantically charged: a peek through the garden fence might
lead an onlooker to think that Holgrave was attempting to woo Phoebe.[30]
Hawthorne's summerhouse in *The House of the Seven Gables* serves an important purpose: its restoration represents the regeneration of the Pyncheon
family with the eventual union between Phoebe and Holgrave. We learn at
the end of the novel that Holgrave is a descendent of Matthew Maule, the wizard who in an earlier era had cursed the house after Colonel Pyncheon wrested
ownership away from Maule. Maule's well, decrepit and dry since the wizard's
time, had infected the whole garden; the ruinous state of the summerhouse

signified the Pyncheon family's ruin. Although small in size, the summerhouse plays an important symbolic role in the narrative.

Hawthorne's summerhouse was rustic, but summerhouse architectural styles ranged from the exotic to the rustic, and everything in between, including Grecian and Gothic. Downing wrote "There is no limit to the variety of forms and patterns in which these rustic seats, arbors, summer-houses, etc., can be constructed by an artist of some fancy and ingenuity."[31] According to *The Horticulturist*, the monthly journal Downing edited, the style of summerhouse depended on the scale and style of the main house. Hence, "classically embellished structures" were only appropriate "in the first class of country residences, where the mansion or villa, [is] in a high style of art." But for "the more humble and simple cottage grounds, the rural walks of the *ferme ornée*, and the modest garden of the suburban amateur," the journal recommended rustic work. [32] Pattern book author and architect Samuel Sloan made this distinction as well, labeling more elaborate structures with refined detail "architectural" summerhouses, to distinguish them from the rustic variety (Sloan also criticized amateur efforts at summerhouse building, calling those not designed by an architect "ridiculous").[33]

Although summerhouses were European or Eastern in architectural inspiration, some observers saw in them a uniquely American character. A summerhouse on the Bronx River in Westchester County, New York, appeared in *Gleason's Pictorial Drawing-Room Companion* on July 9, 1853. The accompanying text praised the builder of the summerhouse for constructing an object of taste and for retreating to the country to beautify it. The *Gleason's* writer noted "One might imagine it to be a Chinese pagoda, on some Eastern river, for it has a foreign look about it that is not at all American." Despite its foreign origins, the writer declared paradoxically that the summerhouse was evidence of American nationalism; he celebrated summerhouses as farm improvements, stating that "To fertilize and improve his farm outright to be the prime temporal object of every owner of substantial soil." The author expansively concluded that "All national aggrandizement, power, and wealth may be traced to agriculture."[34] In other words, summerhouses and their builders participated in the creation of greatness in the nation, even though the summerhouse in the article is Chinese in inspiration. In this short article, the *Gleason's* writer hit on this paradox of summerhouse design: summerhouses can be simultaneously American and exotic. But the contradictions of summerhouse design extended to function and meaning as well. In nineteenth-century prescriptive literature, summerhouses could represent both frivolity and industry.

Writers often suggested wood as the building material for rustic summerhouses. *The Gardener's Monthly* contributor Samuel L. Boardman wrote that the materials for a summerhouse "can be selected from the wood-pile when the crooked limbs are being cut for fuel, or a day or two in the forest will furnish an abundance."[35] But in places where wood was scarce and expensive (as on the prairie), some agricultural periodicals suggested thatch for the roofing of a summerhouse. John M. Smith, a reader from Oskaloosa, Iowa, wrote to *The Gardener's Monthly* in 1859, recommending "slough grass," which was "very abundant in low prairie lands," and which formed "a cheap, substantial and durable roof for outbuildings, as timber is scarce."[36] In locations more suburban than rural, *Woodward's Country Homes* (borrowing from *The Horticulturist*) recommended a more elaborate style of summerhouse, rather than the rustic style appropriate to rural areas.[37]

In the prescriptive literature, the siting of the summerhouse was a matter of great importance to those tastefully improving their properties. In a high-style example from *The Model Architect*, Sloan illustrates a landscape plan of the house and garden and how they relate (figure 3.6). The plan features a fountain and large pool to the rear of the house, beyond which, in a straight line stands the Romanesque summerhouse "in the midst of the grove." Beyond the summerhouse, on an elevated incline on the right is the observatory, "from which we may readily conceive a fine extensive view." Even in a

FIGURE 3.6. "A Country Residence." Samuel Sloan, *The Model Architect: A Series of Original Designs for Cottages, Villas, Suburban Residences, etc.* Philadelphia: E. S. Jones & Co., 1852. Design XXVI. RBR NA7130 S63m*. Courtesy of the Winterthur Library's Printed Book and Periodical Collection.

residence of a man of such means, economy was still a factor. Sloan wrote that the summerhouse was composed of "wood painted white, or if possible of marble."[38] A slightly more modest example of the relationship between house and summerhouse was Isaac Royall's house in Medford, Massachusetts. Martha Lamb's *The Homes of America* described the "unique" summerhouse, located at the "end of a graveled walk" on an "artificial mound." In this case, the summerhouse doubled as an icehouse, demonstrating the practicality of the builder.[39] This arrangement of house / summerhouse was an exceedingly common one in the prescriptive literature of the period. An illustration from Sloan's *Architecture Review and American Builders' Journal* and a "Farmer's House" from Alexander Jackson Davis's *Rural Residences* (1838) demonstrate the ideal relationship of house to summerhouse, one in view of the other.[40] These examples demonstrate that nineteenth-century prescriptive literature was aimed at owners of both elaborate country residences and more modest farmhouses.

Ideally, summerhouses were sited to take advantage of a view.[41] In laying out a garden, views leading from the house to landscape adornments were paramount, as shown by English writer Edward Kemp in an illustration to his book *How to Lay Out Garden*.[42] Sloan suggested that a situation affording many different views, but that was also within sight of the house, was best.[43] An illustration, from Frank J. Scott's book *The Art of Beautifying Suburban Home Grounds of Small Extent* (1870) demonstrates the view from the summerhouse to the house (figure 3.7).[44] This rustic structure has numerous openings to exploit views of both the house and the surrounding landscape. The summerhouse builder was composing the view, directing the occupant's attention to particular objects, in much the same way a landscape painter framed his scene. Art historian Malcolm Andrews explores the tension between inside and outside in landscape painting, and many of his conclusions apply to summerhouse construction: "The presence of an interior determines our relationship with that landscape, which is so often inflected by our sense of the duality 'indoors' and 'outdoors.'"[45] The summerhouse allowed one to be simultaneously inside and outside, with the architecture functioning as mediator between the two.

The proliferation of summerhouse illustrations in prescriptive literature suggests that these structures were in demand by farmers.[46] An 1856 issue of *New England Farmer* published a letter from a reader requesting a plan for a "small and cheap summer-house," to which another reader, Allen W. Dodge, responded with a verbal description of his own summerhouse. Dodge then informed the editor that when he visited in the summer, "we will sit and talk over the past exploits of farming."[47] According to agricultural and horticultural

FIGURE 3.7. View from the summerhouse to the house. Frank Jesup Scott, *The Art of Beautifying Suburban Homegrounds of Small Extent*, New York, 1886 (copyright 1870), p. 107 "Chapter XII, The Lawn." Heading Illustration. RBR SB473 S42. Courtesy of the Winterthur Library's Printed Book and Periodical Collection.

journals, summerhouses also represented industry and morality to nineteenth-century farmers. John M. Smith of Greenville, Illinois, provided drawings of his summerhouse to *The Gardener's Monthly*, writing:

> I have often thought that many persons, living in the country, and with limited means yet with a taste which only needs encouragement to display it, might beautify their homes, and make them loved by their children, if they would only exercise their ingenuity during seasons when active, necessary labor on their farms could not be performed. During the winter months most farmers, particularly those who are not the best supplied with *pecuniary* means, have little actual labor to perform; and that is *the* time to 'fix-up' their homes, and make them loved by their children.[48]

Daniel Harrison Jacques, author of numerous, inexpensive handbooks on a range of topics, agreed. In Jacques's *The Garden: A Pocket Manual of Practical Horticulture*, he wrote that every rural house of "taste" should have "seats, arbors, and other structures of rustic work. . . . They may be cheaply erected, and will add greatly to the out-of-door attractions." [49] "Improvement" to one's property was also an indicator of gentility and taste. As is usually the case with nineteenth-century prescriptive literature, pattern book authors stressed correctness in adornment. In *Practical Landscape Gardening* (1855), G. M. Kern wrote that a "correct and practiced taste" is necessary "to superintend the distribution of such objects in a Garden. . . . Too richly or highly ornamented, it will appear gaudy—too plain will argue poverty—and to be out of place will betray ignorance."[50]

Because of the ephemeral nature of rustic summerhouses, many do not survive. A rustic summerhouse was only estimated to last "from 10 to 15 years without repairs," although if red cedar (the "best" material) was used, twenty years or more could be expected.[51] Bronson Alcott was an amateur builder of rustic shelters for his neighbor and friend, Ralph Waldo Emerson. Alcott also embellished the landscape behind his own house "Hillside" in Concord, Massachusetts (built c. 1688; modified in 1845 by Alcott). In his journal, Alcott wrote of an after-dinner call by Emerson on September 13, 1846, during which the two men sat and talked in the summerhouse; he declared "Worthy place, the arbour, for the reception of the poet as my guest."[52] When Nathaniel Hawthorne purchased "Hillside," Hawthorne called Alcott's summerhouse "a mere skeleton of slender, decaying, tree-trunks, with neither walls nor a roof; nothing but a tracery of branches and twigs, which the next wintry blast will be very likely to scatter in fragments along the terrace."[53] *The Homes of America* reported in 1853 that Alcott's summerhouses were "gradually falling, shattered,—and disappearing."[54] Indeed, Alcott's rustic structures do not survive, and many other rustic summerhouses have been reclaimed by nature.

Some summerhouses, although rustic, were constructed of materials more long-lasting than tree branches and trunks. An illustration from *The Horticulturist* in 1856 shows a rustic summerhouse of iron, which has been "successfully employed." The durability of iron was its advantage: "If it is regularly painted, a permanent structure may be erected that will require no repair."[55] The best examples of surviving iron summerhouses are at Belmont Mansion (1853) in Nashville, Tennessee. On axis with the house is a summerhouse, built circa 1860; the design appeared in Janes, Kirtland & Company's *Illustrated Catalogue of Ornamental Iron Work* in 1870.[56] Scattered on the lawn of Belmont Mansion are a number of other iron summerhouses, all providing views from one to another and back to the house.[57]

Summerhouses appeared as embellishments not only in private gardens, but also in the pleasure grounds of large-scale developments, including resorts. Located in the Shawangunk Mountains near New Paltz, New York, Mohonk Mountain House and its summerhouses demonstrate the principles of sylvan retreat.[58] Alfred and Albert Smiley created Mohonk, beginning in 1869 when Alfred visited the spectacular spot and convinced Albert to purchase the property, which opened for business in 1870. Throughout the picturesque landscape around Mohonk Mountain House are numerous rustic seats and summerhouses (as many as 155 were cataloged in 1917).[59] At this nineteenth-century resort, views were integral to the visitors' experience; to exploit the views, the Smileys constructed both summerhouses and prospect towers. Albert Smiley carefully chose the sites; he declared: "I never take a walk or drive over the estate, but I find some ugly tree to be removed, a new path to be built . . . a vista to be opened . . . , a summerhouse to be built . . ."[60] Mohonk's summerhouses have numerous openings to exploit views of both the Mountain House and the surrounding scenery.

In the late nineteenth century, Mohonk was a vacation spot for many urban and suburban residents. Guests at Mohonk could immerse themselves in nature, although the vastness of the landscape intimidated some. In the early days of Mohonk, the guidebook tells us that "not infrequently guests lost their way on the long tramps, and on one occasion a lady despairing of ever getting home became hysterical and sent up heart-rending shrieks till help came. She was found standing less than two hundred feet from the house."[61] Discovering a summerhouse on a long tramp would signify civilization and reinforce the notion that the hotel guest was not, in fact, in the wilderness.

Landscape architecture like that at Mohonk was good for one's health, according to nineteenth-century notions. *The Illustrated Annual Register of Rural Affairs* advocated summerhouse building to their readers because of the health benefits of outdoor activity. "A seat where girls can sew or read in the fresh open air, will more than pay for itself by the health it will preserve or impart," the *Register* informed its readers.[62] It was the supposed health benefits that made summerhouses appropriate for institutional settings, according to Thomas S. Kirkbride, the influential superintendent of the Pennsylvania Hospital for the Insane and author of a treatise on hospital design. In 1845, Kirkbride described in the hospital's annual report the improvements to the pleasure grounds of that institution. Among the walks, which were placed to maximize views, Kirkbride planned to add "summer-houses, rustic seats, and other objects of interest, to tempt the patients voluntarily to prolong their walks, and to spend a greater portion of their time out of the wards, and engaged in some agreeable occupation." Kirkbride stressed that the health benefit of these pleasure grounds was even greater than one might suppose; even those who "are not capable of realizing their beauties, still have an indistinct recollection of something pleasant in connexion with them."[63] The M'Lean Asylum for the Insane at Charlestown, Massachusetts, had grounds that were "well laid out," with summerhouses. At Hartford's The Retreat for the Insane, there were "extensive gardens and walks . . . for the recreation and health of the inmates that are indulged with this liberty."[64] The summerhouses then functioned as a healthy antidote to the disease within the asylums.

Although Mohonk Mountain House served an entirely distinct clientele—elites on vacation, rather than institutional patients—the notion that recreation out of doors was healthy was paramount in both kinds of landscapes. Engaging language similar to Kirkbride's, the Smileys emphasized both the healthful and moral benefits of time outdoors. The Smileys were Quakers, and gambling and drinking were not allowed on the premises. Indeed, one journalist noted that the only bar at Mohonk was one of clear spring water.[65] In Albert Smiley's words:

> In place of cards, dancing and tippling, we have put before our guests something more desirable, that is a library of good standard works . . . we have entertainments and lectures, and tableaux, charades, etc., and we have a garden of the choicest selection of herbaceous plants in the state. We have spent large sums of money in roads and paths, and we have one hundred and thirty-seven summerhouses, and a large number of settees and seats to entice people out of doors to get enjoyment.[66]

Hence, in Smiley's conception of Mohonk, the outdoors becomes an antidote for evil enticements in a narrative of temperance and morality. The existence of the summerhouses throughout the landscape surely enticed guests out of the confines of the Mountain House and into nature and healthy recreation. Since the view from each summerhouse led to yet another summerhouse, the little buildings assisted the explorer in navigating the complex landscape of Mohonk.

As an ornamented picturesque landscape, Mohonk not only provided an escape for well-heeled city dwellers but also approximated the villa estates of the Hudson Valley elite. Indeed, some of the guests at Mohonk had their own villas, including Edwin C. Litchfield, listed in Mohonk's promotional brochures of the 1880s as a reference for potential guests to contact. Litchfield's Italianate villa Grace Hill (1853–1858), designed by Alexander Jackson Davis, still stands, located in what was then suburban Brooklyn. Influenced by Downing's theoretical books on gardening and horticulture, these nineteenth-century villas were often set within rolling landscapes, punctuated by garden and park structures. At Mohonk, the Mountain House anchors the landscape and provides a visual focus in much the same way a villa does on a private estate. Montgomery Place in Annandale-on-Hudson provides an intriguing comparison to Mohonk. Montgomery Place was originally constructed circa 1802; an addition by Davis was added between 1841 and 1844. During these years in the 1840s, Downing consulted with the owners, the Livingstons and the Bartons, on planning the landscape around the villa. He then published a description entitled "A Visit to Montgomery Place" in his journal *The Horticulturist* in October 1847; Davis provided illustrations. One of Davis's illustrations of *The Cataract* shows a wild landscape with a waterfall to the right, a winding path with climbers to the left, and a picturesque summerhouse overlooking the scene.[67]

While images of Montgomery Place predate Mohonk Mountain House by several decades, there are striking similarities to the scenes created in the Shawangunks by the Smileys. Many Mohonk summerhouses perch high above the Mountain House and lake, similar to the siting of the summerhouse at Montgomery Place. Built of natural materials, these summerhouses both blend into the landscape while simultaneously assisting the viewer in experiencing the landscape by framing and accentuating the view. Another view of a "Rustic Seat" at Montgomery Place, illustrated in Downing's article, resembles any number of such rustic structures at Mohonk. Of course, the sources here are the same, namely, English pattern books such as those by John Claudius Loudon and their American counterparts by Downing and others. In some ways, the Smileys were re-creating the elegant lifestyle of the Hudson Valley estates at Mohonk. In a print included in the Smileys' promotional brochures of the 1880s (figure 3.8), the activities on display are the same that residents and visitors to villas could expect: here we see a couple off on a nature ramble, a couple promenading, ladies gossiping and sewing under the shade of trees, children playing,

FIGURE 3.8.   Mohonk Lake Mountain House. New Paltz, NY: Mohonk Mountain House, 1888.

people enjoying a carriage ride, canoeists on the lake, and guests surveying the landscape from the rustic summerhouses that proliferate at Mohonk.

The Smileys were likely familiar with Downing's writings about villas and their landscapes, as they borrowed the design of one of their most prominent summerhouses, the one at the center of the formal garden next to the Mountain House, from Downing's book on landscape gardening.[68] These similarities to villa landscape design were not lost on contemporary commentators, including the author of an article in the *New York Times* in 1882, who wrote:

> Under Mr. Smiley's fostering care the country about Mohonk is beginning to resemble a great English demesne. Fine carriage roads wind around the bluffs, and to every point at which a fresh view is to be had footpaths lead to the same spots by the most circuitous and picturesque routes. Summer-houses of rough wood and neatly thatched roofs, of all sizes and shapes, are perched like birds' nests on every overhanging rock and in every retired nook. One or two even stand out in the water, securely founded on sunken rocks, serving both as buoys and as retired places for picnickers. There are something over 90 of these houses scattered at different points, and they form one of the most attractive features of the hotel, being at once picturesque, convenient as resting-places for climbers, and delightful resorts for the reader to hide in, sheltered from the sun but allowing the mountain breezes unbroken sway.[69]

What Mohonk Mountain House offered to its visitors was an approximation of the English aristocratic villa and its grounds ("a great English demesne"): a "house" (the hotel) surrounded by a carefully constructed landscape with numerous lookout points.

The existence of summerhouses outside and inside the city points to growing unease with rapid industrialization and urbanization. During the age of pattern books advocating rural life, summerhouses and the landscapes they adorned created a retreat from the city. Constructed landscapes featuring summerhouses in suburban and rural settings provided this counterbalance to urban life.[70] Indeed, the idea of having access to a landscaped park was a selling point not only for Mohonk, but earlier for Llewellyn Park, a Romantic suburb designed by Llewellyn S. Haskell and Alexander Jackson Davis between 1853 and 1857 in West Orange, New Jersey. Based on both English landscape and suburban design principles, Llewellyn Park featured ornamental structures, including a summerhouse perched on a knoll near the entrance gate. This English landscape garden was not solely reserved for the aristocracy, as noted by a contemporary who pointed out that the "fortunate purchaser of two or three acres becomes a virtual owner of the whole five hundred; a plan for which a poor man, for a few thousands of dollars, may buy a country seat that challenges comparison with the Duke of Devonshire's."[71] The Duke of Devonshire's magnificent country house Chatsworth in Derbyshire, England, is surrounded by gardens laid out by Lancelot "Capability" Brown in the 1760s. For middle-class Americans to aspire to live in a Chatsworth-like setting by moving to Llewellyn Park is quite extraordinary.

Summerhouses also appeared in urban locations where they provided respite from the surrounding city. Philadelphia resident G. Albert Lewis remembered nostalgically a Gothic Revival summerhouse located in his family's garden on the city's South Second Street. In this rendering from 1900 (figure 3.9), Lewis recorded how he remembered the summerhouse from his childhood. The structure was the focus of the garden parties of his parents, presumably at mid-century. "When lighted with many Chinese lanterns, and decorated with coloured lamps, [the summerhouse] presented a fairy-like scene, viewed from the parlor windows," Lewis wrote.[72]

That summerhouses provided entrée into a fantasy world of follies was evidenced by Manasseh Cutler's description of the Vauxhalls or public pleasure gardens of the late eighteenth and early nineteenth centuries in America. Nighttime illumination brought city dwellers out to enjoy these places of social and architectural spectacle. Designed in the picturesque manner by Samuel Vaughn, Gray's Garden near Philadelphia was a mystical wonderland enhanced by the inclusion of delightful architectural elements. An advertisement for the garden used summerhouses as a selling point. Dr. Manasseh Cutler, visiting

Figure 3.9. "Summer House in Garden of House, S. Second St." G. Albert Lewis. *The Old Houses and Stores with Memorabilia Relating to Them and My Father and Grandfather*. Philadelphia: G. Albert Lewis, 1900. n. p. The Library Company of Philadelphia.

in July 1787, wrote in his journal that at the end of the alleys, none of which were straight or alike in size or form, were summerhouses, arbors, or bowers, "each of which was formed in a different taste." Chinese bridges, a hermitage, cascades, grottoes, a labyrinth, and a "spacious summer-house" with a Chinese roof and "a beautiful winding staircase" mesmerized Cutler. He wrote, "During the whole of this romantic rural scene, I fancied myself on enchanted ground, and could hardly help looking out for flying dragons, magic castles, little Fairies, Knight-errants, distressed Ladies, and all the apparatus of eastern fable."[73] While wandering amid these delights, Cutler created his own narrative, clearly influenced by his reading of works such as *The Arabian Nights*.

In addition to creating a potentially fantastical literary narrative, summerhouses in urban locales provided city dwellers with contact with nature. For those circumscribed by the city, the garden could be brought to them. An example is "Gilmore's Summer Concert Garden," on Madison Avenue and Twenty-Sixth Street in New York City. The inside, a "vast hippodrome," was transformed into a "glittering pageant" of garden delights, which included "rustic arbors" and "curiously-fashioned rendezvous." In these "rustic nooks," one could listen to music, surrounded by companions in a simulacrum of the suburban garden or the resort landscape.[74] Summerhouses and other rustic structures such as the bridges and seats in New York City's Central Park likewise gave visitors a taste of the country; one observer noted that they were "very suggestive of rural life."[75] Calvert Vaux's designs for rustic embellishments in Central Park were so popular that Kingston, New York, manufacturer Dunne and Company sold replicas based on Central Park designs. Architectural historian Francis R. Kowsky notes that it was in Central Park where "rustic architecture was widely employed for the first time in the United States," and the park's success sparked increased popularity for such structures.[76]

Downing summed up the appeal of summerhouses in American gardens when he wrote in his *Treatise* that rustic seats and structures "have the merit of being tasteful and picturesque in their appearance, and are easily constructed by the amateur, at comparatively little or no expense."[77] As a tastemaker and horticulturist to the Hudson Valley elite, Downing guided middle-class readers on how to project an image of gentility within restricted budgets. Downing himself maintained what biographer David Schuyler has called a "veil of gentility."[78] His house in Newburgh, despite its genteel trappings, was heavily mortgaged, and Downing worked long hours in an office wing, the door of which was hidden behind a bookcase in the library. Downing labored to cultivate the appearance of leisure even while toiling away at projects to maintain his lifestyle. Like the class-conscious farmers reading agricultural periodicals and constructing summerhouses, Downing had his own hermitage on the grounds of Highland Garden in Newburgh, New York (c. 1840s). In "The Home of the Late A. J. Downing," *The Horticulturist* described the hermit-age as "a pretty, rural structure, neatly constructed of rough bark and logs, presenting an attractive object in the walk, and furnishing a cool retreat from the burning heat of our midsummer noons."[79] Hence, Downing, the ultimate proponent of the rustic style in the first half of the nineteenth century, under-stood the aspirations of the American middle class. As a sign of leisure, summer-houses proliferated in the landscape as symbols of gentility for the middle class while also projecting signs of civilization in the landscape.

CHAPTER 4

Towers

The Belvedere and the Panoptic Sublime

Thomas Jefferson gave his estate an Italian name, "Monticello," or "little mountain" and named the higher eminence to the southwest of Monticello, "Montalto," or "high mountain." There he planned to site one of his most ambitious garden follies, an unexecuted prospect tower that would have been visible from the west front of Monticello and from its dome room. In Jefferson's words, the tower's windows would have directed "the line of sight to Monticello." Indeed, the tower would have served as both an eye-catcher in the landscape and a belvedere from which viewers could survey the plantation landscape.[1] In typical Jefferson fashion, he redesigned the tower three times, the first two in the neoclassical style and the last one in the medieval revival style, a design that is simultaneously medievalizing and cubic in its rationalism (figure 4.1). His designs varied in height from 100 feet high for the first tower, which featured a different Roman order on each of its five stories, to 120 feet high for the medieval revival cubic tower, to an enormous 200 feet for a column. As William Beiswanger points out, the column would have been 600 feet above Monticello and almost 1,200 feet above the valley.[2] Jefferson was inspired by eighteenth-century Scottish philosopher Henry Home (better known as Lord Kames), who wrote, "to look down upon objects makes part of the pleasure of elevation."[3]

The notion of the view and its attendant power dynamics in the building type of the belvedere (from *bel vedere* or beautiful view), and prospect towers

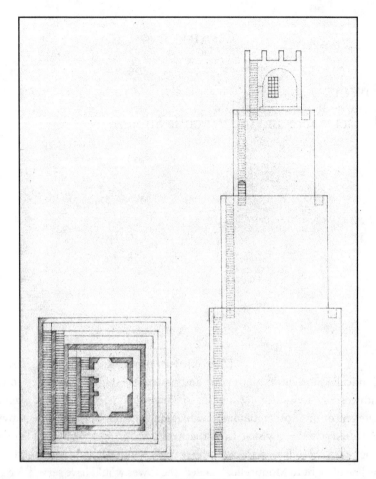

FIGURE 4.1.   Monticello: castellated tower, [1778], by Thomas Jefferson. Coolidge Collection of Thomas Jefferson Manuscripts. Special Collections Jefferson N93; K64. 23.2 × 18.5 cm (9 1/8 × 7 1/4 in.). Collection of the Massachusetts Historical Society. http://www.masshist.org /thomasjeffersonpapers/doc?id=arch_N93.

generally, are subjects largely unexplored by architectural historians of nineteenth-century America.[4] These ornamental structures appeared in England in eighteenth-century landscape gardens, such as Stourhead in Wiltshire, where King Alfred's Tower, designed by Henry Flitcroft, to this day provides the spectator with a panoramic view of the surrounding countryside. Settings for prospect towers in the United States included gardens, parks, rural cemeteries, and tourist attractions: in other words, anywhere an elevated view was desirable. In general, the architectural styles of belvederes ranged from the neoclassical to the more exotic Gothic and Chinese and took the form of many different building types, including lighthouses, pagodas, obelisks, and castellated towers. What they shared in common, however, was the inherent power embodied in looking down from on high.[5]

Art historian Alan Wallach has described this desire to survey extensive views as the "panoptic sublime" in his articles on nineteenth-century American landscape paintings, which often exploit such views.[6] Wallach writes that the term *panoptic* "underscores the connections between vision and power: the ascent of a panorama tower provided the visitor with an opportunity to identify, at least momentarily, with a dominant view—Foucault's 'eye of power.'"[7] To illustrate his thesis, Wallach uses the estate, called Monte Video, of Daniel Wadsworth, a wealthy scion of Connecticut society in the early republic. Wallach argues that Wadsworth was a member of a "declining aristocracy" attempting to maintain its cultural hegemony. Wadsworth built a country house on a mountain near Hartford, Connecticut, and placed a belvedere on an eminence overlooking the spectacular scenery. By doing so, he "acquired for himself the aura of gentility," according to Wallach.[8] Like a true aristocrat, he then opened his estate to the eager public who came to admire the view. Indeed, as Wallach explains, "Monte Video stood for hierarchical relations, for noblesse oblige, for tradition, for timelessness."[9] The visitors who viewed the panoramic scenery from Wadsworth's tower experienced the "panoptic sublime," defined by Wallach as "a sudden access of power, a dizzying sense of having suddenly come into possession of a terrain stretching as far as the eye could see."[10] The development of the belvedere in America shows how the aristocratic tradition of tower building becomes democratized as the century progresses. As picturesque tourism gained popularity for the middle class, towers began to proliferate at tourist attractions. Eventually, the working class gained access to the view with the advent of the public park movement in the United States and the establishment of Central Park in New York City.

Although wealth was a prerequisite for tower building in the aristocratic English tradition, Americans who did not have the means to construct towers still reveled in the heightened view. An image, "View from the Summit of Red Hill" (in New Hampshire) from *Ballou's Pictorial Drawing-Room Companion* (May 19, 1855), illustrates a basic human desire to survey the view from a great height (figure 4.2). If no observation tower existed at any given site, one could pile up stones and use a tree for balanced support to gain the desired extra height. The writer of the Ballou's article described the thrill of the summit from which one looks "down upon vast reaches of land, with hundreds of villages and hamlets, streams, plains, and forests mapped out upon the

FIGURE 4.2. "View from the Summit of Red Hill." *Ballou's Pictorial Drawing-Room Companion*, Boston: M. M. Ballou, VIII:20 (May 19, 1855), p. 312 RBR AP2 G55 F. Courtesy of the Winterthur Library's Printed Book and Periodical Collection.

grandest topographical scale."[11] When the George family gave Georges Hill to Fairmount Park in Philadelphia, Mr. George remarked that the hill, previously only enjoyed by his family, would be open to all. Everyone, "the poor as well as the affluent," enjoys a good, elevated view, he told the crowd at the public opening in 1869.[12]

At Kaaterskill Falls in the Catskill Mountains, an observation platform was built sometime in 1825 or 1826. The platform was decidedly not a folly; it was utilitarian in appearance and had little architectural interest. It is not surprising that landscape painter Thomas Cole elides the wooden structure (which represents the incursion of man into the sublime natural landscape) at the top of the falls in his painting *Kaaterskill Falls* completed in 1826. In contrast, other observation towers took advantage of the popularity of eclecticism and associationism in the architectural design of the nineteenth century. These towers were meant to be looked at, thereby imprinting on the landscape or cityscape a landmark (rather than just a position from whence a prospect might be admired).

In 1828, architect John Haviland designed a tower as part of the Chinese Pagoda and Labyrinth Garden, a pleasure garden in Philadelphia built by Peter A. Brown (figure 4.3). A writer in the contemporary periodical *The Casket* remarked that, "Among all people . . . eminences, whether natural or artificial, that command extensive views of picturesque and beautiful scenery,

FIGURE 4.3. John Haviland, "The Pagoda," in *The Casket*, Philadelphia, 11 (Nov. 1828), p. 509, 1828. RBR AP2 C33. Courtesy of the Winterthur Library's Printed Book and Periodical Collection.

always present peculiar attractions of resort to the inhabitants of thronged and dusty cities." The 110-foot high pagoda was located on Francis's Street and was designed in the "light eastern style." A placard inside the structure explained to the visitor that he or she had entered the "Temple of Confucius." Like visitors to Kew Gardens in London, who, delighted, came upon the Pagoda there (designed by Sir William Chambers in the eighteenth century), Americans examining the exterior and climbing the interior steps to the viewing area were transported to a faraway place: China. In such a manner, Americans were able to co-opt the architecture of the Far East in order to counteract the dearth of a native architectural heritage. What were the benefits of visiting the pagoda? According to *The Casket*, "With the aid of a telescope . . . the visitor . . . can take a survey of the country for a circuit of thirty miles, and enjoy all the pleasures accompanying country life, without subjecting himself to the diseases and perils incident to autumnal decay." In addition, *The Casket* tells us that the view from the Pagoda "will better prepare the mind for its continual struggles in life."[13]

Like Haviland, designers of rural cemeteries took their cues from the aesthetic of the English landscape garden of the eighteenth century. There are differences between the two (the most obvious being the primary function of cemeteries as repositories of the remains of the dead). However, there are many similarities. Both landscapes contain monuments and memorials, often sited as "eye-catchers," inviting the visitor to explore the sculptural and architectural scenery set within a lush landscape laid out in a naturalistic fashion. The funereal function of these cemeteries was complemented by their use as parks, a place for the urban populace to experience nature.[14] The first rural cemetery was Mount Auburn, in Cambridge, Massachusetts (1831). Jacob Bigelow was a driving force behind both the establishment of the cemetery and the architecture sited within it. Bigelow designed the Egyptian Revival entrance gate, as well as the granite fantasy, Bigelow Chapel. Eventually, Bigelow's plan to place a prospect tower on the summit of a hill in the cemetery was realized, with the help of local Boston architect Gridley J. Fox Bryant, who drew up the plans for Washington Tower, completed in 1853 (figure 4.4).[15]

FIGURE 4.4.   "Tower or Observatory" from *Dearborn's Guide Through Mount Auburn* (Boston: Nathaniel S. Dearborn, 1854), Am1854.DEA11573.D.1, p. 1. The Library Company of Philadelphia.

From Washington Tower, tourists still have a spectacular view of Boston; indeed, the building itself functions mainly as a lookout tower. Within its walls is only a winding staircase leading to an outdoor prospect platform. With a little imagination (which nineteenth-century tourists had in abundance), one can transport oneself briefly to medieval times (and create one's own narrative) when climbing the granite steps of the tower. At the summit, one can continue in a melancholy vein on the fleeting nature of life, a reverie encouraged by the views of sentimental monuments to the dead visible in the landscape below. Of course, the tower also has a patriotic impulse, as it is named after President George Washington. Unlike other cemetery structures, such as chapels, gates, mausoleums, and crematoriums, all of which had distinct funereal functions, observation towers in rural cemeteries served the purpose of ornamenting the landscape and providing views for the spectator. They became great tourist attractions. Indeed, as Blanche M. G. Linden notes, a dedication ceremony for Washington Tower was never held, as the tower became a tourist magnet immediately. In many guidebooks, Washington is not even mentioned; the belvedere function is emphasized over the commemoration of Washington.[16]

Lookout towers improved already magnificent views from hilltops. An early nineteenth-century lighthouse-shaped observation tower survives in Portland, Maine. Built by Lemuel Moody in 1807, the Portland Observatory was a maritime signal station located on Munjoy (or Mount Joy) Hill (figure 4.5). Using his telescope, Moody would observe ships coming into the port from afar and raise a signal flag to inform the city's merchants of the ship's approach, thereby facilitating preparation for trade. Moody built the lighthouse-styled tower as a commercial venture. The Portland Observatory also became a tourist attraction immediately. One contemporary writer proclaimed, "From the summit of Munjoy Hill there is a fine view of the city and surrounding country. There is here an observatory or telegraph station, 100 feet high. . . . The White Mountains, eighty miles distant, are plainly visible, and the sight is much aided by a splendid spy-glass, bought at a cost of $500."[17] One writer, a native of Portland, gushed about the beauty of the scenery from the observatory. In "Vacation Rambles," published in *The Ladies' Repository*, Professor Larrabee writes:

To see Portland to advantage, you should ascend the Observatory, on the summit of Munjoy Hill. . . . Such a landscape, combining such variety, so much of the beautiful, the grand, and the sublime . . . I have seen no where else. . . . The beauties of the place . . . are indeed exhaustless. . . . You may look, and observe, and spy with a good glass all day, and yet constantly be finding in the surrounding landscape some new feature of interest.[18]

FIGURE 4.5. "The Portland Observatory." Lemuel Moody, Portland, ME, in *Gleason's Pictorial Drawing-Room Companion* V:13 (Sept. 24, 1853), p. 200, 1807. Courtesy of the Winterthur Library's Printed Book and Periodical Collection.

For Larrabee, variety and extent are what makes the view from the observatory worthwhile.

Prospect towers have proliferated, to this day, at one of the premiere tourist attractions in North America, Niagara Falls, where the tourist trade flourished after the opening of the Erie Canal in 1825. At Niagara, heightened views became more and more accessible to the general public. In 1827, two brothers, Augustus and Peter Porter, built a bridge over some turtle-shaped rocks (called "Terrapin Rocks") from Goat Island along the edge of the Horseshoe Falls at Niagara. Six years later in 1833, they added Terrapin Tower on the American side of the Falls as a way to capitalize on the tourist trade (figure 4.6). Forty-five feet high and ascended by means of a winding staircase within, the stone tower became an instant tourist draw as it provided, according to travel guides, the best vantage point of the falls. Horatio A. Parsons's *Steele's Book of Niagara Falls*, proclaimed "no visiter [*sic*] on either side should presume to leave the Falls without visiting the tower and bridge."[19]

Nineteenth-century descriptions of the Terrapin Tower experience are numerous, as most visitors to the falls visited the precariously placed landmark. Tourists eagerly purchased prints of Niagara Falls as souvenirs of their trip. Those intrepid visitors to Terrapin Tower, who enjoyed the thrill of crossing the bridge to the tower over the rushing water below, wanted to remember their daring and to share it with friends and family at home. According to one

FIGURE 4.6.   "Niagara. [The falls and Terrapin Tower.]" The Miriam and Ira D. Wallach Division of Art, Prints and Photographs: Photography Collection, The New York Public Library. New York Public Library Digital Collections. http://digitalcollections.nypl.org/items/510d47e1-9c5e-a3d9-e040 -e00a18064a99 (accessed November 1, 2018).

contemporary source, thousands of visitors carved their names into the wood-work of the tower, perhaps as a way of declaring their conquest of the site.[20] One tourist, David Clapp, whose diary is preserved at the Winterthur Library, described his sublime experience of Terrapin in 1843: "The almost deafening roar of the water, the trembling of the tower, the clouds of mist, the rainbow on the opposite side, the mighty rush of the rapids above, and the frail foot-path which connected us with the land, each aided in forming a scene which in its effects on the beholder is indescribable and can never be forgotten."[21]

Inherent in the appeal of Terrapin was danger. A writer in *Harper's New Monthly Magazine* noted that at Terrapin, one could lean over the precipice from the observation balcony or climb down to gather shells and pebbles from the edge of the falls. But, he cautioned, "be not over-bold. These waters, appar-ently so gentle, sweep down with a force beyond your power to stem." The writer explained that a man fell from the bridge connecting the tower to Goat Island, and "in the twinkling of an eye" was swept to the edge. Luckily, the man became lodged in some rocks and was pulled to safety.[22] Because of the danger, some visitors were overcome by the experience; a contributor to *The Ladies' Repository* wrote in positive terms of the view from the "overhanging" tower but noted, "it is too overwhelming to be enjoyed, or even endured very long."[23] An anonymous author in the *Southern Literary Messenger* described the tumultuous feelings evoked by the tower's site on the edge of the falls: "Look-ing down into the terrible vortex below, you are made dizzy, and cling to the railing of the Tower for support."[24] Another *Ladies' Repository* writer warned of the future destruction of the tower by the mighty gush of water: "there is reason to apprehend that the point of rock on which the tower stands will it-self yield to the mighty pressure and also plunge down the abyss."[25] This view of Terrapin Tower persisted so much that some accounts of its demise blamed the instability of the tower, insisting that it had to be destroyed (the real rea-son that Terrapin Tower was demolished in 1873 was that a rival attraction had been built at Prospect Point by a relative of the owners of Terrapin).[26]

Of course, the breathtaking scenery of the falls was a source of nationalis-tic pride for Americans who were awestruck by the sublimity of the great won-ders of nature on the North American continent. As Benjamin Silliman wrote in his travel book, *Remarks Made on a Short Tour Between Hartford and Quebec in the Autumn of 1819*, "National character often receives its peculiar cast from natural scenery. . . . Thus, natural scenery is intimately connected with taste, moral feeling, utility and instruction."[27] Published to commemorate George Washington's death, an engraving links Niagara Falls with the future success of the United States by showing the female figure of Columbia, an allegory of prosperity. Literary scholar Elizabeth McKinsey writes "[Columbia] leans on Washington's gravestone . . . while she holds a United States flag with an eagle, now the national bird, superimposed on it . . . [Niagara Falls] represents the American land where Columbia will act out her destiny."[28]

It is useful to examine Terrapin Tower in light of the increasing nationalism of the early to mid-nineteenth century. Many Americans, including the writer James Fenimore Cooper, lamented the lack of architectural heritage in the young republic.[29] However, sites of spectacular natural scenery supplied an antidote to such qualms. Niagara Falls was an important natural landmark for those wishing to distinguish American from European scenery. In the nineteenth century Niagara Falls became a locus for nationalist zeal. Although diminutive in its sublime context, Terrapin Tower provided the viewer with a nationalist narrative that may be lost on today's observers. Terrapin Tower's architectural style plays a crucial role in this narrative.

The architectural style of Terrapin underscores the nationalism inspired by the falls. Like the Portland Observatory, Terrapin Tower takes the shape of a lighthouse, but as one droll writer in *Gleason's Pictorial and Drawing-Room Companion* noted, "The Prospect Tower is only called Lighthouse from analogy, for no other light but that of cigars was ever kindled there that we know of."[30] Make no mistake: no one thought the little building was an actual lighthouse since navigation was obviously impossible at the edge of the falls. But, as the Gleason's correspondent noted, Terrapin Tower looked like a lighthouse.

The choice of the lighthouse type for this prospect tower at Niagara Falls is significant; as John Stilgoe shows in *Common Landscapes of America*, lighthouses represented the new power of the national government in the early republic, as they were constructed not by local authorities but by the federal government. As Stilgoe writes, "But the federal government may well have understood . . . that the towers symbolized its strength and that every man, woman, and child who saw their massiveness might glimpse the permanency and strength of the infant republic."[31] Just a decade before Terrapin Tower was built, the government built a lighthouse at the mouth of the Mississippi. Designed by Benjamin Henry Latrobe and built between 1818 and 1821, this lighthouse was, according to architectural historian Michael W. Fazio, "intended to be not only an aid to navigation but also a great symbol of the wresting of the Louisiana Territory from the French and of the emerging status of New Orleans as the primary port of entry in the United States." Fazio writes that the lighthouse proclaimed the expulsion of the French from the area and the arrival of both immigrants and trade goods to the "vastly expanded American continent."[32]

The construction of such lighthouses represented a major advance for the young republic. In 1832, the engineer and architect Robert Mills wrote in his book *The American Pharos, or Light-House Guide*, "The British government, ever watchful over the interest of commerce, has spared neither expense, time, nor trouble, to secure the safety of the mariner approaching its coasts, or navigating its waters. Our commercial interests are equally important, and demand a corresponding attention from our government."[33] The establishment of lighthouses was crucial if the United States was going to compete with Europe, and Great Britain, in particular. Therefore, in the 1830s, when Terrapin Tower was built, lighthouses held specific meanings in American culture. Sited on the American side of the Falls, Terrapin Tower, although not an actual lighthouse, represented the new power of the United States. And like the mouth of the Mississippi, Niagara Falls was located at another important gateway into the United States; hence, the symbolic lighthouse, a feat of engineering because of its precarious situation, welcomed foreigners to America.

Although a narrative of nationalism is evident at Terrapin Tower, one English tourist had a different interpretation of the tower. Novelist Anthony Trollope wrote:

> I do not quite approve of that tower, seeing that it has about it a gingerbread air, and reminds one of those well-arranged scenes of romance in which one is told that on the left you turn to the lady's bower, price sixpence; and on the right ascend to the knight's bed, price sixpence more, with a view of the hermit's tomb thrown in. But nevertheless the tower is worth mounting, and no money is charged for the use of it. It is not very high, and there is a balcony at the top on which some half dozen persons may stand at ease. Here the mystery is lost, but the whole fall is seen.[34]

Trollope could not extend forgiveness to other structures visible from Terrapin. Across the falls on the Canadian side, he observed the so-called Camera Obscura, which contained a dark room from which one could view a projected image of the falls. Trollope lamented the moneymaking purposes of such "tasteless" buildings that were positioned poorly in the landscape.[35] Why did Trollope forgive Terrapin Tower while lambasting the Camera Obscura? It seems that the very "gingerbread" appearance that Trollope seems to lament may be its redeeming feature. Indeed, it is the design features of Terrapin Tower that lend the structure the associational qualities prized by nineteenth-century commentators. Despite the lighthouse appearance of the tower, Trollope is reminded of the popular tourist attractions of his own homeland. He describes the tourist experience readily available at places such as Kenilworth Castle, which also features towers. The associational elements of architectural design sparked romantic daydreaming.

Other towers at Niagara, including Charles Robinson's pagoda on the Canadian side at Table Rock, lacked the architectural interest of Terrapin Tower. The pagoda was a lattice-work wooden tower placed atop another structure; it is strikingly *not* freestanding, as is Terrapin. Throughout the decades following the construction of Terrapin Tower, observation towers were built both at Niagara Falls and nearby at the Lundy's Lane Battlefield in Ontario, dating from the War of 1812, where a total of five towers were constructed to cater to American and Canadian tourists. The first tower built at Lundy's Lane, called Anderson Tower, was a "crude structure without a cellar and without a stone foundation, and merely consisted of four huge logs placed in the sand, tapering at the top and covered with lattice work. . . . The posts soon decayed, and during a stormy winter night the first observatory collapsed, and was never rebuilt by its owner."[36] Certainly, this rude structure did not have historicized architectural aspirations. The second tower, built by Donald McKenzie in 1846, was more elaborate in that it had a cellar and a stone foundation and some indigenous decoration on the inside. According to the owner's daughter, Jennie McKenzie, "the first storey [*sic*] had shelves around the inside, upon which were placed Indian beadwork . . . moose-hair, bark-work, bullets which were picked up in the gardens at that time, stone specimens, also bows and arrows and different kinds of canes."[37] In total, four wooden and one steel tower were built over the course of the nineteenth century at Lundy's Lane Battlefield. None of these towers participate in the associational *tromp-l'oeil* of Terrapin Tower, however. Hence, the popularity of Terrapin stems not only from its spectacular site, but also from its design. It is an eye-catcher in the landscape: a "lighthouse" where no vessel would ever dare navigate.

The pictorial legacy of Terrapin Tower is enormous. The tower is visible in many depictions of the falls, notably Frederic Church's painting *Niagara* (1857). This painting, with its "message of national hope and expansiveness," embodies the swelling nationalism of the period.[38] However, Church focused, not surprisingly, on the waterfall, rather than the tower (it is just visible across the water). Of course, nineteenth-century landscape paintings are compositions rather than literal transcriptions of particular places. Painters chose what to include in any particular scene, and the claptrap of tourism diminished the sublimity and wild quality of a site. In contrast, photographs and engravings of Niagara highlight, rather than diminish, Terrapin Tower. Perhaps because of its dramatic siting on the brink of the cataract, or perhaps because of its architectural association with nationalist pride in a new nation, Terrapin Tower was remembered through prints and photographs for years to come. Demolished in 1873, the lost tower was so beloved that in 1908, one commentator wrote that the reconstruction of "this ancient landmark" was under consideration at Niagara Falls.[39] Although never rebuilt, the tower piques our interest even today and tells a story about nationalism in early nineteenth-century America.

In addition to the thrill of sublime nature, the tower also gave its visitors a feeling of power. McKinsey writes,

> As an undeniably phallic image defying the waters at the very brink of the precipice, [Terrapin Tower] represented man's ultimate ability to resist and control the forces of Niagara. Standing at its top, common tourists could not only admire the great feats of the bridge- and tower-builders, but could also participate in the elation of conquest to some degree, for there they had the most "commanding" view of the cataract. As the guidebooks all told them, there they would not only be affected by it, they would also in a sense possess it.[40]

At Terrapin Tower, mere visitors became, in their imaginations, *owners* of the spectacular landscape. Such a position "outside of nature, master of what he [the viewer] surveys" is akin to the position "assumed by visitors to the cycloramas or panoramas," notes John F. Sears, but also, Sears writes, "a faintly sacred point of vision that recalls Moses's view of the Promised Land from Mount Pisgah."[41]

Perhaps the most ambitious style for prospect towers in the nineteenth-century United States was the Egyptian Revival and its concomitant building type, the obelisk (a four-sided stone structure tapering to a pyramidal apex). Napoleon's New Eastern campaigns and resultant archaeological finds, along with Jean-François Champollion's deciphering of hieroglyphics in 1822, sparked great interest in ancient Egyptian civilization in both Europe and the United States in the early nineteenth century.[42] American obelisks were first and foremost monuments, most often commemorating military victories, but many were also prospect towers.[43] Examples include Solomon Willard's Bunker Hill Monument (1825–1843) and the Chalmette Monument, attributed to Newton Richards, in New Orleans (c. 1850–1908). Others, such as the Washington Monument (designed by Robert Mills and completed by Thomas Casey) in Washington, DC, commemorated military figures, while still others hailed the military attributes of historical figures, such as the Lincoln Mausoleum designed by Larkin G. Mead and Russell Sturgis in Springfield, Illinois (1869–1874). Obelisks appeared with some frequency in English landscape gardens as ornaments. Thomas Jefferson noted obelisks in the gardens at Lord Burlington's Chiswick House near London, at Alexander Pope's garden at Twickenham, and at the Leasowes in Shropshire. Although Jefferson was critical of the obelisk in Chiswick in particular, describing it as "of very ill effect," he designed an obelisk for his own graveyard monument, which was erected in 1833.[44] Why co-opt the architecture of ancient Egypt in grandiose statements of national identity, such as the Washington Monument? Historian Joy M. Giguere explains that since the 1790s, Americans "appropriated" Egyptian forms "to articulate to the rest of the world the nation's identity as the modern beneficiary of antiquity's greatest achievements."[45]

English garden obelisks tend to be solid like their ancient Egyptian prototypes, but their American counterparts were often hollowed out and built on a much larger scale, allowing the obelisks to function as prospect towers. The expansive quality of the view was paramount. The view from the Saratoga Monument (1877–1882), an obelisk designed by Jared Clark Markham in Schuylerville, New York, to commemorate the American defeat of the British at Saratoga during the Revolutionary War (figure 4.7), allowed one to see "the entire region between Lake George, the Green Mountains, and the Catskills."[46] The Saratoga Battle Monument is quite eclectic in its associationism: it is an obelisk with Gothic Revival ornamentation and statues of American military leaders.[47] Architectural historian John Zukowsky first noted the curiously hollow nature of American obelisks in an article in *Art Bulletin* in 1976. Zukowsky attributes the dual function of monument and belvedere to the desire of nineteenth-century American tourists to view the landscape from an aerial perspective as part of a popular expansionist philosophy expressed in the phrase "manifest destiny." In this reading of obelisks, height equals power, and an expansive view, even if it does not encompass the frontier literally, suggests manifest destiny.[48]

Although the towers described thus far were available to middle-class tourists, by the 1850s and 1860s, the elevated view became more accessible to the working class. "The People's Park" at Birkenhead, England, inspired Frederick Law Olmsted, codesigner of Central Park. Birkenhead Park was created for the public, a rarity in England at the time, when access to large expenses of landscaped grounds were limited to aristocrats, who on occasion, in acts of *noblesse oblige*, allowed visitors.[49] On a visit to Birkenhead in May 1851, Olmsted and other park patrons sought shelter from the rain in a pagoda "on an island approached by a Chinese bridge." The sight of this little gathering inside a garden folly impressed on Olmsted's mind the democratization of landscape that a public park represented. Olmsted noted that he was "glad to observe that the privileges of the garden were enjoyed about equally by all classes." While some people had servants and carriages, "a large proportion were of the common ranks" and some were "evidently the wives of very humble laborers."[50]

Olmsted's conception of Central Park was also open in terms of access, although as Roy Rosenzweig and Elizabeth Blackmar have shown, Olmsted

FIGURE 4.7.   Exterior view of the Saratoga Battle Monument in the Village of Victory near Schuylerville, New York. New York State Archives. Education Dept. Division of Visual Instruction. Instructional lantern slides, 1911–1925, A3045-78, Lantern slide D47_ShE, Box 17.

thought of the park as an institution that could inculcate gentility within working class visitors; hence, he favored behavioral codes in line with the genteel activity of promenading as opposed to the sports and recreational activities of the masses.[51] Nevertheless, with the opening of Central Park, people of all social classes were able to experience the delight in elevation and the power inherent in the view from above at Belvedere Castle, built between 1867 and 1871 and designed by Calvert Vaux (figure 4.8). Vaux was an English architect who came to the United States to partner with landscape gardener Andrew Jackson Downing; he codesigned Central Park with Olmsted. The Romanesque Revival tower is made of stone, reminiscent of medieval castle architecture. The castle becomes part of the landscape itself, as it seems to grow

FIGURE 4.8.   "The Observatory, Central Park, N. Y." The Miriam and Ira D. Wallach Division of Art, Prints and Photographs: Picture Collection, The New York Public Library. New York Public Library Digital Collections. http://digitalcollections.nypl.org/items/510d47e2-8b5d-a3d9-e040 -e00a18064a99 (accessed November 1, 2018).

organically from the natural rock on which it is placed. Although the building looks like a fortification, its elaborate style was originally nothing more than a shell with open window frames and doors. Its sole purpose was to provide an excellent prospect of Central Park through a series of viewing platforms and to ornament the landscape. The view from the castle takes in a large extent of the park, giving the castle its "Belvedere" name.[52]

As for the democratization of the view, Olmsted himself explained his intentions in codesigning Central Park: "It is one great purpose of the Park to supply to the hundreds of thousands of tired workers, who have no opportunity to spend their summers in the country, a specimen of God's handiwork that shall be to them, inexpensively, what a month or two in the White Mountains or the Adirondacks is, at great cost, to those in easier circumstances."[53] Whether working class visitors consciously participated in the panoptic sublime is unknown, but for the first time, they had access to the view afforded by an elevated folly. A 1906 postcard, "The Observatory, Central Park, N.Y.," suggests that not all visitors to Belvedere Castle were interested in the view of the Central Park landscape. The postcard instead highlights the social power inherent in the view. People occupy the many lookout platforms throughout the belvedere, but not all gazes point outward to the landscape. Most conspicuous is a man striking a casual pose, leaning against the parapet in a relaxed position with his legs crossed. Although the view behind him is beautiful, he is looking inward at the people crossing the large terrace of the belvedere. The viewer's gaze is likewise directed at the two main figures in the postcard, slightly off-center, a woman and young girl who promenade across the broad expanse.

Indeed, not every belvedere user realized that the gaze flowed in both directions. Belvederes functioned in the landscape as eye-catchers, directing the viewer from one lookout to the next and back again. At Fairmount Waterworks in Philadelphia, where a number of belvederes dotted the landscape overlooking the Schuylkill River, some visitors were unaware of being the object of curious gazes. In 1875, one publication (*A Century After: Picturesque Glimpses of Philadelphia and Pennsylvania*) observed, "There are those, too, who consider an arbor on a hill the very place for a little quiet flirtation, as if privacy was nowhere so certain as in such a spot. But getting up on a pedestal is never the safest way to avoid being seen, and the doings on the hill-top may come to be proclaimed on the house-top (see figure 4.9)."[54] The belvedere, then, becomes a locus for romantic trysts and perhaps even transgressive sexual behavior, viewed in turn by the voyeur in another belvedere. Indeed, Victorian Americans were not as prudish as our contemporary popular culture imagines, as Karen Lystra shows in her book *Searching the Heart: Women, Men, and Romantic Love in Nineteenth-Century America*.[55] The architecture of the belvedere functions as a frame around the bodily interactions of the lovers on view. The author of *A Century After* also notes that the camera obscura in the nearby pleasure grounds of Lemon Hill reveals the activities of young lovers: "Fred and Georgiana . . . have just discovered a pretty nook in the shrubbery . . . when lo! From the terrible lens of the camera, a complete picture of

ARBOR ON BASIN.

FIGURE 4.9. "Arbor on Basin" from *A Century After: Picturesque Glimpses of Philadelphia and Pennsylvania*, Philadelphia: Allen, Lane and Scott and J. W. Lauderbach, 1875. Am1875 Century 13899. Q p. 30. The Library Company of Philadelphia.

the transaction is projected on the field of vision."[56] This radical shift in power dynamics from "viewer" to "viewed" reveals the spectacle of modern life in nineteenth-century America and the importance of the belvedere as a building type embodying a modern kind of panoptic vision.

Jefferson's proposed Montalto prospect tower offered its owner a chance to experience the "panoptic sublime." In the entry in *Keywords* on "Eminence," landscape historian Therese O'Malley states that siting structures on high terrain "offered visual command of an estate." "Such surveillance," she notes, "was a vital part of maintaining the plantation labor system of large slave popula- tions."[57] Although never constructed, Jefferson's tower would have emphasized the power of the plantation's owner. Architectural historian Dell Upton has ar- gued that enslaved people were able to subvert the power hierarchies at south- ern plantations, but the siting of the Montalto tower at a distance from the vegetable garden, vineyard, and other working spaces at Monticello would have set the tower apart.[58] With a telescope, the viewer in the tower would have been able to watch the goings-on in the plantation landscape, while the people on the ground, without the benefit of magnifying instruments, would have been the object of a one-way, panoptic gaze. Jefferson's prospect tower highlights the in- herent power in height. However, in the nineteenth century, towers were not always the purview of the elites, and hence the panoptic vision splinters and shifts. When towers became open to the public, we no longer had a single, powerful man of wealth gazing down at those beneath him both figuratively and literally. Belvedere Castle in Central Park tells the story of democratization with the arrival of the public park, a place where people of all social classes have access to landscape ornaments and their views. Other belvederes, and Terrapin Tower in particular, tell an associational story of national striving while high- lighting the spectacular beauty of wondrous natural sites in a narrative of nationalism.

CHAPTER 5

Ruins

The Nineteenth-Century Delight in Decay

On his 1788 visit to Wilhelmsbad, Hanau, Germany, Jefferson discovered a "clever" ruin resembling the "remains of an old castle." In the margin of his notes, Jefferson drew the cruciform ground plan as well as the plan of the circular room in the upper story. He described four "little square towers" at the corners that functioned as platforms for observing the view. Presumably these drawings and notes were for his own future reference in designing ruins at Monticello, an indulgence he never pursued. Shifting unceremoniously in his notes, he then declared that he preferred the ruin at Hagley Park in Worcestershire, England, a place he had visited during his garden tour in 1786.[1] Again, he doodled in the margin a drawing of Hagley Castle, one of the most well-known sham ruins of the English landscape garden tradition. Built for Lord Lyttelton and designed by Sanderson Miller in 1747–1748, the medieval-looking, ruinous castle at Hagley Park attracted a great deal of attention in the eighteenth century. Poet and landscape gardener William Shenstone described the castle in 1749 as consisting "of one entire Tow'r and three stumps of Tow'rs with a ruined wall betwixt them."[2] This pseudomedieval ruin was full of associations, and the sight of it would send the viewer into rapturous flights of fancy. One contemporary observer imagined visitors would contemplate "what sieges it had sustained,—what blood had been spilt upon its walls."[3] Artificial garden ruins allowed viewers to imagine heroic deeds of bygone eras. A ruin is the ultimate folly in that it serves purely as a landscape ornament. In a new nation as rational and enlightened as the United States, who would build a ruin? Indeed, the sight of any kind of ruin in the landscape of the new republic was jarring to say the least. When Alexis de Tocqueville visited upstate New York in 1831, he came upon the ruins of a habitation on an island in Oneida Lake that to him appeared completely untouched, a true American wilderness. Amid the new growth of vegetation, he discerned fences, a hearth, a chimney, a cabin. His response—"What! already in Ruins!"—reveals the common idea that America was too new to have ruins of any kind.[4]

But the desire for ruins was intense. Ruins aged the American landscape, thereby conferring a cultural status equivalent to Europe's architectural heritage. Gardeners and architects indulged this desire for age by building purpose-built ruins in America. Ruins fulfilled a need for a physical heritage beyond pure nature. Purpose-built ruins in the nineteenth-century United States were rare, but they did exist. When Americans built ruins, oftentimes their pragmatism ironically led them to rebuild the ruins as permanent structures. Beyond ruin follies, though, existed a larger culture of ruins among writers and tourists who sought out actual ruins from America's past to visit and to ponder. Places such as Fort Ticonderoga became sites of pilgrimage for tourists fascinated by the allure of ruins with a history to reveal. And in the visual culture of the nineteenth century, Americans projected their desire for ruins onto natural scenery; cave openings became Gothic pointed arches, and, in the paintings of the Hudson River School, trees bent overhead to form irregular, but clearly discernable, arches—ruins in the landscape. Transcendentalist Margaret Fuller participated in this hunt for ruins in nature; in viewing the arched rock at Mackinac Island in Michigan, she wrote that "these natural ruins may vie for beautiful effect with the remains of European grandeur."[5] This larger context of ruin fascination in American visual culture proves that although purpose-built ruins were rare in the United States, the desire for ruins was pervasive.

Scholars have argued for two distinct interpretations of ruins. On the one hand, some argue that nineteenth-century ruins express a kind of cultural anxiety. For instance, Sarah Burns contends that the ruins in Thomas Cole's paintings express Jacksonian anxiety and fear of personal failure. More recently, Nick Yablon writes that nineteenth-century pictures of ruins (even those of cities destroyed by fire) "were not necessarily expressions of cultural pessimism or nihilism, or even of antipathy toward modernity or urbanism as such." Since the seventeenth century, he suggests, ruins have "elicited pleasure as much as gloom." Certainly, in English examples, one can find both purely pleasurable ruins, as well as ruins-as-political-statements, suggesting the conflicts and anxieties of the age.[6]

In the eighteenth century, English garden designer and author Batty Lang-
ley popularized ruins in his book, *New Principles of Gardening* (1728). Purpose-
built ruins began to appear in English landscape gardens. In the nineteenth
century, William Gilpin, the English clergyman and champion of the picturesque, sought out authentic ruins. In his travel book describing the English
countryside, *Observations on Several Parts of the Counties of Cambridge, Norfolk,
Suffolk, and Essex* (1809), Gilpin juxtaposed completed buildings with their ruinous counterparts (figure 5.1). According to Gilpin, ruins gained a picturesque advantage for three reasons: ruins created irregularity in general form
with infinite variations; regularized architectural elements, including windows and arches, become irregular in ruin; and colors from weather stains
and the growth of plants, including moss, weeds, and ivy, break straight lines
and contribute to the picturesque effect. On ruins, Gilpin writes: "It is not
every man who can build a house that can execute a ruin. To give the stone its
mouldering appearance—to make the widening chink run naturally through all
the joints—to mutilate the ornaments—to peel the facing from the internal
structure—to show how correspondent parts have once united, though now
the chasm runs wide between them—and to scatter heaps of ruin around with
negligence and ease, are great efforts of art; much too delicate for the hand of
a common workman; and what we very rarely see performed."[7] In the Age of
Sensibility, to view an authentic ruin was to engage vicariously with the senti-
ments of the ruin's former inhabitants. In his book *Observations on Modern Gardening* (1770), Thomas Whately notes that "All remains excite an enquiry into
the former state of the edifice . . . and certain sensations of regret, of venera-
tion, or compassion, attend the recollection." Although Whately acknowledges that real ruins work best in sparking an imaginative reverie, he also
notes that sham or "fictitious" ruins can likewise create weaker, but similar,
emotions.[8]

One such designed ruin is the so-called Grotto (1836) built by Nicholas Biddle
for his Andalusia estate on the Delaware River near Philadelphia (figure 5.2).[9]
Biddle was a prominent financier and president of the Second Bank of the
United States. He engaged Thomas Ustick Walter to renovate his federal-style
house Andalusia into a Greek Revival temple overlooking the river. At the
bottom slope of a graceful lawn sits the Grotto. This extant structure, also
designed by Thomas Ustick Walter, takes the form of a Gothic ruined chapel.
Apparently, in the age of rampant eclecticism in American architecture, neither
architect nor client was troubled by the contradiction of placing a ruined
Gothic chapel as a picturesque eye-catcher from the temple front of a Greek
Revival villa.[10] Although built as a ruin, the little chapel is now fully enclosed,

FIGURE 5.1. "Ruin Illustrated with Regard to its General Form," from *Observations on Several Parts of the Counties of Cambridge, Norfolk, Suffolk, and Essex*, London: T. Cadell and W. Davies, 1809. Is Gilp 3910.0 p. 122. The Library Company of Philadelphia.

FIGURE 5.2.   Thomas Ustick Walter, The Grotto, Andalusia, 1836. Photograph by author.

functioning as a vault for the Biddle family; indeed, such is often the fate of purpose-built ruins which have managed to survive until the present time.

In the early 1840s, John Church Cruger built a ruinous chapel on an island in the Hudson River near Barrytown and placed within and about it several large Maya artifacts that his friend and travel author John Lloyd Stephens had given him.[11] Stephens had acquired Maya artifacts in Yucatán and displayed artifacts of carved wood and pottery in a "panoramic exhibition [which] showed the glories of ancient civilizations and bonded Egypt and Central America" before they were destroyed by a fire soon after their arrival in New York.[12] However, a few stones had been delayed in transit, thereby avoiding the blaze, and Stephens gave these objects to Cruger. The stones were displayed around the Romanesque Revival ruin for about eighty years until Cruger's daughters sold them in the early twentieth century to the American Museum of Natural History in New York, where they now reside. The assistant curator of anthropology at the museum at the time, Herbert J. Spinden, wrote an article detailing the history of the stones soon after their integration into the museum's collection, noting how in their setting on Cruger's Island, the "carved blocks of gray limestone from Yucatán showed in startling contrast against the dark background of lichened slabs from the native ledges."[13]

Imagine how curious a sight to travelers on the Hudson—a ruined chapel decorated with these fantastic and exotic stone objects. In the company of Andrew Jackson Downing, the Swedish novelist Frederika Bremer observed the stones, noting their affinity to Egyptian statuary:

> On . . . a point projecting into the river, has a ruin been built, in which are placed various figures and fragments of walls and columns, which have been brought from the remarkable ruins lately discovered in Central America or Mexico. The countenances and the headdresses resembled greatly the heads of Egyptian statues. I was struck in particular with a sphinx-like countenance, and a head similar to that of a priest of Isis. The ruin and its ornaments, in the midst of a wild, romantic, rocky, and wooded promontory, was a design in the best taste.[14]

Not all travelers recognized the correct origin of the stones, however; *New England: A Handbook for Travellers* noted that the "picturesque and truly ancient ruin" on the island was "imported from Italy."[15] Whether viewers thought the objects were Central American, Egyptian, or Italian, they seemed to understand that the stones did not belong on Cruger's Island and that they had come from elsewhere. The greatest irony of Cruger's Folly is, of course, that these stones were removed from their original location in the ruins of the ancient Maya cities of Uxmal and Kabah to reside in a faux ruin in the pleasure garden of a well-to-do American on the Hudson River.[16]

The ruined gateway to Hollywood Cemetery on Cherry Street in Richmond, Virginia, is likewise out of place (figure 5.3); how could the American landscape sport a medieval ruin? Likely designed by local architect Henry Exall "in the form and semblance of a ruined tower," the gateway was completed in 1877.[17] Like Biddle's Grotto, the Hollywood Cemetery gatehouse's existence as a ruin came to an end; in 1897 Marion J. Dimmock enclosed the ruin to create a finished chapel for the cemetery. Practicality triumphed over aesthetics, and today only a portion of the ruin survives.[18] Illustrated in an inset alongside the entrance in C. Poindexter's *Richmond: An Illustrated Hand-Book and Guide with Notices of the Battle-Fields* is the Monument of Confederate Dead (designed by Charles Henry Dimmock and dedicated in 1869), a pyramid that in other period depictions is often covered in plant life, much like the ruined gatehouse.[19] These two ruins evoke wildly different periods of architectural history, Gothic and Egyptian, and yet are united in their ruinous states.

For the Gothic style in particular, literature, especially historical romances, played a large role in popularizing ruins. In its square form, pointed arches, stone construction, and ragged roofline, Hollywood's gatehouse tower resembled Dryburgh Abbey, Scottish poet and novelist Sir Walter Scott's resting

FIGURE 5.3.   "Hollywood Entrance and Soldiers' Monument." Charles Poindexter, *Richmond: An Illustrated Hand-book and Guide with Notices of the Battlefields*. Richmond, VA: J. L. Hill Print, 1896. RB115337. The Huntington Library, San Marino, CA.

place. Ruins associated with Scott provided visitors with material for plaintive musings about historical incidents. In the following passage, Downing explained the allure of Gothic architecture by invoking British history and fiction. Although he does not specifically mention Scott, it is likely he has the Scottish Romantic poet and novelist in mind:

> The ideas connected in our minds with Gothic architecture are of a highly *romantic* and *poetical* nature, contrasted with the classical associations which the Greek and Roman styles suggest. Although our own country is nearly destitute of ruins and ancient time-worn edifices, yet the literature of Europe, and particularly of what we term the mother country, is so much our own, that we form a kind of delightful ideal acquaintance with the venerable castles, abbeys, and strong-holds of the middle ages. Romantic, as is the real history of those times and places, to our minds their charm is greatly enhanced by distance, by the poetry of legendary superstition, and the fascination of fictitious narrative.[20]

Places such as Kenilworth Castle, featured in Scott's novel *Kenilworth* (1821), became part of the British grand tour, the itinerary of which many American artists and writers followed, including Downing on his 1851 trip to Great Britain. Books such as *Landscape Illustrations of the Waverley Novels: with Descriptions of the Views* (London, 1832) featured images of ruins associated with Scott and his writings. American painters including Thomas Cole, Asher B. Durand, John Casilear, and Sanford Gifford visited Kenilworth and made sketches or oil paintings of the ruins.[21] More so than complete buildings, ruins suggest a narrative, one that can be constructed by the viewer. Indeed, ruins are inherently narrative structures. In Lilly Martin Spencer's painting *Reading the Legend* (1852), a couple reads a book while a ruinous castle appears in the background, conjured up from their imaginations. How popular was Sir Walter Scott in Richmond, where the ruined gatehouse to Hollywood Cemetery stood? Scholar Emily B. Todd analyzed the borrowing records of a Richmond library between 1839 and 1860 and found that antebellum readers "binged" on Scott's series of Waverley novels: "These library borrowing records suggest that patrons read the novels as a collection—often entering (for days and days) historical worlds created by Walter Scott."[22]

An American version of Melrose Abbey, a ruined medieval building featured in Scott's long narrative poem, *The Lay of the Last Minstrel* (1805), is Washington Irving's home Sunnyside in the Hudson Valley (1835–1837). Irving and his friend, landscape painter George Harvey, transformed an old farmhouse into a picturesque cottage for Irving. Irving had visited Scott at his home Abbotsford in Scotland and emulated Scott's baronial manor not in scale but in conception and in details. In the essay "Abbotsford" (1835), Irving describes visiting Sir Walter Scott at Abbotsford.[23] Most relevant to our discussion is that Irving visited the ruins of Melrose Abbey, located near Abbotsford. From Melrose, Irving took some clippings of the ivy home to New York and later planted the ivy on Sunnyside's walls. Sunnyside, then, became a combination of house and ruin, covered with plant life. George Inness's painting of Sunnyside shows the little cottage almost consumed by nature, a picturesque object of delight (figure 5.4). A winding path leads to Irving's door through the landscape Irving designed in the English style. By creating a house-as-ruin, Irving was conferring age on the landscape. As he noted in his sketch "The Voyage," the scene of a "mouldering ruin of an abbey overrun with ivy" was "characteristic of England."[24] Hence, Irving borrowed the notion of age to apply to America's untamed landscape. As Alice P. Kenney and Leslie J. Workman write in their seminal essay "Ruins, Romance, and Reality: Medievalism in Anglo-American Imagination and Taste, 1750–1840": "Therefore, although they read the same books, English readers learned from them what to look for in their historic

FIGURE 5.4.   George Inness (1825–1896), *Sunnyside*, 1850–1860, oil on canvas, Historic Hudson Valley, SS.79.34. Historic Hudson Valley, Pocantico Hills, NY.

surroundings, while American readers learned how to make their surroundings look more historic."[25]

Inspired by Mount Auburn Cemetery, the founders of Woodlawn Cemetery in Everett, Massachusetts, laid out their cemetery in the mid-nineteenth century.[26] The chief designer was Henry Weld Fuller, a member of the Massachusetts Horticultural Society. Many of the founders and trustees of Woodlawn also served on the Mount Auburn board. And like Mount Auburn, Woodlawn also had an observation tower, called the "Great Tower" (figure 5.5), described in an address at the consecration of the cemetery on July 2, 1851:

> [A] rustic winding-tower of rocks—seventy feet in diameter at the base—has been commenced, and raised about twenty feet, to constitute an observatory of a picturesque and striking character. This is to be covered with ever-green ivy, and with moss and climbing roses, between which visitors may wind their way, ascending to the top.[27]

After its completion, Fuller described the tower in his guide to the cemetery, as a "massive pile of rocks."[28] Another guidebook writer called it a "ponderous pile."[29] Visitors ascended the thirty-foot tower by means of a spiral walk.

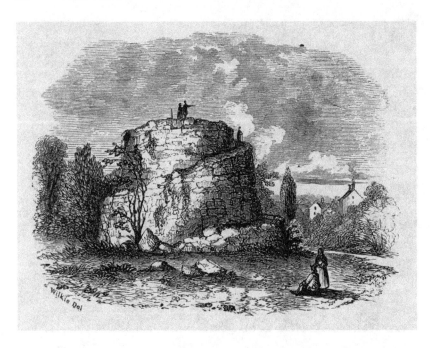

FIGURE 5.5. "Rock Tower," in the Woodlawn cemetery in North Chelsea and Malden. Following page 44, in Fuller, Henry Weld, 1810–1889. *The Woodlawn Cemetery in North Chelsea and Malden*. Boston: Higgins and Bradley, 1856. F74.M2 F85 1856. Image 6.8 × 9.2 cm; including text 8 × 9.2 cm. Collection of the Massachusetts Historical Society.

Unlike the intact and formidable granite construction of Washington Tower at Mount Auburn, Woodlawn's "Great Tower" appears ruinous.[30] Fuller writes "It does not now appear like a modern structure; and when its interstices are filled with ferns and mosses, and its huge bowlders [*sic*] are bound together by countless cords of woodbine and ivy, and its baldness covered by green leaves and lichens and relieved by running roses, it will seem still more like a relic of ancient times."[31] Ruins encouraged visitors to ponder the effects of time and weather on man-made structures, with attendant thoughts on human mortality, an activity well suited to the cemetery setting. The tower was also a belvedere, providing views of the ocean to the east. But this structure was not only a ruin; it was a hybrid of a ruin and rockwork, a popular garden ornament. It is likely that Fuller had consulted Andrew Jackson Downing's *A Treatise on the Theory and Practice of Landscape Gardening* (1841) in which Downing declares that once rockwork is formed, "creeping, and alpine plants, such as delight naturally in similar situations, may be planted in the soil which fills the interstices between the rocks," a description similar to Fuller's own.[32]

What is interesting about Woodlawn's Great Tower is its presence in a cemetery, since the building serves no obvious funereal function.[33] Perhaps Fuller realized this incongruity. He writes, "What an altar for Mount Moriah! . . . Probably, in time, it [the tower] will form only the foundation for some high observatory; but, while remaining in its present unpolished grandeur, it may well remind us of the altar of Abraham, and of his unfaltering faith. Here, then, let us rekindle our faith in God, and renew our good resolves."[34] By linking the tower with Abraham's dutiful attempt to sacrifice his son Isaac on Mount Moriah, Fuller is creating a narrative about this architectural folly in order to legitimize the presence of a pleasurable garden structure in a sacred location. Abraham's story is particularly relevant to the formation of a cemetery. The anonymous author of the *Guide to Laurel Hill Cemetery Near Philadelphia* (1847) notes that Christians will find inspiration in the "patriarchs of Israel," who present to us "a spirit of reverence and solicitude for the burial-places of their dead." Quoting Abraham on his acquisition of a burying place for his wife Sarah in the book of Genesis, the writer uses Abraham as an example worth imitating in the formation of nineteenth-century cemeteries.[35] Fuller likewise associates the Great Tower, located on Moriah Avenue within the cemetery, with Abraham, although most tourists would probably have enjoyed the tower not for any religious narratives referenced by Fuller, but for the view toward the ocean to the east and the meadows and forests surrounding Woodlawn.

In the Hudson Valley, Matthew Vassar added a miniature replica of the ruins of prehistoric Stonehenge in his estate Springside in Poughkeepsie, originally designed by landscape gardener Andrew Jackson Downing in 1850–1852. In his book *Vassar College and Its Founder* (1867), historian and writer Benson J. Lossing described the scene at Springside: "Look up to the left . . . and see, on the summit of this high knoll, how weird appear those huge upright stones, standing here like palisades, and there like solitary sentinels guarding some mysterious spot. This is called Stonehenge because of its suggestiveness of those strange remains of the Druids found at a place of that name in England."[36] Perhaps a picturesque garden folly from the pages of Scottish garden designer John Claudius Loudon's book *An Encyclopedia of Cottage, Farm and Villa Architecture and Furniture*, inspired Vassar. Loudon illustrates "a huge imitation of Stonehenge" at Alton Towers in Staffordshire, England, and although Vassar's Stonehenge is on a much smaller scale, the resemblance is noteworthy.[37] Today, visitors to the Springside site can view the remains of the Stonehenge ruins, toppled blocks of stone engulfed in plant life.

Stonehenge was one of the most popular English ruins in the nineteenth century, attracting American landscape painters. Thomas Cole included an intact Stonehenge-like circle of rocks in part two of his Course of Empire series, *The Pastoral or Arcadian State* (1834). In 1882, William Trost Richards painted Stonehenge, about which he wrote: "It has that pathetic look which is peculiar to all human work which has reverted to Nature. Architectural enough to be a ruin, and as rude and moss covered as though ages ago it had been left by some glacier."[38] Images of Stonehenge appeared in American visual culture throughout the nineteenth century, including a view from an article by John Harris Morden entitled "Engla-Land and the Abiding Memorials of its Antiquity," which appeared in *Potter's American Monthly* in 1875. The mystery of the origins of Stonehenge fascinated readers. In the article, Morden wrote "In viewing Stonehenge, we are almost willing to credit the strange old legend which tells how Merlin, or Merdhin, the magician, flew away, bearing the stones from Curragh of Kildare, Ireland." After listing the many theories about Stonehenge, including English architect Inigo Jones's idea that it was a "Roman temple of the Tuscan," Morden concluded that the accepted theory credits the Druids with the construction of Stonehenge, a common belief in the nineteenth century.[39]

American ruins were not necessarily purpose-built structures; sometimes they were natural forms that resembled architecture. Ruinous pointed arches abounded in nineteenth-century literature and visual culture. Hudson River School artists projected the Gothic arch onto the American landscape in paintings such as Thomas Cole's *Kaaterskill Falls* of 1826 in which the cave behind the waterfall (a popular nineteenth-century tourist attraction in New York State's Catskill Mountains) takes the shape of a yawning Gothic arch of earth at the top of the painting. Indeed, there are numerous examples of Gothic arches in paintings of the American landscape by artists of the Hudson River School. These painted arches function as Gothic ruins in the landscape, at times tinged with Gothic terror of the literary kind. Although these ruins are not follies, their existence on the literary page or the painted canvas points to a larger cultural fascination with ruined architecture. They represent a search for ruins in the American landscape.

American interest in natural Gothic arches derives from a similar impulse in nineteenth-century European art and literature. The German Romantic landscape painter, Casper David Friedrich (1774–1840), mirrors the natural arch with its architectural equivalent in his painting *Abbey in the Oak Forest* (1809–1810), in which a procession of monks moves toward a fragmented abbey with a Gothic arched entryway. Above the abbey's pointed arch, the tree branches almost bend into the shape of an arch. Art historian Karl Whittington has characterized the painting as one of many "deathscapes" (paintings depicting "open graves, cemeteries, and churchyards often in winter and ruin") by Friedrich.

In opposition to transcendent and hopeful interpretations of the painting, Whittington adheres to the notion that the painting is unabashedly "depressing," "a meditation not on transcendence but on death itself."[40] Gnarled and leafless trees surround the figures within the shadowy landscape. Here the Gothic arch acts as a liminal portal between life and death, and the Gothic equates with nature. Indeed, nineteenth-century observers saw Gothic architecture as organic. In *The Deerslayer* (1841), James Fenimore Cooper imagines that forests inspired the Gothic builders:

> The arches of the woods, even at high noon, cast their sombre shadows on the spots, which the brilliant rays of the sun that struggled through the leaves contributed to mellow, and, if such an expression can be used, to illuminate. It was probably from a similar scene that the mind of man first got its idea of the effects of Gothic tracery and churchly hues; this temple of nature producing some such effect, so far as light and shadows were concerned, as the well-known offspring of human invention.[41]

However, Michael Makarius points out that "this notion can just as well be turned on its head; the whole attraction of the ruin lies in its almost allowing a product of nature to be perceived as a human artifact."[42]

Indeed, in the nineteenth-century United States, geological features resembling architecture became tourist attractions, especially caves which functioned as natural "ruins" in the landscape. A good example is in Glens Falls, New York, the so-called Cooper's Cave. Named after James Fenimore Cooper (1793–1851) and featured in his most successful novel in the Leatherstocking series, *The Last of the Mohicans* (1826), this cave was a tourist attraction even before Cooper visited in 1824.[43] In 1798, Timothy Dwight visited the falls and declared that the "prevailing appearance here is that of sublimity," as the water falls in "great sheets, or violent torrents." He continued, "The wildness is extreme, the variety endless, and the beauty intense. From some pictures, which I have seen, I should believe Salvator Rosa might have exhibited this group of objects with advantage . . ."[44] In 1813, the *Gazetteer of the State of New York* described how the cascades flowed over the large rock islands in the river, creating "long excavations or caverns, presenting arched subterranean passages of considerable extent, evidently worn by the water."[45] When Cooper visited, the cave was exposed due to the seasonal low-water point.[46] Cooper was so impressed with the wild surroundings, he reportedly declared "I must place one of my old Indians here."[47] According to his daughter, Susan Fenimore Cooper, Cooper spent time studying the area closely "with a view to accurate description at a later hour."[48] Cooper subsequently had a copy of *The Last of the Mohicans* sent to his traveling partner Edward Smith-Stanley, writing that the two had been there "in the caverns at Glens falls [sic], and it was there that I determined to write the book, promising him a Copy."[49]

The cave at Glens Falls is a Gothic ruin at the center of the novel. Cooper's description of the cave highlights the verticality of the fissure, calling to mind the elongated proportions of the Gothic arch in architecture: "At the farther extremity of a narrow, deep, cavern in the rock, whose length appeared much extended by the perspective and the nature of the light by which it was seen, was seated the scout [Hawk-eye], holding a blazing knot of pine."[50] Cooper has borrowed various conventions of earlier Gothic novels in the cave scene. First and foremost is the cave itself. Cave settings were prevalent in Gothic novels, "even to the point of absurdity," according to Allen Grove. In his scholarly introduction to the popular anonymous British novel *The Cavern of Death* (1794), Grove highlights the popularity of caverns by listing the numerous titles featuring the words "cave" or "cavern."[51] In the United States, Charles Brockden Brown used a mysterious cave setting in his early American novel *Edgar Huntly* (1799). What make caverns particularly suitable to Gothic stories are the inherently sublime qualities of these natural spaces: dimness and obscurity, irregularity in form, and a palette naturally limited to dark colors. In *A Philosophical Enquiry into the Origin of Our Ideas of the Sublime and Beautiful* (1757), Edmund Burke characterized the sublime as encompassing terror caused by obscurity, vastness, and power, while he associated the beautiful with pleasure and procreation. Early American painters exploited the Burkean sublime in paintings of caves. Both Washington Allston's *Donna Mencia in the Robber's Cavern* (1815) and Rembrandt Peale's *The Court of Death* (1820) feature caves—mysterious, subterranean spaces where either bandits lurk or allegorical figures representing human disasters reside.

Cooper uses these elements of the Burkean sublime to great advantage in *The Last of the Mohicans*. For instance, the cave in the story has more than one outlet, and this abundance of thresholds makes the cave both eminently escapable and simultaneously penetrable (ultimately, the Hurons will indeed enter the cave). Earlier, in a particularly Radcliffean moment of suspense, we read that "A spectral looking figure stalked from out the darkness behind the scout, and seizing a blazing brand, held it towards the further extremity of their place of retreat. Alice uttered a faint shriek, and even Cora rose to her feet, as this appalling object moved into the light . . ."[52] The figure is revealed to be their ally, Chingachgook, but in that moment, the indistinct spaces of the cave allow for the possibility of the intrusion of the supernatural in the form of a specter. When Duncan Heyward assures Alice that he will examine the "security of [her] fortress," he is superficially assuaging her fears because the cave is about as safe to a young heroine as any Gothic castle. The prototype, of course, is Ann Radcliffe's castle in her Gothic novel *The Mysteries of Udolpho* (1794). In the castle of Udolpho, Gothic heroine Emily is imprisoned and confronted with any number of frightful experiences in the multitudinous chambers (Cooper's cave likewise contains various spaces). The cave serves as a refuge from the forest haunted by Native American "savages," but the cave is as Gothic as the rest of the wilderness. It is the transposition of the Gothic castle to the New World. As Donald A. Ringe suggests, the caves in *The Last of the Mohicans* are "the wilderness counterparts of the castles, rooms, and subterranean labyrinths familiar from Gothic fiction . . ."[53] Ringe rightly points out that the cave is "the classic Gothic enclosure."[54] In his correspondence with his patron Daniel Wadsworth in 1828 regarding a painting of a cave, Cole outlined his opinion on caves as natural features: "Though a cave may be a gloomy object in Nature—a *view* of its entrance gives rise to those trains of pensive feeling and thought that I have always found the most exquisitely delightful—The poets often speak of caves, and grottos as pleasing objects, and I do not know why the painter may not think as the poet—It is a cool retreat during the Noon-day heats . . ."[55] This quotation highlights two distinct interpretations of caves, the gloomy Gothic cave and the cool grotto, a common feature in landscape gardens.

Like caves, trees also took the shape of ruinous Gothic arches. There are numerous examples of trees bending to form an arched canopy in the forests depicted on Hudson River School canvases. But in American landscape paintings, Gothic arches more often represent the presence of God in nature. For example, Durand's painting *Early Morning at Cold Spring* (1850), referred to as *Sabbath Bells* in the nineteenth century after a line from a William Cullen Bryant poem, presents the viewer with a solitary figure situated off-center beneath trees with branches tilting inward to create a noticeable pointed arch. Durand innovated the use of the vertical format in American landscape paintings, thereby accentuating the upward thrust of the Gothic arch. In the era of Transcendentalism, Durand believed that nature was an appropriate place for worship. In a letter, he writes, "To-day again is Sunday. I do not attend the church service, the better to indulge reflection unrestrained under the high canopy of heaven, amidst the expanse of waters."[56] Worthington Whittredge (1820–1910) adopted the vertical format for his paintings of interior forest scenes, such as *The Old Hunting Grounds* of 1864 (figure 5.6). In *Book of the Artists*, Henry T. Tuckerman notes that the "silvery birches . . . lean towards each other as though breathing of the light of other days."[57] Art historian Anthony Janson points out that Whittredge's painting is "a complex realization of William Cullen Bryant's poetry."[58] Indeed, the painting is a visualization of Bryant's "A Forest Hymn" (1825) in which Bryant writes, "The Groves were God's first

FIGURE 5.6. Worthington Whittredge, *The Old Hunting Grounds*, 1864. 36 1/4 × 27 1/8 in. (92.1 × 68.9 cm). Oil on canvas. Gift of Barbara B. Millhouse. 1976.2.10. Courtesy of Reynolda House Museum of American Art, affiliated with Wake Forest University.

temples."[59] Paintings of tree boughs forming a pointed Gothic interior are common in Hudson River School paintings; art historian Kevin Avery has called the works of Sanford Robinson Gifford (1823–1880) "woodland 'naves,'" an apt architectural metaphor especially evident in Gifford's *Kauterskill Falls* of 1871.[60]

Looking more closely at Whittredge's painting we see beneath that arched canopy a ruined canoe, thereby highlighting the painting's title, *The Old Hunting Grounds*. Whittredge's painting acknowledges that this land at one time provided sustenance for the Native Americans who lived among these birch trees and hunted in the birchbark canoe; the old canoe is a wistful reminder of their presence here. This pleasant Romanticism has a darker subtext, however, because it glosses over the fact that many Americans believed that Native Americans would become extinct. According to Barbara B. Millhouse, "The comforting belief that nature functions in continuous cycles of renewal and decay supported the notion that white people usurping the place of the Indian is as inevitable and irreversible as the young birches replacing the old gnarled trees."[61] The painting then has two competing ruins: the ragged Gothic arch of trees suggests divinity, while the canoe represents nostalgia for the past tinged with the potential loss of Native people due to notions of Manifest Destiny and the federal policy of Indian removal.

How do we reconcile these two divergent interpretations of the American wilderness—the dark and frightening Gothic forests of Cooper's novels and the contemplative and serene scenes of Durand, Whittredge, and Gifford? Perhaps the two visions of nature are not so different. Matthew Sivils explains:

> It is tempting to view Transcendentalism and the American Gothic as conflicting literary movements. After all, Emerson's healing, uplifting, divine woods seem a far cry from the dark wildernesses found in the Gothic texts. Upon closer consideration, however, they might be said to share some important commonalities . . . [they both] promote the idea that mankind ultimately dictates the moral atmosphere of the natural world.[62]

In upstate New York, tourists could experience both the terrifying sublime and the calm, reassuring Transcendental landscape. Washington Irving describes wild scenery in the Catskill Mountains as typically sublime:

> The interior of these mountains is in the highest degree wild and romantic; here are rocky precipices mantled with primeval forests; deep gorges walled in by beetling cliffs, with torrents tumbling as it were from the sky; and savage glens rarely trodden excepting by the hunter.[63]

But while the Catskills and the Hudson River Valley could be sublime, they could also be beautiful, in Burkean terms. An Englishman named John Fowler traveled the Hudson by steamboat in 1830 and wrote "I was so hurried on from the sublime to the beautiful, that before the image of one had impressed itself upon the mind, the other appeared to take possession, and every successive change but deepened the thrill of admiration and rapture."[64] In general, landscape tourists were "not seeking a wilderness experience," but rather a comfortable tour of sites familiar from their readings of history and literature.[65]

Another example is Dover Stone Church in Dover Plains, New York, in the Hudson Valley region. This natural cave opening mimics the shape of a Gothic pointed arch, and tourists visited to see the interior cavern with its "pulpit" (a rock ledge). A local literary journal *The Poughkeepsie Casket* described the Dover Stone Church in 1838:

> [The Church] is formed by a large fissure in a rock on the margin of a mountain which rises abruptly from the plain. . . . The 'Church' has two apartments; the inner is the larger, being about seventy feet in length. They are separated from a huge mass of rock, which seems to have been detached from above, and has been aptly termed the *pulpit* . . . a staircase leads to extensive ledges at a height of thirty feet, forming commodious galleries overlooking the body of the "Church" below. Altogether, this natural excavation is so formed as to give, very readily, to the beholder the idea of a temple of worship.[66]

By 1877, this site had welcomed thousands of visitors, according to the *General History of Duchess County from 1609–1876, Inclusive* (1877).[67] In 1876, Benson Lossing documented the Dover Stone Church as a tourist site with his pamphlet *The Dover Stone Church*.[68] Thomas Cole's friend and fellow landscape painter Asher B. Durand (1796–1886) visited the Dover Stone Church in 1847 and completed three studies of the area in preparation for his oil canvas *Dover Plains, Duchess County, New York* (1848). Durand's rendering (figure 5.7) highlights the cave opening as a ruined Gothic arch.[69]

The Dover Stone Church was also a site of nationalistic pride; such age-old rock formations conferred legitimacy on the American landscape. In the eighteenth century, at the dawn of American nationhood, European scholars characterized the continent and its wildlife as young and even inferior compared to Europe. The French naturalist Comte Georges-Louis de Buffon argued that American species were inferior in size to those of Europe, stating that American animals were degenerate due to a hostile environment. The superior attitude of some Europeans sparked Thomas Jefferson's interest in natural history, which became an intellectual pursuit of many Americans in the late eighteenth and nineteenth centuries; these pursuits were often tinged with the nationalistic desire to prove the Europeans wrong.[70] The heyday of American landscape painting was also a time of exciting new geological discoveries. As Barbara Novak has written, "With every geological discovery America grew older. Geological time, transcending exact chronology, was infinite and thus potentially mythical." From this point of view, Novak continued, "the 'nature' of the New World was superior to the 'culture' of the old."[71] Thus, the popularity of the Dover Stone Church is part of this larger desire for Americans to showcase the age and respectability that a Gothic ruin could bestow on the Hudson Valley landscape, both in terms of natural and cultural history. The fact that this particular geological formation would be reimagined

FIGURE 5.7.   Asher Brown Durand, "Dover Stone Church," Dover Plains, New York; c. 1847: Graphite and white gouache on gray paper, mounted on card; sheet (paper): 14 × 10 in. (35.6 × 25.4 cm). Gift of Miss Nora Durand Woodman, New-York Historical Society, 1918.125.

by writers and tourists as a Gothic arch suggests the power of literature on the nineteenth-century imagination, since it was largely the writings of Gothic novelists that spurred the revival of medieval architecture.

Observers applied that imaginative reverie to American ruins as well. Ruins with patriotic associations held particular curiosity. Benson Lossing explained the appeal of such ruins: "Broken arches and ruined ramparts are always eloquent and suggestive of valiant deeds, even where their special teachings are not comprehended; but manifold greater are the impressions which they make when the patriotism we adore has hallowed them." Upstate New York's Fort Ticonderoga, the eighteenth-century fort in use during the French and Indian War and captured by the Americans at the start of the Revolutionary War, became a popular tourist attraction in the nineteenth century, despite its dilapidated state. Lossing illustrates his visit to this "relic of the revolution" in his book *Pictorial Field-Book of the Revolution* (1850–1852). In the background, the forlorn ruins provide a backdrop for the picturesque tourists in the foreground (figure 5.8). Lossing sketched the ruins just before sunset, and in describing them he imagines the events that took place there; he notes the "rickety steps" that Colonel Ethan Allen ascended and the door at which Allen demanded the surrender of the British captain. Later in the evening on the day of his visit, Lossing returned to the ruins to witness them by moonlight. He writes, "All was hushed, and association, with its busy pencil, wrought many a startling picture." Just then, he is indeed startled by a footstep; Lossing's daytime guide to the ruins, an octogenarian Revolutionary War veteran named Isaac Rice, had also returned, as he claimed he always did, by moonlight. Lossing's description of his visit to Ticonderoga shares much in common with Irving's visit to Melrose Abbey in Scotland in 1817. Escorting Irving

FIGURE 5.8. "Ticonderoga at Sunset," in Benson J. Lossing, *Pictorial Field-Book of the Revolution*, vol. 1 (New York: Harper & Brothers, 1851), 127.

on his tour was Melrose's caretaker, Johnny Bower, who reminds Irving that, according to Scott, the best time to view the abbey was by moonlight. Indeed, darkness and obscurity, features of the Burkean sublime, enhanced the experience of ruins. Like visitors to other spots hallowed by history and literature, including Kenilworth Castle, tourists would imagine the events that had occurred there, much like Lossing did at Ticonderoga.[72]

Another American ruin of great interest in the nineteenth century was the Old Stone Mill or "Newport Ruin" in Newport, Rhode Island, believed by some in the nineteenth century to have been built by twelfth-century Norsemen (figure 5.9). Others argued that Governor Benedict Arnold (an ancestor of the famous traitor) built the structure in the Colonial era. Located in Touro Park and now believed to be a Colonial-era copy of a seventeenth-century windmill in Chesterton, England, the building took hold of the nineteenth-century popular imagination.[73] Characters in James Fenimore Cooper's novel *The Red Rover* (1827–1828) speculated about its origins, and Cooper described it as a "small circular tower, which stood on rude pillars, connected by arches, and might have been constructed, in the infancy of the country, as a place of defence [sic], though is it far more probable that it was a work of a less warlike nature."[74] Henry Wadsworth Longfellow featured the tower in his poem, "The Skeleton in Armour" (1841). Previous to writing the poem, Longfellow had studied Scandinavian literature, planned lectures at Harvard on the topic, and then visited Fall River, Massachusetts, to see a skeleton discovered by workmen leveling a hill in Fall River in 1831. The skeleton, wearing a metal breastplate, was that of a Native American.[75] However, nineteenth-century historian Jared Sparks argued that the skeleton was a Norseman, cementing the notion that Vikings had come to the New World before Columbus. Longfellow fabricated a Romantic biography for the dead Norseman:

> [I have] prepared for the press another original ballad. . . . It is called 'The Skeleton in Armour,' and is connected with the old Round Tower at Newport. The skeleton really exists. It was dug up near Fall River, where I saw it some two years ago. I suppose it to be the remains of one of the old North sea-rovers, who came to this country in the tenth century. Of course I made the tradition myself; and I think have succeeded in giving the whole a Northern air.[76]

In Longfellow's poem, the skeleton is that of a Norseman who flees across the ocean in order to marry his beloved against her father's wishes. Landing in what is now Newport, the Norseman builds his love "a lofty tower"—the Newport Ruin—where they live until her death, at which time he buries her beneath the tower. Devastated by the loss, the Norseman wears his armor to

FIGURE 5.9. "Morning Promenade in Front of the Old Mill at Newport," in *Frank Leslie's Illustrated Newspaper*, vol. VIII, No. 197 (Sept. 10, 1859), bottom of p. 231. RB499751. The Huntington Library, San Marino, CA.

the forest where he falls on his spear, thereby explaining the location of his remains miles away from Newport.[77] With strokes of his pen, Longfellow created a worthy narrative of romance and adventure to explain the presence of this mysterious ruin in Newport. The poem was a huge success; wrapped in Romanticism, the ruin likewise became a sensation. The image in *Frank Leslie's Illustrated Newspaper* in 1859 shows the Newport Ruin as a backdrop for a genteel morning promenade. Evening promenades were equally charming. One guidebook author tells us "[The Old Stone Mill] is a pretty sight on a summer's evening, this green spot, dotted with moving figures sauntering up and down under the grim shadow of this picturesque ruin. By moonlight it is superb."[78] The supposed Scandinavian origin of the tower piqued the public's curiosity and fulfilled a craving for novelty. Years later, in 1881, wealthy New Yorker Catherine Lorillard Wolfe built a house named Vinland in Newport to celebrate the city's hypothesized Viking heritage. Designed by Peabody and Stearns in an interpretation of Norse architecture with "rough-faced brownstone laid in random ashlar with contrasting smooth-textured brownstone trim," the house featured "sea dragons, Nordic ornament, and even Viking heads." In the library of the house, a painting by Walter Crane illustrated the construction of the tower.[79]

In the nineteenth century, the power of ruins derived from the larger interest in nature and nationalism in American culture. Ruins suggested that the architectural hubris of humankind will be consumed, and that nature will reign triumphant, a common theme in Hudson River School painting; the most famous example is perhaps Cole's *Desolation* (1836) from his *Course of Empire* series. Because ruins are often overgrown, ruins embody the idea that architecture and nature are inseparable. In Cole's painting, *Lake with Dead Trees (Catskill)* (1825), no buildings appear, but the painting depicts a haunted, eerie landscape of nature in ruins, perhaps an implicit reference to the destruction of nature caused by the lumber and tourism industries in the Catskills, as Kenneth Myers has suggested.[80] Art historian Sarah Burns notes "The lake . . . is closed off on all sides. There is no way out of this graveyard, haunted by the ghosts of trees."[81] While Cole noted that America had no ruins in his "Essay on American Scenery" (1836), the American landscape did have age, and primeval, old growth forest becomes a replacement for the architectural ruins of human habitation and civilization. That American scenery was superior to European scenery was a rallying cry of nationalism in the mid-nineteenth century. Indeed, a review of Jasper Cropsey's *Evening at Paestum* in 1856 (figure 5.10) is a case in point. In the painting, a spectacular sunset leaves in semi-darkness the ruins of a Greek temple in all its moldering glory. The reviewer in *Frank Leslie's Illustrated Newspaper* writes:

> We will close with the little gem by Mr. Cropsey, entitled "Evening at Paestum." Its treatment is tranquil, its effect solemn yet attractive. . . . We understand that Mr. Cropsey contemplates taking up his residence abroad. This we regret, for if he carrys [*sic*] this intention into effect, he

FIGURE 5.10. Jasper Francis Cropsey, *Evening at Paestum*, 1856. Oil on panel, 9 1/2 × 15 1/2 in. Frances Lehman Loeb Art Center, Vassar College, Gift of Matthew Vassar, 1864.1.21.

will bury his American genius and individuality in the ruins of ancient art. There is not an example of one of our artists going abroad who has been improved. . . . If our prairies, hill sides, meadows, mountains, valleys, savannahs, and extensive coasts—our calms and storms, and beautiful and sublime in nature, afford no school for artists, then let them break their palettes in despair, and think no more of art.[82]

The suggestion that travel and study abroad would crush the American exceptionalism of Cropsey's art highlights the heightened nationalism of the period. The reviewer wants Cropsey to paint scenes of American scenery rather than the ruins of the Old World. But Hudson River School painters had been fascinated by ruins since the movement's inception. One of the paintings that launched Thomas Cole's career, *View of Fort Putnam* (1825), shows the ruins of this Revolutionary War fort in the distance, situated like a medieval castle on a steep promontory. Fort Putnam was a popular tourist destination in the nineteenth century, not just for the view but for the ruins themselves. N. P. Willis's book *American Scenery* (1840) popularized William Bartlett's view of the Hudson Highlands from Fort Putnam, with the ruins visible to the right side of the composition in the print (figure 5.11). Consequently, many landscape painters painted this panoramic scene. In Bartlett's view and in most

Figure 5.11. "View from Fort Putnam (Hudson River)," from N. P. Willis, et. al., *Forest, Rock and Stream* (Boston: Estes and Lauriat, 1886), following p. 64.

subsequent paintings, the ruins are clearly evident on the right side of the composition.

However, John Ferguson Weir's *View of the Highlands from West Point* in 1862 is a bit different. Weir replaces the ruins with a large boulder. The artist has situated the viewer below the ruins, excluding the decayed structure from the scene. Why does Weir choose to omit the ruined fort? The ruined walls of the fort have been replaced by a large rock, covered by moss and creeping plant life, suggesting that nature and architecture have become one. This panorama of the Hudson Highlands, uniquely American, fulfills the desire, articulated by the critic in *Frank Leslie's Illustrated Newspaper*, for American artists to paint American scenes. The magnificence of the scenery lies not necessarily in the ruinous remains of man's mark on the landscape, but in the landscape itself. Weir is thus fulfilling Cole's charge in the latter's "Essay on American Scenery," in which Cole instructs Americans to admire their own landscape despite that American scenery is "destitute of . . . vestiges of antiquity." According to this nationalistic view, the ruins are not necessary for the scene to be worthy of being painted.[83]

However, despite these echoes of nationalism in nineteenth-century discourse, the desire for man-made ruins in European architectural styles could

FIGURE 5.12.   "Design for a Summer-House in the Grecian Style," in "Garden Decorations," *The Gardener's Monthly* 111:8 (August 1861), 236. The Library Company of Philadelphia.

not be suppressed. Just five years after Cropsey exhibited his painting of Greek ruins, a curiously similar image appeared in the pages of the journal *The Gardener's Monthly*. This Greek Revival summerhouse (figure 5.12), with its roof "formed of rough boards," its pediment "covered with bark," and its columns formed of "trunks of trees with the bark on" is the ultimate ruin for the American landscape.[84] It is part nature, part man-made, and in a style that recalls the glories of a civilization which Americans, with their democratic ideals, sought to emulate. The temple in the garden suggests that the landscape gardener has tamed the American wilderness. The similarities between Cropsey's painted ruin and the design in *The Gardener's Monthly* highlight the connections between landscape painting and picturesque landscape theory. In nineteenth-century America, artists and landscape gardeners created ruins, real and imagined, for pleasurable contemplation; these ruins often contained deeper cultural meanings in an age when Americans were searching for a national identity.

Conclusion

Thomas Jefferson and the signers of the Declaration of Independence had called for a new government in 1776. By the hundredth anniversary of this seminal event in US history, it was time for citizens to celebrate the nation's progress and reflect on its place in the world. The International Exhibition of Arts, Manufactures, and Products of the Soil and Mine, more popularly known as the Philadelphia Centennial, was a World's Fair that provided this opportunity. The Philadelphia Centennial opened on May 10, 1876, in Philadelphia's Fairmount Park and attracted ten million visitors until the fair closed in November. According to historian Robert W. Rydell, the organizers "sought to challenge doubts and restore confidence in the vitality of America's system of government as well as in the social and economic structure of the country," during the tumultuous period of Reconstruction.[1] While the fair was going on, Philadelphia became the locus for patriotic events. An estimated 250,000 people flocked to Philadelphia to celebrate the Fourth of July at Independence Hall in 1876. Recalling Charles Willson Peale's patriotic efforts during the Revolution, triumphal arches festooned Chestnut Street for the multiday celebration.[2] At the stroke of midnight on the fourth, "there went up from the crowd such a shout as had never been heard in Philadelphia before."[3] Souvenirs of the Centennial, including Robert Newell's *Old Landmarks and Relics of Philadelphia*, documented Philadelphia-area buildings associated with historical events, perpetuating myths about the Edwards-Womrath summerhouse, for instance (figure 2.1).

A bird's-eye view of the Centennial fairgrounds shows us the scale of the World's Fair, with its attractively landscaped grounds and impressive architecture (figure C.1). At the vanishing point, we behold a prominent American flag, a spindly metal prospect tower, and a pavilion. For 25 cents, members of the public ascended the iron tower (visible in a close-up photograph in figure I.1) to take in its self-advertised 30-mile view. Architectural historian Clay Lancaster describes the tower, located on Georges Hill, as "a rectangular structure contracting slightly towards the top, consisting of an open framework of slender iron members . . ."[4] According to *Magee's Centennial Guide of Philadelphia* (1876), Georges Hill was "the highest natural elevation in the city, being 210 feet above high-tide," offering expansive views of both the Centennial grounds and the city of Philadelphia.[5] Architectural historian Bruno Giberti explains that opportunities to view the fair from on high allowed spectators to participate in the spectacle of modern life:

FIGURE C.1. "Bird's eye view, Centennial Buildings, Fairmount Park, 1876. Philadelphia." The Miriam and Ira D. Wallach Division of Art, Prints and Photographs: Print Collection, The New York Public Library. New York Public Library Digital Collections. http://digitalcollections.nypl.org/items/510d47d9-7d82-a3d9-e040-e00a18064a99 (accessed November 4, 2018).

The overview combined the functions of surveillance and spectacle; it restored the primacy of the gaze and the controlling relationship of the few to the many (both aspects of surveillance) while putting the individual observer on full display to the crowd below (the classic spectacle). Also like the vista, the overview implied a position of power; it was by definition, by virtue of height, a privileged look. It provided a superior kind of comprehension, which was not available to a person on the ground. This ostensibly privileged look was democratically extended to all who climb the stair or pay for the elevator.[6]

Thousands of visitors stopped at Georges Hill daily "to delight the eyes with the marvelous beauty of the landscape [and] rest their wearied limbs under the shadow of its tasteful pavilion."[7]

A showcase for American industry, the fair famously featured the enormous Corliss Engine on display in Machinery Hall. But smaller machines attracted attention as well. The Singer Manufacturing Company had its own pavilion or exhibition building, constructed in the "Gothic cottage style," and "topped off with handsome finials [and] open timber-work and decorations."[8] At a cost of $20,000, the pavilion was certainly elaborate. A polychromatic Mansard roof hovered over an elaborate verandah, giving the pavilion the architectural vocabulary of popular domestic architecture of the period.[9] The architect, James Vandyke, hailed from Elizabeth, New Jersey, home also of the company's huge factory. Visitors to the building's reception parlor added their names to a register, in the hopes of winning the "two millionth machine" manufactured by the company.[10] In July 1876, 3,631 employees of the Singer Sewing Machine Company made an "industrial excursion" to the pavilion. *The Scientific American* encouraged such excursions to educate factory workers who were encouraged to make reports on what they had learned at the Centennial.[11]

After the death of Isaac Singer (1811–1875), his business partner and attorney Edward Clark (1811–1882) became president of the Singer Manufacturing Company in September of the same year as the Philadelphia Centennial.[12] Far from the shores of the Schuylkill River in Philadelphia, Clark was busy building his own tower, as different from the iron tower on Georges Hill as one could imagine. New York architect Henry Hardenbergh (1847–1918) designed this fanciful folly named Kingfisher Tower on the shores of Otsego Lake in Cooperstown, New York (figure C.2). Hardenbergh's best known designs are the Dakota Apartment Building (1884) and the Plaza Hotel (1907), the former commissioned by Clark in his other role as a land developer in New

FIGURE C.2.   Kingfisher Tower, Cooperstown, New York, September 6, 1908. Arthur J. Telfer, glass plate negative, 5 × 7 in (h × w). Fenimore Art Museum, Cooperstown, NY. Gift of Arthur J. Telfer, Smith and Telfer Photographic Collection, 5-07, 885.

York City.[13] Clark engaged Hardenbergh to design a number of buildings in his wife's hometown of Cooperstown. One such project was a picnicking house located directly on Otsego Lake in what Clark called the "Swiss Chalet" style. In front of the picnicking house, Clark constructed the pseudomedieval Kingfisher Tower; the main purpose of this tower, according to Clark, was to "beautify the lake."[14] The tower also functioned as a belvedere, offering beautiful views of the unspoiled landscape of Otsego Lake, made famous in James Fenimore Cooper's novels as "Glimmerglass."

Kingfisher Tower is located on Point Judith, 2 miles north of Cooperstown on the east side of Otsego Lake, which is 9 miles long and 1.5 miles wide. One can see the tower from the shores of Cooperstown or catch glimpses of it also through the trees on Lakeside Road.[15] The tower occupies a footprint of 20 square feet and rises to a height of approximately 60 feet. The "miniature castle," as Clark called it, comes complete with pointed arch windows, stained glass, loophole windows, machicolated parapets, ramparts, and, believe it or not, a solid oak portcullis and tiny drawbridge, which at one time connected the structure to the causeway.[16] Over time, Kingfisher Tower has become an important landmark on Otsego Lake. Kingfisher Tower anchors our experience of the lake or, as Clark asserts, "it forms an objective point in the scene presented by the lake and surrounding hills," and it draws tourists away from the Baseball Hall of Fame to view the tower from the water.[17] Indeed, as soon as the tower was completed, summer tourists enjoyed close-up views on steamboat tours.

After the locals started calling Kingfisher "Clark's Folly," Clark wrote a newspaper article to justify his building of Kingfisher Tower. First, Clark noted the belvedere function of the tower, writing that through the "numerous openings and loopholes with which the walls are pierced, a fine panoramic view of the lake and country can be obtained." Clark also wrote that he built Kingfisher Tower "simply by a desire to beautify the lake and add an attraction which must be seen by all who traverse the lake or drive along its shores. They whose minds can rise above simple notions of utility to an appreciation of art joined to nature, will thank him for it."[18] Clearly, Clark believed that the lake needed improvement, that nature could be perfected by man. Similar issues often arise with nineteenth-century landscape paintings. For instance, scholars such as Nancy K. Anderson have argued that painters of the American West sometimes elaborate on their subject matter, the actual landscape of the West, although they would have us believe that they are *transcribing* the views, rather than creating semifictional ones.[19] Clark and his architect were similarly constructing a fantasy landscape when they added Kingfisher Tower to the scenery of Otsego Lake. Whereas before the tower was built, the landscape was distinctly *American* as a pristine, completely natural place, the tower *improved* on nature. And as Clark asserted, anyone who can appreciate that buildings can be more than simply utilitarian, will understand his motivations.

In addition to the aesthetic function of the tower, there was an economic purpose. An early historian of Cooperstown notes that Clark had the tower built "to furnish work for many in the community who were out of employment" in the period following the financial crisis of the Panic of 1873.[20] If Clark's purpose was to provide jobs for local workmen, this points to the multiple functions of the tower and Clark's manifold motivations in building it. Kingfisher Tower is a landscape ornament with historical associations, linking the United States with the medieval past of Europe; for its owners, the tower provides a view of the lake; for tourists, it provides a curious punctuation to an otherwise natural landscape; for workers, it sparked employment, if only temporarily.

Just as Clark intended, the tower "gives a character of antiquity to the lake," likening this long, narrow lake to the German Rhine, dotted with castles.[21] Nicholas Fox Weber, biographer of the Clark family, declares that Clark "saw this act of architectural patronage as a service to the larger public, opening American eyes to the finest of European style."[22] Clark was not the first prominent Cooperstown resident to bring European styles to the shores of Otsego Lake. James Fenimore Cooper had Gothicized his home Otsego Hall in an attempt to educate his countrymen in the architectural styles of Europe.[23] At first, Kingfisher seems paradoxical—why build a European-style tower in America when the nation is celebrating its Centennial? But on closer examination, one sees that Clark and Hardenbergh decorated some of the colorful earthen tiles on the orange roof of Kingfisher Tower with stars, a reference to the American flag. Kingfisher Tower co-opts European architecture and blends it with American nationalist sentiment.

Although early modernism was starting to challenge historicism in American architecture in 1876, historicized follies remained popular for decades after the Centennial, even as metal towers—the architectural cousins of the Eiffel Tower—began to proliferate. Historian Nick Yablon tells us that follies "did not become widespread until the Gilded Age."[24] Of course, this statement is not entirely true, but Yablon's point that follies proliferated in the Gilded Age—and beyond—is accurate. Sometimes these buildings had more than one function. A good example is the water tower at Earlescourt, Edward Earle's development of cottages built in 1886–1887 in Narragansett, Rhode Island. The image of the tower shown in figure C.3 appeared in both *Scientific American, Architects and Builders Edition* in March 1887 and in *Scientific American* in August 1888. Designed by the Constable Brothers of New York City, the tower's chief function was to supply water to the development by means of the attached windmill. *Scientific American* notes that the tower departs from "the common plan of such structures," and displays "novelty and boldness." Rather than design a nondescript tower in the functionalist mode, the architects created a pseudomedieval tower of stone with a wooden superstructure featuring a large griffin, a fantastic mythical creature, half lion and half eagle. The magazine notes that the tower fulfills its function as an "ornamental addition to the landscape."[25] Indeed, the tower serves the dual purpose of water tower and landscape ornament, although the latter function overshadows the former, in that the tower is quite fanciful, a detail not lost on the twentieth-century photographer Walker Evans. Evans wrote of the quirky Narragansett landmark: "The battlemented, shingled water tower . . . might have been the result of a visit to Rhode Island by William Beckford, Horace Walpole, Ludwig of Bavaria, or all three."[26] Here Evans refers to two eccentric writers of Gothic fiction, Beckford and Walpole, each of whom built houses full of Gothic imagination. Beckford's Fonthill Abbey (1796–1812) was a monstrous conglomeration of pinnacles and towers, while Walpole's Strawberry Hill (1749–1777) was a dainty plaything castle in comparison. Ludwig of Bavaria was the nineteenth-century king of Bavaria responsible for the creation of

A WINDMILL TOWER AND WATER TANK AT NARRAGANSETT PIER, R. I.

CONSTABLE BROTHERS ARCHITECTS.

FIGURE C.3. "A Windmill Tower and Water Tank at Narragansett Pier, R. I., Constable Brothers Architects." *Scientific American Architects and Builders Edition*. III:3 (March 1887): 45–47.

Germany's Neuschwanstein Castle, the supposed prototype for Disneyland's Cinderella Castle, a narrative folly of a different sort.

Stone lookout towers were especially popular at the turn of the century. Rockford Tower (1899–1900) in Wilmington, Delaware, is a water tower made partly from stones reclaimed from local farm walls. The Norman-style tower looks "like a pile of rocks that has stood for centuries," expressing the value of historicized architecture planted in the American landscape.[27] Castle Craig frowns defiance on an eminence overlooking Meriden, Connecticut. Built in 1901, the round, crenellated tower, offering "one of the finest panoramic views in the world," was a gift of Walter Hubbard to Hubbard Park.[28] On Prospect Hill in Somerville, Massachusetts, stands a "tower of roughly hewn granite," built in 1903 to mark the spot where historical events of the American Revolution took place.[29] Not all prospect towers were stone; "Copper King" Thomas Lawson wrapped an unsightly iron standpipe (1900) visible from his home Dreamwold in Scituate, Massachusetts, in wood and shingles in 1902 to create an attractive medieval revival folly. He sent an architect to Europe to study examples of towers to hide the utilitarian function of the standpipe.[30] Like the Narragansett Tower, the Lawson Tower was a fanciful belvedere with a decidedly mundane purpose.

A stone tower overlooks Mohonk Mountain House in the Shawangunk Mountains of New York. The architectural partnership of Allen & Collens designed the tower to memorialize Albert K. Smiley (1828–1912). Sky Top Tower (1920–1923) was the fourth observatory on the spectacular overlook. The Gothic Revival tower appears as if "growing out of the rock that nature placed there," as the stone was quarried from the site.[31] As discussed in chapter 3, the Quaker owners, the Smiley family, forbade guests from drinking and dancing. The Smileys often characterized Mohonk in pseudomilitaristic language. One Mohonk publication describes Sky Top Tower as a "watch-tower" and Mohonk as a "morally embattled" Citadel.[32] Built to commemorate the golden anniversary of Albert and Eliza Smiley in 1907, the Testimonial Gateway functioned as a fortified entrance. Like the sham castellation of Blaise Castle in England, the medievalized fortifications at Mohonk highlight the narrative possibilities of architectural follies. Here we have Sky Top tower—is it a prospect tower for the pure enjoyment of Mohonk guests, or is it a symbolic watchtower guarding the sacred precinct of the Mountain House from the evil influences of the outside world?[33]

A completely different, but no less dramatic, landscape unfolds beneath another stone tower, The Watchtower at Desert View (1933), perched on the edge of the South Rim of the Grand Canyon (figure C.4). Architect Mary Elizabeth Jane Colter designed the tower to resemble, in her words, a prehistoric Indian watchtower. She explained her motivations in a guidebook she wrote to respond to questions by tour guides and bus drivers who brought the curious to the building. She cites as sources the towers built by ancestral Puebloans at Mesa Verde and Hovenweep. In colorful language, she describes the scenery and siting of such towers which "play 'hide and seek' among boulders in the arroyos; chase each other up the rugged sides of cliffs; hang to the very brink of the canyon walls; and scramble to the slanting crowns of monolithic rock pinnacles. We cannot but question what it is all about!"[34] Colter designed her watchtower to blend in with the landscape to "create no discordant note against the time-eroded walls of this promontory" and to provide a

FIGURE C.4.   "The Watchtower at Desert View." Brian C. Grogan, creator, 1994. 10. WATCH
TOWER, FACING N., East Rim Drive, between South Entrance Road and park boundary, Grand
Canyon, Coconino County, AZ, HAER ARIZ,3-GRACAN, 6–10. Library of Congress, Prints and
Photographs Division, HABS.

spectacular view. She decided that no style of modern architecture using
modern materials would be appropriate, creating an "unsolvable dilemma,"
until the idea of the watchtower provided a resolution.[35] Colter's comment
highlights the fact that follies are more successful when historicized. Therefore, Colter designed a new ruin for an ancient landscape. But the ruin is even
more "sham" than one might realize at first glance; Colter tells us that "the
whole building has a steel framework hidden away in it that would do credit
to a modern office building."[36] The irony here leaves us breathless; a sham ruin
based on prehistoric Native American architecture hiding a metal skeleton. The
Centennial Tower meets Kingfisher Tower, indeed.

Private gardens in the so-called Country Place Era at the turn of the century
continued to feature architectural adornments to provide delight and respite
to garden enthusiasts. At Henry Francis du Pont's estate Winterthur in Delaware, follies dot the landscape here and there. Marian Coffin designed the
Winterthur gardens, which included a summerhouse and umbrella seat purchased from a nearby nineteenth-century estate named Latimeria.[37] Downing had praised Latimeria, home of China Trader John Latimer, in his 1850
edition of *A Treatise on the Theory and Practice of Landscape Gardening.*[38] By

moving Latimeria's garden ornaments to his estate, du Pont integrated the nineteenth-century folly tradition into his twentieth-century garden; his house is, of course, a similar hodgepodge of past and present, full of period rooms representing other times and places.

Even as High Modernism started to eclipse historicism in the mid-twentieth century, follies held interest in some quarters. Philip Johnson (1906–2005) completed his iconic Glass House in New Canaan, Connecticut, in 1949. Between 1948 and 1999, Johnson developed the land around the house into a picturesque wonderland with numerous follies. In 1991, Johnson commented that the experience of the Glass House was not only about his residence: "To me, the house is a park. To me, the whole experience is a park in which there are, indeed, monuments or occasions or accidents or things by nature and things that I've placed there that create a place."[39] One folly, the Monument to Lincoln Kirstein (the Lincoln Kirstein Tower, 1985), commemorated the life of Johnson's Harvard classmate and cofounder of the New York City Ballet (figure C.5). Situated within view of the Glass House on a man-made pond, the folly was both an abstract sculpture and a belvedere with steps leading to the top. In *The Philip Johnson Glass House: An Architect in the Garden*, Maureen Cassidy-Geiger describes the tower as "a choreographed ascent, Gothic ruin, and Bauhaus staircase," suggesting the extreme eclecticism and evocative quality of Johnson's design.[40] Breaking free of the International Style, some of Johnson's landscape buildings are downright playful and decidedly postmodern. Inspired by his friend Frank Gehry's unorthodox use of chain-link fence and Robert Venturi's abstract historicism, Johnson designed the Ghost House in 1984. The Ghost House is a transparent folly constructed of chain-link on a deserted foundation Johnson had discovered on his property. The chain-link created, in Johnson's words, an "indoor-outdoor effect" appropriate to folly design in which indoors and outdoors flow together seamlessly.[41]

Johnson's interest in the picturesque dated back to his boyhood. At age twelve, his parents allowed him to wander around Paris alone. Fortuitously, he discovered the Parc des Buttes Chaumont, "still the greatest romantic park in the world," as he called it.[42] The French engineer, J. C. A. Alphand, designed the park in 1867 during Napoleon III's Second Empire (1851–1870) when Alphand served as Director of Parks, Bridges, and Roads under Eugene Haussmann. When the commissioners of Fairmount Park in Philadelphia sent the park's superintendent Russell Thayer abroad in 1879 to report on the major parks of Europe, Thayer visited Buttes Chaumont and noted the follies. He wrote, "On the summit of the highest butte is situated a small ornamental Corinthian pavilion, which resembles the temple of Vesta at Tivoli."[43] Years later Johnson remembered the "fake caverns, and little bridges, a little fake

FIGURE C.5. Monument to Lincoln Kirstein, by Philip Johnson, Philip Johnson's Glass House, New Canaan, CT, 1985. Photograph by author.

mountain, and a little lookout on top," the last a reference to the Corinthian pavilion that Thayer had noted. The park's design clearly inspired Johnson's interest in the picturesque.[44] Another inspiration was a landscape painting in Johnson's collection, *The Burial of Phocion* (1648–1649) by Nicolas Poussin. Johnson displayed the painting in a place of honor in his Glass House.[45] Both the Parisian park and the Poussin painting feature classical temples. These two historical precedents for buildings set naturally within landscapes had a lasting impact on Johnson's twentieth-century psyche.

In the late twentieth century, follies enjoyed a resurgence that continues to this day. For an exhibition at the Leo Castelli Gallery in New York and the James Corcoran Gallery in Los Angeles, curator B. J. Archer invited architects to design follies, a theme first conceived on a visit to Stourhead in 1977.[46] As post-modernism gained traction, follies were the perfect antidote to the stringent orthodoxy of high modernism. Follies are useless, outrageous, and above all, historicized, in direct contrast to the functionality, clean lines, and ahistoricism of the International Style. As Archer explains, follies "violated the tenets of the architect in the recent past."[47] At the same time, follies are sympathetic to postmodernist theory, in that they incorporate "narrative and fantasy, irony and wit."[48] The exhibition catalog begins with a reprint of Edgar Allan Poe's sketch "The Landscape Garden" (1842, later expanded into "The Domain of Arnheim"), in which the narrator's friend, "the young Ellison," inherits a vast sum of money. With this windfall, Ellison indulges in landscape gardening. Poe's narrator declares the landscape garden "the fairest field for the display of invention, or imagination . . ."[49] Archer imagines that Ellison's garden was "no doubt to be punctuated with follies."[50]

What follows Poe's sketch are contemporary folly designs, including some by the architect Bernard Tschumi (b. 1944), who began experimenting with follies in 1979 with his project *20th Century Follies*. To Tschumi, follies provide "a critical laboratory for architecture."[51] At the time of the 1983 exhibition, Tschumi had just won the competition to design the Parc de la Villette, which was completed in 1985 in Paris. Philip Johnson and Mark Wigley included the design in their landmark exhibition *Deconstructivist Architecture* at the Museum of Modern Art in New York in 1988. Tschumi's contribution to the history of follies is substantial, but one does not go to the Parc de la Villette hoping to encounter historicized follies of the eighteenth and nineteenth-century variety. Rather, Tschumi's follies are outrageous in new and startling ways. Tschumi placed his follies (or *folies*) at intersections of a grid placed over reclaimed industrial land. Instead of blending in with the landscape, these follies stand out with their bright red color and deconstructivist design, made up of "dismembered" cubes that appear to have been blown apart and put back together haphazardly. In the end, Tschumi creates, in his own words, "follies in the park: freestanding structures linked by broken galleries that twist through a fractured topography."[52] Tschumi disrupts the serenity of Stourhead and Stowe in favor of warping distortion; even so, Tschumi's structures similarly provide delight and suspense for the viewer, keeping with the centuries-old tradition of folly building.

Over the last several decades, follies have continued to fascinate contemporary architects and curators. Examples of folly exhibitions include *Functional Follies: 20 Architectural Objects of Delight*, commissioned by the Savannah College of Art and Design for its twentieth anniversary in 1999 and *Follies: Fantasies in the Landscape* at the Parrish Art Museum in Southampton, New York, in 2001.[53] In 2017, an exhibition at Olana, Frederic Church's house in Hudson, New York, showcased architectural designs inspired by a summerhouse in an 1886 landscape plan. Other than its location, no documentary evidence for the summerhouse has surfaced, so the architects had free rein to design ingenious folly concoctions in the Olana landscape.[54] In 2018, the Winterthur Garden opened an exhibition, *Follies: Architectural Whimsy in the Garden*, consisting of seven new follies added to Winterthur's existing collection. The new follies were in styles ranging from "Chinese" to "Gothic," a clear nod to the historicism and exoticism of the traditional folly.[55] Contemporaneous with the Winterthur exhibition in 2019, the Storm King Art Center featured an exhibition called *Mark Dion: Follies*. Mark Dion is a contemporary artist who has been creating follies for decades. Dion's follies encompass everything from lemonade stands to field stations, often with messages that spur environmental action.[56]

While an overview of these exhibitions shows that many contemporary folly designs share very little stylistically with the follies of the picturesque age, replicas and near-replicas also inhabit our world today. A recent article in *Architectural Digest*, "Inside Architecture's New Classicism Boom," includes Philip J. Liederbach's design for a not-quite-identical copy of Samuel McIntire's two-story neoclassical Derby Summerhouse (1793), now located at Glen Magna Farms in Danvers, Massachusetts.[57] Years earlier, in 1993, the documentary filmmaker Ken Burns (b. 1953) recreated exactly—"to the millimeter"— Thomas Jefferson's neo-Palladian brick summerhouse at Monticello behind his house in Walpole, New Hampshire. Burns uses the structure as a sylvan retreat—it is located in an apple orchard—a place to get away from the outside world, a place of quiet reflection away from the ringing telephone.[58] At the time of construction, Burns was beginning work on his Thomas Jefferson documentary. An interviewer asked him why he recreated Jefferson's summerhouse, to which Burns replied:

It's interesting. There is a wonderful structure, a 13-by-13-foot brick structure without doors, but four huge, triple hung Palladian windows, that Jefferson anchored one of his vegetable garden in Monticello with. He called it the garden pavilion. And before I began actively to work on the Thomas Jefferson film, I built an exact replica, down to the bricks and the windows, and every dimension is exactly the way it was in Monticello. In part because I felt that it was a way of calling him, celebrating him, asking him to be present for us. I don't mean that in a "channeling" kind of way. I mean only that we ensure that we have a future when we find ways to honor the past. And for me, one of the ways to honor the past came in building this magnificent garden pavilion, which I'm looking at right now out of my office window.[59]

Burns got his folly building right—in some ways at least. He places the summer-house in a spot visible from the window of his house. He understands the purpose of the summerhouse as an escape from the overt sociability of the house with its technological intrusions. But to say that his summerhouse is "exactly" the same as the one that Jefferson inhabited is not entirely true. The little brick summerhouse on the edge of the vegetable garden at Monticello is a "conjectural reconstruction" of Jefferson's actual design, "based on archae-ological remains and Jefferson's specifications."[60] Built in 1984, the building is a best guess at what existed there in Jefferson's time, when a strong wind rep-utably brought the little summerhouse down in the 1820s.[61]

Eighteenth and nineteenth-century follies come in all shapes and sizes with a plethora of styles from which to choose. These sometimes rambunctious, os-tensibly useless structures continue to fascinate us, years after the picturesque as a landscape theory might have faded away. An article, "Not for Sale: Gazebo w/ Writer Fully Attached," in the *New York Times* in 2002 captures the enduring pleasure these little buildings give us. The author, novelist Gary Krist, retreated to a backyard gazebo to write, slightly away from his Bethesda home. Channel-ing Mark Twain and Washington Irving, Krist used the gazebo as a work space. He mentions gazebos are "not meant to be used as workplaces," so he is un-aware of the tradition of the summerhouse as a place for the production of nar-rative. He writes that his gazebo "is unlike a porch or a quiet corner of the neighborhood Starbucks. It is a wonderful hybrid, somewhere between inside and outside, shelter and exposure, civilization and wild nature (well, as wild as Bethesda gets)." It is this "ambiguity" that Krist likes best about his backyard ga-zebo. He thinks of the gazebo as "a place uniquely conducive to the making of art, balancing, on the one hand, the Romantic impulse toward communion with raw nature and, on the other, the Classical ideals of detachment and aesthetic distance."[62] Here Krist taps into the appeal of follies: their meanings are multiva-lent, they spark creativity, whether written or visual, and they draw us to them to enjoy their prospects and contemplate both the world around us and the pas-sage of time. In the nineteenth century, these diminutive buildings embodied complex ideas of national identity. So, although metal prospect observatories like the one on Georges Hill at the Philadelphia Centennial became popular in the modern era, associationist towers such as Kingfisher tell stories through their style and location. Indeed, little buildings tell big stories.

NOTES

Introduction

1. Jane Austen, *Northanger Abbey* (1818; Toronto: Bantam Books, 1985), 65.

2. Gwyn Headley, *Architectural Follies in America* (New York: Wiley, 1996), 1–2.

3. John Fleming, Hugh Honour, and Nikolaus Pevsner, *The Penguin Dictionary of Architecture and Landscape Architecture*, 5th ed. (London: Penguin Books, 1998), 197.

4. Sir Geoffrey Jellicoe, Susan Jellicoe, Patrick Goode, and Michael Lancaster, eds., *The Oxford Companion to Gardens* (Oxford: Oxford University Press, 1986), 192. On American follies, see Clay Lancaster, *Architectural Follies in America; or Hammer, Sawtooth and Nail* (Rutland, VT: C. E. Tuttle, 1960); May Brawley Hill, *Furnishing the Old-Fashioned Garden: Three Centuries of American Summerhouses, Dovecotes, Pergolas, Privies, Fences & Birdhouses* (New York: Harry N. Abrams, 1998); and Headley, *Architectural Follies in America*. Both Headley and Lancaster cover a wide range of unusual buildings (beyond garden follies and ruins). Hill's book is a useful source for images, as is M. Christine Klim Doell, *Gardens of the Gilded Age: Nineteenth-Century Gardens and Homegrounds of New York State* (Syracuse: Syracuse University Press, 1986). On the influence of foreign cultures on American garden design, see Raffaella Fabiani Giannetto, ed., *Foreign Trends in American Gardens: A History of Exchange, Adaptation, and Reception* (Charlottesville: University of Virginia Press, 2016).

5. Spiro Kostof, *A History of Architecture: Settings and Rituals* (New York: Oxford University Press, 1985), 553.

6. Edward Malins, *English Landscaping and Literature, 1660–1840* (London: Oxford University Press, 1966), 51. See also Kenneth Woodbridge, *Landscape and Antiquity: Aspects of English Culture at Stourhead 1718–1838* (Oxford: Clarendon, 1970), 30–37. Scholars have challenged the *Aeneid* interpretation of Stourhead, and the garden has become, in Oliver Cox's words "an iconographical battlefield" of competing interpretations. Cox provides a succinct overview of the garden's historiography and then shows how contemporary visitors to Stourhead failed to mention any holistic, iconographical narratives in direct contradiction to most scholarly interpretations. Oliver Cox, "A Mistaken Iconography? Eighteenth-Century Visitor Accounts of Stourhead," *Garden History* 40, no. 1 (Summer 2012): 98–116.

7. On the politics of eighteenth-century English landscape, see Tom Williamson, *Polite Landscapes: Gardens and Society in Eighteenth-Century England* (Baltimore: Johns Hopkins University Press, 1995), 61–65. See also John Martin Robinson, *Temples of Delight: Stowe Landscape Garden* (London: National Trust, 1990). On the Temple of Liberty, see Chris Brooks, *The Gothic Revival* (London: Phaidon Press, 1999), 54–55; and Michael J. Lewis, *The Gothic Revival* (London: Thames and Hudson, 2002), 19–20.

8. Thomas Cole, "Essay on American Scenery," in *American Art 1700–1960. Sources and Documents*, ed. John W. McCoubrey (Englewood Cliffs, NJ: Prentice-Hall, 1965), 108.

9. Alison had published his *Essays on the Nature and Principles of Taste* in 1790, but it was the second edition of 1811 that received widespread attention. On architectural associationism, see John Archer, "The Beginnings of Association in British Architectural Esthetics," *Eighteenth-Century Studies* 16, no. 3 (Spring 1983): 241–264 and Dale Townshend, *Gothic Antiquity: History, Romance, and the Architectural Imagination* (Oxford: Oxford University Press, 2019), 45–88. On associationist theory and American landscape painting, see Ralph N. Miller, "Thomas Cole and Alison's Essays on Taste," *New York History* 37 (July 1956): 281–299; Earl A. Powell III, "Thomas Cole and the American Landscape Tradition: Associationism," *Arts Magazine* 52, no. 4 (April 1978): 113–117; Angela Miller, *The Empire of the Eye: Landscape Representations and American Cultural Politics, 1825–1875* (Ithaca, NY: Cornell University Press, 1993), 79–80; Rebecca Bedell, *The Anatomy of Nature: Geology and American Landscape Painting, 1825–1875* (Princeton, NJ: Princeton University Press, 2001), 94–98; and Rachael Ziady DeLue, *George Inness and the Science of Landscape* (Chicago: University of Chicago Press, 2004), 123–124, 134–135.

10. Cole, "Essay," 108. The sublime is an aesthetic category encompassing power, height, obscurity, infinity, and terror, as defined by Edmund Burke in *A Philosophical Enquiry Into the Origin of Our Ideas of the Sublime and Beautiful*, first published in 1757 (Edited by Adam Phillips, Oxford: Oxford University Press, 1990).

11. Sometimes utilitarianism and nationalistic iconography merge in a single structure, such as a design for a standpipe at the Philadelphia Water Works erected by Birkinbine & Trotter around 1855. A masonry base with buttresses and a Gothic pointed arch entrance supported an iron tower with a spiral staircase leading to an observation platform. The standpipe was both a utilitarian scientific advancement and a belvedere. A cast-iron statue of George Washington was to grace the top of the tower in an obvious act of national boosterism (it was never added; the tower stood until 1932). *Gleason's Pictorial Drawing-Room Companion* published the proposed design in 1853 and noted that "this structure will form one of the notable curiosities in the vicinity of the city of brotherly love, an object of much scientific interest." The strange combination of modern materials, Gothic Revival design, and neoclassical sculpture did not seem to bother the Gleason's correspondent. "Philadelphia Water Works," *Gleason's Pictorial Drawing-Room Companion* IV:13 (March 26, 1853): 201; and Calder Loth and Julius Trousdale Sadler Jr., *The Only Proper Style: Gothic Architecture in America* (Boston: New York Graphic Society, 1975), 130.

12. The architectural and landscape history of America's first century of nationhood is understudied. While individual designers such as Andrew Jackson Downing, Calvert Vaux, and Frederick Law Olmsted have been the subjects of scholarship in recent years, currently there are no scholarly overviews of nineteenth-century American garden and park architecture. For an analysis of mid-Atlantic outbuildings in the eighteenth century, see Michael Olmert, *Kitchens, Smokehouses, and Privies: Outbuildings and the Architecture of Daily Life in the Eighteenth-Century Mid-Atlantic* (Ithaca, NY: Cornell University Press, 2009).

13. It is not clear if the summerhouse in Linscott's painting ever existed or whether it derives solely from Linscott's imagination. However, the summerhouse is stylistically accurate to the mid-nineteenth century. On Linscott, see Arthur L. Eno Jr. and

Thomas A. Smith, eds., *The Middlesex Canal: Prints by Louis Linscott* (Billerica, MA: Middlesex Canal Association, 1978).

14. Quoted in Sandra A. Babbidge, *Bremo Fountain Temple: Monument to John Hartwell Cocke and the Temperance Movement* (Charlottesville: School of Architecture, University of Virginia, 1989), 1–5, 17. See also K. Brooke Whiting, *Gen. J. H. Cocke's Vanishing Legacy: The Gardens and Landscape of Bremo* (Richmond: The Garden Club of Virginia, 2000). On the temperance movement in the South, see Ian R. Tyrrell, "Drink and Temperance in the Antebellum South: An Overview and Interpretation," *The Journal of Southern History* 48, no. 4 (November 1982): 485–510.

15. Babbidge, *Bremo Fountain Temple*, 4, 8.

16. On nationalism, see Benedict Anderson, *Imagined Communities: Reflections on the Origin and Spread of Nationalism* (London: Verso, 1993); Eric J. Hobsbawm and Terence O. Ranger, eds., *The Invention of Tradition* (Cambridge: Cambridge University Press, 1983); and Miller, *Empire of the Eye*. The idea of nationalism is paradoxical in that it bolsters one large unifying idea of nationhood within a community that comprises heterogeneous citizenry. According to Yael Tamir, "An inquiry into the nature of these terms will reveal an irony hovering over the study of nationalism: the more we struggle to provide an adequate definition of nation, and the more we learn about the emergence of nations and about the origins and development of nationalism, the less credible is the nationalist image of nations as homogeneous, natural and continuous communities of common fate and descent. Yet, it is precisely this image that nurtures the unique power of nationalism." Yael Tamir, "The Engima of Nationalism," *World Politics* 47, no. 3 (April 1995): 420. Historian Carroll Smith-Rosenberg discusses the lack of coherence when we discuss the term *identities*, which are "layered, fluid, changing, often contradictory, their forms dependent on where and in relation to whom they are constituted." Carroll Smith-Rosenberg, *This Violent Empire: The Birth of an American National Identity* (Chapel Hill: University of North Carolina Press for the Omohundro Institute of Early American History and Culture, 2010), 17. In this book, we shall see that follies were often the privilege of the wealthy elites. In some instances, enslaved people built follies for plantation landscapes; in others, immigrant labor was key. Middle-class farmers built summerhouses as way to proclaim their own status. European Americans used follies to promote their own particular heritage and place within the country's history, whether it was Scandinavian-American or New England Brahmin. Each folly has its unique place in its particular setting while often contributing to larger themes of nationalism.

17. For a definition of the picturesque, see Therese O'Malley, *Keywords in American Landscape Design* (New Haven, CT: National Gallery of Art in association with Yale University Press, 2010), 501–509.

1. The English Landscape Garden in America

1. See George Green Shackelford, *Thomas Jefferson's Travels in Europe, 1784–1789* (Baltimore: Johns Hopkins University Press, 1995), 43–63; Ross Watson, "Thomas Jefferson's Visit to England, 1786," *History Today* 27, no. 1 (January 1977): 3–13; Marie Kimball, *Jefferson and the Scene of Europe 1784 to 1789* (New York: Coward-McCann, 1950), 127–158; Richard Guy Wilson, "Jefferson and England," in *Thomas Jefferson Architect: Palladian Models, Democratic Principles, and the Conflict of Ideas*, eds. Lloyd DeWitt and

Corey Piper (Norfolk, VA: Chrysler Museum of Art, 2019), 42-50; and Andrea Wulf, *Founding Gardeners: The Revolutionary Generation, Nature, and the Shaping of the American Nation* (New York: Alfred A. Knopf, 2011), 35–57.

2. Quoted in Christopher Thacker, *The History of Gardens* (Berkeley: University of California Press, 1979), 183.

3. Quoted in Elizabeth Barlow Rogers, Elizabeth S. Eustis, and John Bidwell, *Romantic Gardens: Nature, Art, and Landscape Design* (New York: Morgan Library and Museum, 2010), 18. See also Thacker, *History of Gardens*, 181–197.

4. Therese O'Malley, *Keywords in American Landscape Design* (New Haven: National Gallery of Art in association with Yale University Press, 2010), 341–344.

5. A visitor to Monticello, who did not know the name of this feature, described Jefferson's ha-ha as follows: "As we approached the house we rode along a fence which was the only one of the kind I ever saw. Instead of being upright, it lay upon the ground across a ditch, the banks of the ditch raised the rails a foot or two above the ground on each side of the ditch so that no kind of grazing animals could easily cross it, because their feet would slip between the rails. It had just the appearance of a common post and rail straight fence, blown down across a ditch." Quoted in O'Malley, *Keywords*, 342. Later, around 1820, James Fenimore Cooper built a ha-ha on his grounds near Scarsdale, New York. Blake Nevius, *Cooper's Landscapes: An Essay on the Picturesque Vision* (Berkeley: University of California Press, 1976), 65.

6. Thomas Jefferson, "Notes of a Tour of English Gardens," in *The Papers of Thomas Jefferson*, eds. Julian P. Boyd and Mina R. Bryan (Princeton, NJ: Princeton University Press, 1954), 9:371. Also available at the Founders Online at http://founders.archives.gov/documents/Adams/01-03-02-0005-0002-0001; in John Dixon Hunt and Peter Willis, eds., *The Genius of the Place: The English Landscape Garden 1620–1820* (Cambridge, MA: MIT Press, 1988), 333–336; and in Edwin Morris Betts, ed., *Thomas Jefferson's Garden Book, 1766–1824* (Charlottesville, VA: Thomas Jefferson Memorial Foundation, 1999), 111–114.

7. Adams later annotated his copy, now in the Boston Public Library. Adams's copy is available online in the internet archive at https://archive.org/details/observationsonmo00what/page/n1/mode/2up.

8. Jefferson, "Notes," 369.

9. Thomas Whately, *Observations on Modern Gardening*, 4th ed. (London: T. Payne, 1770), 116–117.

10. Jefferson, "Notes," 369.

11. Jefferson, "Notes," 369.

12. William Beiswanger, "The Temple in the Garden: Thomas Jefferson's Vision of the Monticello Landscape," *Eighteenth-Century Life* VIII, no. 2 (January 1983), 176. Jefferson also lists as sources Pallado, Gibbs, and Spon. Jefferson had purchased Kent's book in Williamsburg, Virginia in December 1778.

13. Beiswanger, "Temple in the Garden," 176. For the full specifications, see Frederick Doveton Nichols, *Thomas Jefferson's Architectural Drawings, Compiled and with a Commentary and a Check List* (Boston: Massachusetts Historical Society, 1961), no. 6.

14. Quoted in Rogers, Eustis, and Bidwell, *Romantic Gardens*, 16; see also p. 81. Lord Cobham's Stowe is Pope's exemplar of his conception of genius.

15. Timothy Mowl, *Gentlemen and Players: Gardeners of the English Landscape* (Stroud: Sutton Publishing, 2004), 95.

16. On grottoes generally, see Naomi Miller, *Heavenly Caves: Reflections on the Garden Grotto* (New York: George Braziller, 1982).

17. Anonymous, "An Epistolary Description of the Late Mr. Pope's House and Gardens at Twickenham (1747)," in Hunt and Willis, eds., *The Genius of the Place*, 249–250. The Wilderness refers to "a planned arrangement of trees that contained an understory of vegetation, often set within a regularly defined space." The Wilderness was usually located in a remote part of the garden. O'Malley, *Keywords*, 669.

18. James A. Bear Jr. and Lucia C. Stanton, eds., *Jefferson's Memorandum Books: Accounts, with Legal Records and Miscellany, 1767–1826*, vol. I (Princeton, NJ: Princeton University Press, 1997), 247–249. For an analysis of Jefferson's plan, see Beiswanger, "Temple in the Garden," 171–2. The Stourhead inscription has recently been restored: https://www.nationaltrust.org.uk/stourhead/features/restoring-the-grotto-quote.

19. Beiswanger, "Temple in the Garden," 172–173.

20. Whately, *Observations*, 178.

21. Rudy J. Favretti, "Thomas Jefferson's 'Ferme Ornée' at Monticello," *Proceedings of the American Antiquarian Society* 103, no. 1 (1993): 19.

22. Wulf, *Founding Gardeners*, 39.

23. Jefferson, "Notes," 371.

24. Jefferson, "Notes," 370.

25. Quoted in Peter Martin, *The Pleasure Gardens of Virginia from Jamestown to Jefferson* (Princeton, NJ: Princeton University Press, 1991), 145.

26. Wulf, *Founding Gardeners*, 57. Adams wrote that one English garden was "full of rare shrubs and trees, to which collection America has furnished her full share." Quoted in Martin, *Pleasure Gardens of Virginia*, 148.

27. Thomas Jefferson, "Jefferson's Hints to Americans Travelling in Europe, 19 June 1788," https://founders.archives.gov/documents/Jefferson/01-13-02-0173.

28. Jefferson to William Hamilton, July 1806, in Betts, *Thomas Jefferson's Garden Book*, 323.

29. Elizabeth Barlow Rogers, *Landscape Design: A Cultural and Architectural History* (New York: Harry N. Abrams, 2001), 240.

30. Frederick Doveton Nichols and Ralph E. Griswold, *Thomas Jefferson: Landscape Architect* (Charlottesville: University Press of Virginia, 1978), 76.

31. Jefferson, "Notes," 371.

32. John Adams, "Notes on a Tour of English Country Seats, &c., with Thomas Jefferson, 4–10? April 1786," http://founders.archives.gov/documents/Adams/01-03-02-0005-0002-0001.

33. Wulf, *Founding Gardeners*, 48.

34. Beiswanger, "Temple in the Garden," 175. Lightning destroyed the original Lord Cobham statue in 1957; the replica is from 2001.

35. Dorothy Stroud, *Capability Brown* (London: Faber and Faber, 1975), 52; quoted in Beiswanger, "Temple in the Garden," 175.

36. William Hosley, *Colt: The Making of an American Legend* (Amherst: University of Massachusetts Press in Association with the Wadsworth Atheneum, Hartford, 1996), 140–141. Many of the objects from Armsmear now reside in the Colt Collection at the Wadsworth Atheneum. See also Phillip M. Johnston, "Dialogues between Designer and Client: Furnishings Proposed by Leon Marcotte to Samuel Colt in the 1850s," *Winterthur Portfolio* 19, no. 4 (Winter 1984): 257–275. Elizabeth Colt left Armsmear as

a home for elderly women, a function it retains to this day; she left the grounds, known today as Colt Park, to the city of Hartford.

37. Hosley, *Colt*, 145.

38. Martha J. Lamb, ed., *The Homes of America* (New York: D. Appleton, 1879), 181.

39. Henry Barnard, *Armsmear: The Home, The Arm, and the Armory of Samuel Colt: A Memorial* (New York: Alvord, Printer, 1866), 94. See also M. E. W. S., "The Homes of America, VII—Armsmear," *The Art Journal for 1876*, vol. 2, (New York: D. Appleton, 1875), 321–325.

40. Barnard, *Armsmear*, 97.

41. Hosley, *Colt*, 146–149. This colt was later moved to the dome of the new armory, rebuilt in 1868. Hosley, 149.

42. Hosley, *Colt*, 145. Armsmear was open for invited groups; the American Association of Medical Superintendents visited in 1870. Hosley, 146.

43. Carol Grove, *Henry Shaw's Victorian Landscapes: The Missouri Botanical Garden and Tower Grove Park* (Amherst: University of Massachusetts Press in Association with Library of American Landscape History, 2005), 7–8. See also Carol Grove, "Aesthetics, Horticulture, and the Gardenesque: Victorian Sensibilities at Tower Grove Park," *Journal of the New England Garden History Society*, 6 (Fall 1998): 32–41.

44. Shaw owned eleven slaves until 1853 when he began hiring Bohemian immigrants. Grove, *Henry Shaw's Victorian Landscapes*, 47–48, 195, n. 14.

45. Grove, *Henry Shaw's Victorian Landscapes*, 11.

46. Grove, *Henry Shaw's Victorian Landscapes*, 98.

47. Grove, *Henry Shaw's Victorian Landscapes*, 46–47, 50.

48. Grove, *Henry Shaw's Victorian Landscapes*, 120.

49. Grove, *Henry Shaw's Victorian Landscapes*, 84.

50. Grove, *Henry Shaw's Victorian Landscapes*, 141. See also "The Largest Hotel in the World," *Scientific American 3*, no. 26 (December 22, 1860): 403. The ruins are popular now as a backdrop for weddings and can be reserved for $1,000 for that purpose. https://www.towergrovepark.org/the-ruins-1/ (accessed September 1, 2018).

51. According to landscape historian Elizabeth Barlow Rogers, "This apparent attempt to deprive the English of the distinction of having originated their own garden style, and the resentment of this on the part of the English, illustrates the historic rivalry between the two countries." Rogers, *Landscape Design*, 261. See also Eleanor P. DeLorme, *Garden Pavilions and the 18th Century French Court* (Woodbridge, Suffolk: Antique Collectors' Club, 1996).

52. Quoted in Dora Wibenson, *The Picturesque Garden in France* (Princeton, NJ: Princeton University Press, 1978), 42.

53. Monique Moser, "Paradox in the Garden: A Brief Account of *Fabriques*," in *The Architecture of Western Gardens: A Design History from the Renaissance to the Present Day*, eds. Monique Moser and Georges Teyssot (Cambridge, MA: MIT Press, 1990), 263.

54. Michael Symes, "The Concept of the 'Fabrique,'" *Garden History* 42, no. 1 (Summer 2014): 121.

55. Moser, "Paradox in the Garden," 278.

56. Diana Ketcham, *Le Désert de Retz: A Late Eighteenth-Century French Folly Garden. The Artful Landscape of Monsieur de Monville* (Cambridge, MA: MIT Press, 1994), 4.

57. Ketcham, *Le Désert de Retz*, 1. *Le Désert de Retz* was full of follies: "two classical ruins (The Temple of Pan and the Broken Column), a medieval ruin (the Gothic church), a classical temple (the Temple of Repose), a Chinese pavilion, a Tartar tent, an obelisk, a pyramid, a tomb, a rustic bridge, a thatched-roof cottage, a hermitage, a dairy, an open-air theater, and a grotto." Ketcham, *Le Désert de Retz*, 4–5.

58. Thomas Jefferson to Maria Cosway, 12 October 1786. https://founders .archives.gov/documents/Jefferson/01-10-02-0309. For an analysis of the architectural implications of Jefferson's relationship with Maria Cosway, see Ralph G. Giordano, *The Architectural Ideology of Thomas Jefferson* (Jefferson, NC: McFarland, 2012), 83–89; and for a description of Jefferson's visit to *Le Désert de Retz*, what he likely saw there, and the Broken Column's influence on his own designs, see Ketcham, *Le Désert de Retz*, 5–8. Beiswanger notes that the structures Jefferson saw in gardens on the European continent "should not be considered any less important an influence on Jefferson than English examples." Beiswanger, "The Temple in the Garden," 180.

59. Quoted in Rogers, *Landscape Design*, 262.

60. Rogers, *Landscape Design*, 262.

61. David Hays, "Carmontelle's Design for the Jardin de Monceau: A Freemasonic Garden in Late-Eighteenth-Century France," *Eighteenth-Century Studies* 32, no. 4 (Summer 1999): 458.

62. Hays, "Carmontelle's Design," 457.

63. Quoted in Bernd H. Dams and Andrew Zega, *Pleasure Pavilions and Follies in the Gardens of the Ancient Régime* (Paris: Flammarion, 1995), 135–136. See also David L. Hays, "'This is Not a *Jardin Anglais*': Carmontelle, The Jardin de Monceau, and Irregular Garden Design in Late-Eighteenth-Century France," in *Villas and Gardens in Early Modern Italy and France*, eds. Mirka Beneš and Dianne Harris (Cambridge: Cambridge University Press, 2001), 294–326.

64. On Le Petit Versailles, see Kevin Risk, *Valcour Aime Plantation Garden: 'Le Petit Versailles,'* Cultural Landscape Report (Baton Rouge, LA: Louisiana State Dept. of Culture, Recreation, and Tourism, Office of Cultural Development, Division of Historic Preservation, 2002); Roulhac B. Toledano, "Louisiana's Golden Age: Valcour Aime in St. James Parish," *Louisiana History: The Journal of the Louisiana Historical Association* 10, no. 3 (Summer 1969): 211–224; and Marc R. Matrana, *Lost Plantations of the South* (Jackson: University Press of Mississippi, 2009), 180–183. The house burned in 1920; remnants of the garden still exist.

65. Risk, "Valcour Aime Plantation Garden," 8.

66. Quoted in Risk, "Valcour Aime Plantation Garden," 8.

67. On the Petit Trianon, see Pierre Arizzoli-Clémentel Emmanuel Ducamp, *Views and Plans of the Petit Trianon at Versailles* (Paris: A. de Gourcuff, 1998).

68. Risk, "Valcour Aime Plantation Garden," 9.

69. Risk, "Valcour Aime Plantation Garden," 11.

70. Quoted in Risk, "Valcour Aime Plantation Garden," 12. Risk notes that "Aime's garden cannot be fully appreciated without acknowledging the contributions of the slaves who made such an extravagant creation possible. The prominent mountain and its subterranean icehouse, as well as the ornamental lagoon and its meaning *riviere*, represent mammoth feats of hand excavation, and Aime's journal indicates that his 'workers' were responsible for both the excavation and ongoing maintenance

of the garden. The 1860 Slave Census for St. James Parish lists Aime's holdings as 127 slaves, making him one of the largest slaveholders in the parish." Risk, "Valcour Aime Plantation Garden," 67. The role African Americans played in creating gardens for elites in the eighteenth and nineteenth centuries is enormous, especially on plantations in the antebellum American South. For a case study of the contributions of one African American gardener, see Myra B. Young Armstead, *Freedom's Gardener: James F. Brown, Horticulture, and the Hudson Valley in Antebellum America* (New York: New York University Press, 2012). Armstead analyzes and contextualizes the diary of James F. Brown (1793–1868), a former fugitive slave who became master gardener for the Verplanck family in the Hudson Valley. See also Richard Westmacott, *African-American Gardens and Yards in the Rural South* (Knoxville: University of Tennessee Press, 1992).

71. "The table was often set for twenty or thirty people, and he served delicacies produced on the plantation which were rarities for the area. Coffee is reported to have been grown in the greenhouse, and from his own grapes, wines were produced. Fine cheeses, tobacco for cigars, rice, tropical fruit were also available." Toledano, "Louisiana's Golden Age," 216–217.

72. Quoted in Risk, "Valcour Aime Plantation Garden," 13. The entirety of Ripley's comments can be found in Eliza Ripley, "A Visit to the Valcour Aime Plantation," *Social Life in Old New Orleans: Being Recollections of my Girlhood* (New York: D. Appleton, 1912), 182–190 and Eliza Ripley, "A Visit to the Valcour Aime Plantaion," in Frank De Caro and Rosan Augusta Jordan, eds., *Louisiana Sojourns: Travelers' Tales and Literary Journeys* (Baton Rouge: Louisiana State University Press, 1998), 134–138. On the taste for Chinese garden ornaments, see O'Malley, *Keywords*, 187–191 and Judy Bullington, "Cultivating Meaning: The Chinese Manner in Early American Gardens" in *Global Trade and Visual Arts in Federal New England*, eds. Patricia Johnston and Caroline Frank (Durham: University of New Hampshire Press, 2014), 157–179.

73. For a description of the ornamental garden features, see Risk, "Valcour Aime Plantation Garden," 15–16; Toledano, "Louisiana's Golden Age," 215–216; and Matrana, *Lost Plantations of the South*, 180–182.

74. Constance A. Webster, "Bonaparte's Park: A French Picturesque Garden in America," *Journal of Garden History* 6, no. 4 (1986), 330. On Point Breeze, see Webster, "Bonaparte's Park"; Constance A. Webster, "Recreating an American Landscape: Artistic and Literary Images of Joseph Bonaparte's Park at Point Breeze, New Jersey," *Journal of the New England Garden History Society* 4 (Spring 1996): 13–21; and Patricia Tyson Stroud, *The Man Who Had Been King: The American Exile of Napoleon's Brother Joseph* (Philadelphia: University of Pennsylvania Press, 2005).

75. Rogers, *Landscape Design*, 261, 263; Webster, "Bonaparte's Park," 346, n. 13.

76. Webster, "Bonaparte's Park," 337–340.

77. Webster, "Bonaparte's Parks," 342–345.

78. Quoted in Patricia Tyson Stroud, *The Emperor of Nature: Charles-Lucien Bonaparte and His World* (Philadelphia: University of Pennsylvania Press, 2000), 36–37.

79. Stroud, *Emperor of Nature*, 59.

80. A painted view of Point Breeze from circa 1820 captures the belvedere. Attributed to Charles Lawrence, the painting is in the collection of the Art Institute of Chicago (1987.170).

81. E. M. Woodward, *Bonaparte's Park and The Murats* (Trenton, NJ: MacCrellish & Quigley, 1879), 42–43.

82. Quoted in Webster, "Recreating an American Landscape," 17.

83. Noël Dorsey Vernon, "Adolph Strauch: Cincinnati and the Legacy of Spring Grove Cemetery," in *Midwestern Landscape Architecture*, ed. William H. Tishler (Urbana: University of Illinois Press in association with the Library of American Landscape History, 2000), 5–24.

84. Rogers, *Landscape Design*, 259–260. See Patrick Bowe, "Pückler-Muskau's Estate and Its Influence on American Landscape Architecture," *Garden History* 23, no. 2 (Winter 1995): 192–200. On the influence of German and German-speaking landscape designers in the United States, see Blanche M. G. Linden, "Nineteenth-Century German-American Landscape Designers," *SiteLINES: A Journal of Place* 1, no. 2 (Spring 2006): 9–11; and Gert Gröning, "Parks and International Exchange," *SiteLINES: A Journal of Place* 1, no. 2 (Spring 2006): 11–13.

85. Noël Dorsey Vernon, "Strauch, Adolph," in *Pioneers of American Landscape Design*, ed. Charles A. Birnbaum (New York: McGraw-Hill, 2000): 384–388.

86. John Clubbe, *Cincinnati Observed: Architecture and History* (Columbus: Ohio State University Press, 1992), 314–317.

87. Catherine E. Kelly, *Republic of Taste: Art, Politics, and Everyday Life in Early America* (Philadelphia: University of Pennsylvania Press, 2016), 124–125.

88. Kelly, *Republic of Taste*, 127–128.

89. Aaron V. Wunsch, "Woodlands Cemetery," Historic American Landscape Survey (HALS) No. PA-5 (Washington, DC: National Park Service, US Department of the Interior, 2003–2004), 8.

90. Quoted in Wunsch, "Woodlands Cemetery," 8.

91. Kelly, *Republic of Taste*, 130. See also Sarah Chesney, "The Root of the Matter: Searching for William Hamilton's Greenhouse at The Woodlands Estate, Philadelphia, Pennsylvania," in *Historical Archaeology of the Delaware Valley, 1600–1850*, eds. Richard Veit and David Orr (Knoxville: University of Tennessee Press, 2014), 273–296; and Richard J. Betts, "The Woodlands," *Winterthur Portfolio* 14, no. 3 (Autumn 1979): 213–234.

92. James A. Jacobs, "Addendum to The Woodlands," HABS No. PA-1125, Historic American Building Survey (HABS) (Washington, DC: National Park Service, US Department of the Interior), 2.

93. Timothy Preston Long, "The Woodlands: A Matchless Place" (MA thesis, University of Pennsylvania, 1991), 48.

94. Wunsch, "Woodlands Cemetery," 30–31. Manasseh Cutler provides a description of his experience of the house and gardens at The Woodlands in 1803. "Visit of Manasseh Cutler to William Hamilton at The Woodlands," *Pennsylvania Magazine of History and Biography* 8 (1884): 109–110.

95. Long, "The Woodlands," 140–141. A visitor to The Woodlands described the grotto: "a little further on, you come to a charming spring, some part of the ground is hollowed out where Mr Hamilton is going to form a grotto, he has already collected some shells." Quoted in O'Malley, *Keywords*, 328.

96. Kelly, *Republic of Taste*, 131.

97. Kelly, *Republic of Taste*, 139–140.

98. Kelly, *Republic of Taste*, 141.

99. Kelly, *Republic of Taste*, 147.

100. Kelly *Republic of Taste*, 156.

101. Kelly, *Republic of Taste*, 12. In the nineteenth century, the garden at The Woodlands was transformed into a rural cemetery, suggesting the interchangeability of picturesque landscapes.

102. Adams, "Notes on a Tour of English Country Seats."

103. For many elites like Jefferson, the English garden and its follies were exactly what the United States needed. Some tried to argue that American gardens rivaled those of the English. Princess Caroline Laetitia Murat, Joseph Bonaparte's grandniece, who was born in Bordentown, wrote: "As I look back, an old woman, through this long vista of years, it seems to me that I have seen nothing on this side of the Atlantic [in Europe] than can in any way compare to Point Breeze, and the remembered scenes of my childhood." Princess Caroline Murat, *My Memoirs* (London: Eveleigh Nash, 1910), 38. Quoted in Webster, "Recreating an American Landscape," 13. Other observers begged to differ. In 1839, the Philadelphia financier Nicholas Biddle recorded in his journal: "He [Joseph Bonaparte] spent so much money at Point Breeze he says because he was in hopes of bringing his family over to live here and he wished them to see that they had here something better than there is anywhere in Europe, and he thinks he has accomplished it, and that there is no establishment like Point Breeze in Europe. This seems to me an illusion for altho' he has a fine park yet the house is not worthy of the grounds." Quoted in Edward Biddle, "Joseph Bonaparte As Recorded in the Private Journal of Nicholas Biddle," *Pennsylvania Magazine of History and Biography* 55, no. 3 (1931): 222.

2. Temples

1. Vol. 30 of the Campbell Collection at the Historical Society of Pennsylvania contains news clippings from the turn of the century, including "A Frankford Landmark: The Womrath Mansion With its Historic Associations" and "Frankford's 'Declaration' Tradition." Rev. S. F. Hotchkin describes the summerhouse in 1893 as follows: "The striking feature of the grounds is an old but well-preserved and strongly-built summer-house. It is an octagon, with octagonal roof surrounded by a balustrade, while an ornamental finial crowns the centre. It is a remarkable and stylish building of an old fashion, seldom seen to-day. A little piazza encircles it, having circular pillars to uphold the roof. It is painted white and stands on a pleasant eminence. It is not a mere arbor, but entirely enclosed and has six glass windows. The sides are ceiled with wood and the top is plastered. There is an ornamented cornice, and the two doors opposite each other are paneled. It is an interesting antique . . ." Rev. S. F. Hotchkin, *The Bristol Pike* (Philadelphia: George W. Jacobs, 1893), 17–18. Both the mansion and the summerhouse have been demolished.

2. *Old Landmarks and Relics of Philadelphia* comprises six volumes of photographs by Robert Newell and Sons, published for the Philadelphia Centennial (available in the Historical Society of Pennsylvania). See also Kenneth Finkel and Susan Oyama, *Philadelphia, Then and Now: 60 Matching Photographic Views from 1859–1952 and from 1986–1988* (New York: Dover Publications in cooperation with the Library Company of Philadelphia, 1988), 110. The summerhouse was known well enough to warrant a stereograph, also by Robert Newell and Sons. The stereograph is in the collection of the Historical Society of Pennsylvania.

3. The myth continues to this day. See Jack McCarthy, "Persistent History," July 4, 2012, accessed August 11, 2016, http://hiddencityphila.org/2012/07/letter-from-the -northeast/. The story gained some credence in 1916 when a letter by Edwards's niece Fanny Saltar was published in "Fanny Saltar's Reminiscences of Colonial Days in Philadelphia, Contributed by Mrs. E. B. Hoskins," *The Pennsylvania Magazine of History and Biography*, XL, (1916): 187–198. According to Saltar: "One day when Mr. Jefferson was on a visit to my uncle, they walked up to this summer-house. He looked around and said: 'This is the spot on which the signers of the Declaration of Independence dined the day they signed the Declaration,'" 198.

4. Joyce Appleby, *Thomas Jefferson* (New York: Henry Holt, 2003), 45.

5. It has been suggested that Jefferson's monopteros may have been a design, not for a building, but for a shelf clock in temple form. See Thomas M. Allen, *A Republic in Time: Temporality & Social Imagination in Nineteenth-Century America* (Chapel Hill: University of North Carolina Press, 2008), 57–58.

6. On the Montpelier icehouse, see Donna C. Dodenhoff, "The View from Montpelier: James Madison's Configuration of the Ideal Republican Landscape," *Journal of the New England Garden History Society* 9 (Fall 2001): 1–10.

7. *The First Jubilee of American Independence: and Tribute of Gratitude to the Illustrious Adams and Jefferson* (Newark, NJ: M. Lyon, 1826), 39.

8. Andrew Burstein describes the celebrations in Newark, New Jersey, on this day in his book *America's Jubilee: How in 1826 A Generation Remembered Fifty Years of Independence* (New York: Alfred A. Knopf, 2001), 239, 243–245.

9. Quoted in Harold D. Eberlein and Cortlandt van Dyke Hubbard, "The American 'Vauxhall' of the Federal Era," *Pennsylvania Magazine of History and Biography* 68, no. 2 (April 1944): 165.

10. Eberlein and Hubbard, "American 'Vauxhall,'" 171.

11. Later, Paca signed the Declaration of Independence and became governor of Maryland.

12. Barbara Wells Sarudy, *Gardens and Gardening in the Chesapeake 1700–1805* (Baltimore: Johns Hopkins University Press, 1998), 22.

13. Joseph Manca, "Cicero in America: Civic Duty and Private Happiness in Charles Willson Peale's Portrait of 'William Paca'," *American Art* 17, no. 1 (Spring 2003): 84, 69.

14. Manca, "Cicero in America," 78.

15. Manca, "Cicero in America," 79.

16. Jane Mork Gibson and Robert Wolterstorff, "The Fairmount Waterworks," *Philadelphia Museum of Art Bulletin* 84, no. 360/361 (Summer 1988): 12.

17. John P. Sheldon, "A Description of Philadelphia in 1825," *Pennsylvania Magazine of History and Biography* LX, no. 1 (January 1936): 75. For an analysis of visitors' accounts of the Philadelphia Waterworks, see Philip Stevick, *Imagining Philadelphia: Travelers' Views of the City from 1800 to the Present* (Philadelphia: University of Pennsylvania Press, 1996), 72–86.

18. Thirty years after the opening of the Waterworks, rustic summerhouses appeared in the pleasure grounds, greatly contrasting with the earlier temples Graff had designed. Gibson and Wolterstorff, "Fairmount Waterworks," 38. One of the rustic pavilions was recreated in metal on its original spot in the early twenty-first century.

19. The sculptures are entitled *Male Figure Emblematic River Schuylkill in its Improved State* (1825) and *Female Ditto Emblematic of the Water Works* (1825).

20. Arthur S. Marks, "Joining the Past to the Present: William Rush's Emblematic Statuary at Fairmount," *Proceedings of the American Philosophical Society* 157, no. 2 (June 2013): 225–226.

21. Charles Coleman Sellers, "William Rush at Fairmount," in *Sculpture of a City: Philadelphia's Treasures in Bronze and Stone*, ed. Nicholas B. Wainwright (New York: Walker Publishing, 1974), 12–13.

22. Marks, "Joining the Past to the Present," 226, n. 97.

23. Thomas Hamilton, *Men and Manners in America*, vol. 1 (Edinburgh: William Blackwood, 1833), 339–340.

24. William Beiswanger, "The Temple in the Garden: Thomas Jefferson's Vision of the Monticello Landscape," *Eighteenth-Century Life*, VIII, no. 2 (January 1983): 170.

25. Beiswanger, "Temple in the Garden," 184. Henry D. Gilpin, a visitor to Monticello in 1827, writes "there is an eminence where Mr. Jefferson had erected a little Grecian temple & which was a favourite spot with him to read & sit in—we stood on the spot, but a violent storm some years since blew down the temple & no vestiges are left." Merrill D. Peterson, ed. *Visitors to Monticello* (Charlottesville: University Press of Virginia, 2006), 112. The temple was actually Palladian rather than Grecian.

26. On Belfield, see James A. Butler, *Charles Willson Peale's 'Belfield': A History of a National Historic Landmark, 1684–1984* (Philadelphia: La Salle University Art Museum, 2009); Emily T. Cooperman, "Belfield, Springland and Early American Picturesque: The Artist's Garden in the American Early Republic," *Studies in the History of Gardens and Designed Landscapes* 26, no. 2 (2006): 118–131; Diane Newbury, "'But That Garden Now Became His Hobby-Horse': Charles Willson Peale and His Garden at Belfield," *Journal of the New England Garden History Society*, 4 (Spring 1996): 38–47; Therese O'Malley, "Charles Willson Peale's Belfield: Its Place in American Garden History," in *New Perspectives on Charles Willson Peale: A 250th Anniversary Celebration*, eds. Lillian B. Miller and David C. Ward (Pittsburgh: University of Pittsburgh Press, 1991), 267–282; Jessie J. Poesch, "Mr. Peale's 'Farm Persevere': Some Documentary Views, *Proceedings of the American Philosophical Society* 100, no. 6 (December 17, 1956): 545–556; Carl Eaton Soltis, *The Art of the Peales in the Philadelphia Museum of Art: Adaptations and Innovations* (Philadelphia: Philadelphia Museum of Art in Association with Yale University Press, 2017), 212–219; David C. Ward, "Charles Willson Peale's Farm Belfield: Enlightened Agriculture in the Early Republic," in *New Perspectives on Charles Willson Peale: A 250th Anniversary Celebration*, eds. Lillian B. Miller and David C. Ward (Pittsburgh: University of Pittsburgh Press, 1991), 282–301.

27. Quoted in Newbury, "'But That Garden Now Became His Hobby-Horse,'" 46.

28. James Henry, *Sketches of Moravian Life and Character* (Philadelphia: J. B. Lippincott, 1859), 207.

29. Quoted in Charles B. Sanford, *Thomas Jefferson and His Library: A Study of His Literary Interests and the Religious Attitudes Revealed by Relevant Titles in his Library* (Hamden, CT: Archon Books, 1977), 86. Jefferson to Robert Skipwith, August 3, 1771, in Jefferson, *The Papers of Thomas Jefferson*, vol. 1, ed. Julian P. Boyd (Princeton: Princeton University Press, 1950), 79.

30. Charles Willson Peale to Thomas Jefferson, March 2, 1812, in Peale, *The Selected Papers of Charles Willson Peale and His Family*, vol. 3, ed. Lillian B. Miller, (New Haven,

CT: Yale University Press, 1991), 149. Peale also wrote to Jefferson, "Your favorite pursuit, Gardening, is also becoming my favorite amusement." Charles Willson Peale to Thomas Jefferson, August 19, 1812, *Selected Papers of Charles Willson Peale*, vol. 3, 165.

31. Quoted in Charles Coleman Sellers, *Mr. Peale's Museum: Charles Willson Peale and the First Popular Museum of Natural Science and Art* (New York: W. W. Norton, 1980), 83.

32. Peale, *Selected Papers of Charles Willson Peale*, vol. 3, 606. Quoted in Newbury, "'But That Garden Now Became His Hobby-Horse,'" 41.

33. Peale, *Selected Papers of Charles Willson Peale*, vol. 3, 216.

34. Peale, *Selected Papers of Charles Willson Peale*, vol. 5, 382.

35. Peale, *Selected Papers of Charles Willson Peale*, vol. 3, 729.

36. Peale, *Selected Papers of Charles Willson Peale*, vol. 3, 202.

37. Julia Sienkewicz, "Citizenship by Design: Art and Identity in the Early Republic" (PhD dissertation, University of Illinois at Urbana-Champaign, 2009), 221.

38. See Paul Staiti, *Of Arms and Artists: The American Revolution through Painters' Eyes* (New York: Bloomsbury, 2016), 11–62.

39. Staiti, *Of Arms and Artists*, 45.

40. "Celebration of the Arrival George Washington in Philadelphia," *Pennsylvania Packet*, Philadelphia, December 4, 1781, in Peale, *Selected Papers of Charles Willson Peale*, vol. 1, ed. Lillian Miller, (New Haven, CT: Yale University Press, 1983), 365–366.

41. The key primary source that describes this temple is "Account of the Grand Federal Procession in Philadelphia," *American Museum* (July 1788): 57–75. For an analysis of the iconography of the Grand Federal Procession, see Dietmar Schloss, "The Nation as Spectacle: The Grand Federal Procession in Philadelphia, 1788," in *Celebrating Ethnicity and Nation: American Festive Culture from the Revolution to the Early 20th Century*, eds. Jürgen Heidekin, et al. (New York: Berghahn Books, 2001), 44–62. See also Laura Rigal, "'Raising the Roof': Authors, Spectators and Artisans in the Grand Federal Procession of 1788," *Theatre Journal* 48, no. 3 (1996): 253–277.

42. Schloss, "Nation as Spectacle," 52.

43. "Account of the Grand Federal Procession," 59–60.

44. On Bush Hill, see Mark E. Reinberger and Elizabeth McLean, *The Philadelphia Country House: Architecture and Landscape in Colonial America* (Baltimore: Johns Hopkins University Press, 2015), 236–241.

45. Elizabeth Milroy discusses the Federal Procession in *The Grid and the River: Philadelphia's Green Places, 1682–1876* (University Park, PA: Pennsylvania State University Press, 2016), 98–103.

46. Milroy, *Grid and the River*, 101.

47. "Account of the Grand Federal Procession," 59–60.

48. Sienkewicz, "Citizenship by Design," 186. Peale claimed that his garden was so overrun with tourists on Sundays that he had to restrict admission to weekdays in order to exclude less desirable visitors. Sienkewicz, "Citizenship by Design," 215–216.

49. Sienkewicz, "Citizenship by Design," 216.

50. Architecture was of great interest to Brown. See Alan Axelrod, *Charles Brockden Brown: An American Tale* (Austin: University of Texas Press, 1983), 100–104. According to William Dunlap, author of *The Life of Charles Brockden Brown* (1815), Brown "would for hours be absorbed in architectural studies, measuring proportions with

his compasses, and drawing plans for Grecian temples or Gothic cathedrals, monasteries or castles . . ." Quoted in Axelrod, *Charles Brockden Brown*, 101.

51. The summerhouse in *Wieland* was not Brown's first folly invention in his literary work. In the fragment "Signior Adini" (1797), Brown describes a summerhouse similar to the one in *Wieland* in placement within the landscape. This summerhouse "was erected on the verge of an abrupt descent, whose bottom was laved by the river. The opposite bank, which for some miles was uniformly towering and steep, fell away when it came in from off this promontory, as if it were on purpose to allow us the spectacle of the setting sun, and a limited but charming prospect of fields and meadow." Quoted in Robert Lawson-Peebles, *Landscape and Written Expression in Revolutionary America* (Cambridge: Cambridge University Press, 1988), 235; see also p. 239. Axelrod suggests that Wieland's temple is a "reaction to the extremity of wilderness experience . . . Wieland, all but destroyed by his missionary endeavors, erects a symbol of classical order at the end of the wilderness that had debililtated him." Axelrod, *Charles Brockden Brown*, 66. Jeffrey Andrew Weinstock has described Mettingen as "a haunted liminal space positioned on the border between the real and the fantastic and defined by its isolation and strangeness." Jeffrey Andrew Weinstock, *Charles Brockden Brown* (Cardiff: University of Wales Press, 2011), 37. Peter Kafer argues that the site of Mettingen and its temple on the banks of the Schuylkill was formerly occupied by a settlement created by a radical religious group in the 1690s where the Schuylkill River and Wissahickon Creek meet. Kafer includes his own photograph of the spot as it appeared in 1999. The site of the radical group's "tabernacle" built in 1694 would have been in ruins in Brown's time. Peter Kafer, *Charles Brockden Brown's Revolution and the Birth of American Gothic* (Philadelphia: University of Pennsylvania Press, 2004), 112, 114, 117. See also n. 13 and n. 17, Kafer, *Charles Brockden Brown's Revolution*, 227–228, for parallels between the "tabernacle" and Wieland's temple.

52. Charles Brockden Brown, *Wieland or the Transformation, An American Tale*, eds. Sydney J. Krause and S. W. Reid (1798; Kent, OH: Kent State University Press, 1988), 12.

53. Brown, *Wieland*, 11.

54. Brown, *Wieland*, 12.

55. Brown, *Wieland*, 17, 11.

56. Lawson-Peebles, *Landscape and Written Expression*, 231.

57. Larry Kutchen, "The 'Vulgar Thread of the Canvas': Revolution and the Picturesque in Ann Eliza Bleecker, Crèvecoeur, and Charles Brockden Brown," *Early American Literature* 36, no. 3 (2001): 411–412.

58. Brown, *Wieland*, 19.

59. I explore the collision of neoclassical and Gothic architecture in my chapter "Gothic Monticello: Thomas Jefferson's Garden Narratives," in Kerry Dean Carso, *American Gothic Art and Architecture in the Age of Romantic Literature* (Cardiff: University of Wales Press, 2014), 9–28.

60. Brown, *Wieland*, 24.

61. Jane Tompkins, *Sensational Designs: The Cultural Work of American Fiction 1790–1860* (Oxford: Oxford University Press, 1985), 50. Or as David Smith writes, "Initially a space of religious zealotry and isolation, the newly established temple morphs into a Gothic locus of danger and mystery, after which his children attempt to transform the temple into a site of Enlightenment-esque education and art." Smith concludes that "the temple's resistance to sanitizing attempts to remove the Gothic aura of vio-

lence reflects Brown's uncertainty in enlightened rationalism to defeat the superstitions of the past." David Smith, "The Gothic Temple: Epistemology and Revolution in Charles Brockden Brown's *Wieland*," *Gothic Studies* 18, no. 2 (November 2016): 2–3.

62. Brown, *Wieland*, 33.

63. Jennifer Harris, "At One with the Land: The Domestic Remove—Charles Brockden Brown's *Wieland* and Matters of National Belonging," *Canadian Review of American Studies/Revue canadienne d'études américaines* 33, no. 3 (2003): 200.

64. Benson J. Lossing, *Mary and Martha: The Mother and the Wife of George Washington* (New York: Harper and Brothers, 1886), 324–325.

65. Natalie Spasskey et. al., *American Paintings in the Metropolitan Museum of Art*, vol. II, ed. Kathleen Luhrs (New York: The Metropolitan Museum of Art, 1985), 90. See also Bruce Weber, *Every Kind of a Painter: The Art of Thomas Prichard Rossiter (1818–1871)* (Garrison, NY: Boscobel House and Gardens, 2015), 17–19; Katherine Manthorne and John W. Coffey, *The Landscapes of Louis Rémy Mignot: A Southern Painter Abroad* (Washington, DC: Smithsonian Institution Press for the North Carolina Museum of Art, 1996); Barbara J. Mitnick, ed. *George Washington: American Symbol* (New York: Hudson Hills Press, 1999), 65; and Angela D. Mack and Stephen G. Hoffius, eds., *Landscape of Slavery: The Plantation in American Art* (Columbia, SC: University of South Carolina Press, 2008), 102–105.

66. Thomas Prichard Rossiter, *Description of the Picture of the Home of Washington After the War Painted by T. P. Rossiter and L. R. Mignot* (New York: D. Appleton, 1859).

67. Maurie D. McInnis addresses the issue of slavery's relationship to outbuildings in Charleston, South Carolina, in the antebellum period, arguing that the Gothic Revival style appears not in residences but only in backlot buildings, including follies, concluding that the style was not selected for "mere fancy, for the style and its local association resonated with deeper ideological beliefs. The Gothic Revival was a physical manifestation of [Charleston's elite slaveowners'] belief that slavery was a natural component of their Christian society." Maurie D. McInnis, *The Politics of Taste in Antebellum Charleston* (Chapel Hill: University of North Carolina Press, 2005), 197, 238–239.

68. Joel T. Fry, "America's 'Ancient Garden': The Bartram Botanic Garden, 1728–1850," in *Knowing Nature: Art and Science in Philadelphia, 1740–1840*, ed. Amy R. W. Meyers (New Haven, CT: Yale University Press, 2011), 60, 76.

69. Joel T. Fry, "John Bartram and His Garden: Would John Bartram Recognize His Garden Today?," in *America's Curious Botanist: A Tercentennial Reappraisal of John Bartram, 1699–1777*, eds. Nancy E. Hoffmann and John C. Van Horne (Philadelphia: The American Philosophical Society, 2004), 170–171. Thank you to Joel T. Fry for sending me the materials used here about Bartram's Garden.

70. Viator, "Philadelphia Surroundings," *The Pennsylvania Farm Journal* 12, no. 9 (December 1852): 270. "Arbors" are shaded shelters consisting of latticework covered with vegetation. See O'Malley, "Arbor," *Keywords*, 86–91.

71. A Massachusetts Subscriber, "Trees and Pleasure Grounds in Pennsylvania," *The Horticulturist* 5, no. 6 (December 1850): 253–254.

72. Thomas Meehan, *The American Handbook of Ornamental Trees* (Philadelphia: Lippincott, Grambo, 1853), 123.

73. The Washington myth extended to the Womrath summerhouse; in 1893, Rev. S. F. Hotchkin tells us that "Washington is said to have taken tea here." Hotchkin, *Bristol Pike*, 18.

3. Summerhouses

1. Quoted in James C. Kelly and William M. S. Rasmussen, *The Virginia Landscape: A Cultural History* (Charlottesville, VA: Howell Press, 2000), 70.

2. Thomas Jefferson to William Carmichael, 26 December 1786. Accessed October 9, 2018, https://founders.archives.gov/documents/Jefferson/01-10-02-0489.

3. William S. Harwood, "Luxurious Hermits: Asceticism, Luxury and Retirement in the Eighteenth-Century Garden," *Studies in the History of Gardens and Designed Landscapes* 20, no. 4 (2000): 276–278. In New York's Hudson Valley, there was another country house called "The Hermitage" belonging to Charles Coffey Alger (1809–1875) of the Hudson Iron Corporation. Myra B. Young Armstead, *Freedom's Gardener: James F. Brown, Horticulture, and the Hudson Valley in Antebellum America* (New York: New York University Press, 2012), 63. On the history of hermits, see Gordon Campbell, *The Hermit in the Garden: From Imperial Rome to Ornamental Gnome* (Oxford: Oxford University Press, 2013).

4. Thomas Jefferson, "Notes of a Tour through Holland and the Rhine Valley," *The Papers of Thomas Jefferson*, ed. Julian P. Boyd, vol. 13, March 7 to October 1788 (Princeton, NJ: Princeton University Press, 1956), 17, accessed September 12, 2018, https://founders.archives.gov/documents/Jefferson/01-13-02-0003.

5. Christopher Thacker, *The History of Gardens* (Berkeley: University of California Press, 1979), 215. A real hermit occupied a hermitage at the Elias Hasket Derby Farm in Peabody, Massachusetts. In 1820, Eliza Southgate described "a venerable old man" with "a prayer book" seated at "an old table which, like the hermit, seemed moulding to decay." Quoted in Therese O'Malley, "Hermitage," *Keywords in American Landscape Design* (New Haven: National Gallery of Art in association with Yale University Press, 2010), 355. On the rustic hermitage, see also John E. Crowley, *The Invention of Comfort: Sensibilities and Design in Early Modern Britain and Early America* (Baltimore: Johns Hopkins University Press, 2001), 208–216.

6. Harriet Martineau, *Retrospect of Western Travel*, vol. 2 (London: Saunders and Otley, 1838), 226.

7. Patrick McGreevy, *Imagining Niagara: The Meaning and Making of Niagara Falls* (Amherst: University of Massachusetts, 1994), 48–49.

8. William Salmon provides this definition of the term rustic in his book *Pallado Londinesis* (1734). Quoted in W. Barksdale Maynard, *Architecture in the United States, 1800–1850* (New Haven: Yale University Press, 2002), 101. The terms "summerhouse" and "hermitage" were not exactly interchangeable but overlapped a great deal. Summerhouses came in a range of styles, whereas hermitages in gardens tended to be rustic.

9. W. Barksdale Maynard, "Thoreau's House at Walden," *The Art Bulletin*, 81, no. 2 (June 1999): 315.

10. Downing also described James Arnold's summerhouse in New Bedford, Massachusetts as a hermitage. Maynard, "Thoreau's House at Walden," 316. Downing had his own "hermitage" on the grounds of his home Highland Garden, in Newburgh, New York, discussed at the end of this chapter.

11. Andrew Jackson Downing, *The Architecture of Country Houses* (1850; New York: Da Capo Press, 1968), v.

12. Andrew Jackson Downing, *A Treatise on the Theory and Practice of Landscape Gardening, Adapted to North America; with a View to the Improvement of Country Residences*, 4th ed. (New York: George P. Putnam, 1850), 454, 460.

13. David Schuyler, *Apostle of Taste: Andrew Jackson Downing, 1815–1852* (Baltimore: Johns Hopkins University Press, 1996), 2. Using Angela Miller's *The Empire of the Eye* as an interpretative framework, David Wall argues that "this dissemination of a shared American identity [promoted by both landscape artists and Downing] was the product of a narrowly defined northeastern social and political imperative to cement [what Miller calls] a 'cultural endeavor directed at consolidating a middle-class social identity utterly bound up with the civilizing mission.'" David Wall, "Andrew Jackson Downing and the Tyranny of Taste," *American Nineteenth Century History* 8, no. 2 (June 2007): 188.

14. On how social class intersects with gardening and horticulture, see Tamara Plakins Thornton, *Cultivating Gentlemen: The Meaning of Country Life Among the Boston Elite, 1785–1860* (New Haven: Yale University Press, 1989) and Cheryl Lyon-Jenness, *For Shade and for Comfort: Democratizing Horticulture in the Nineteenth-Century Midwest* (West Lafayette, IN: Purdue University Press, 2004).

15. Elizabeth Cromley, "A Room with a View," in *Resorts of the Catskills* (New York: St. Martin's Press, 1979), 18. The entry in *Keywords* on summerhouses lists the three purposes of summerhouses: providing shelter, commanding a view, and terminating a view. O'Malley, "Summerhouse," *Keywords*, 600–601.

16. "Rustic Adornments," *The Gardener's Monthly*, II, no. 11 (November 1860): 338.

17. Francis R. Kowsky notes that Hibberd's "audience was the new English middle class, which felt that good taste demanded that they have examples of rustic design in their homes and gardens." Francis R. Kowsky, *Country, Park, and City: The Architecture and Life of Calvert Vaux* (New York: Oxford University Press, 1998), 116.

18. Shirley Hibberd, *Rustic Adornments for Homes of Taste* (London: Groombridge & Sons, 1870), 368. Jay Appleton's "Prospect-Refuge Theory" helps explains why human beings desire both wide-open views and shelter when experiencing a landscape. He writes, "Habitat theory postulates that aesthetic pleasure in landscape derives from the observer experiencing an environment favourable to the satisfaction of his biological needs. Prospect-refuge theory postulates that, because the ability to see without being seen is an intermediate step in the satisfaction of those needs, the capacity of an environment to ensure the achievement of *this* becomes a more immediate source of aesthetic satisfaction." Jay Appleton, *The Experience of Landscape* (London: Wiley, 1975), 73.

19. Hibberd, *Rustic Adornments*, 368–369.

20. Maynard, "Thoreau's House at Walden," 303–325.

21. Quoted in Barbara Finney, "Washington Irving's Cockloft Summerhouse: Literature Transformed into Architecture" *Nineteenth Century* 26, no. 1 (Spring 2006), 25. Jasper Cropsey was probably the artist of the landscape painting. For the full story of the replica, see Finney, "Washington Irving's Cockloft Summerhouse," 23–28. See also Constance M. Greiff, *Lost America: From the Mississippi to the Pacific* (Princeton, NJ: Pyne Press, 1971), 226.

22. The summerhouse is extant but has been moved to the campus of Elmira College, where today visitors can take a tour and view an exhibition on Twain in a nearby building. Francis Whiting Halsey identifies the architect of the summerhouse as Alfred H. Thorp. Francis Whiting Halsey, ed., *Authors of our Day in their Homes, Personal Descriptions and Interviews* (New York: James Pott, 1902), 32.

23. Quoted in Lorraine Welling Lanmon, *Quarry Farm: A Study of the "Picturesque,"* (Elmira, NY: Elmira College Center for Mark Twain Studies at Quarry Farm, 1991), 3.

24. Quoted in Lanmon, *Quarry Farm*, 17. At the time of the summerhouse's construction, octagons were popular thanks to Orson Fowler's book *A Home for All; or, the Gravel Wall and Octagon Mode of Building* (1848). On literary tourism and Quarry Farm, see Hilary Iris Lowe, "Commemorating Writers' Workplaces: The Case of Mark Twain's Study and Quarry Farm," in *From Page to Place: American Literary Tourism and the Afterlives of Authors*, eds. Jennifer Harris and Hilary Iris Lowe (Amherst: University of Massachusetts Press, 2017), 125–145.

25. Lanmon notes that she knows of no octagonal pilot houses. Lanmon, *Quarry Farm*, 28, n. 51.

26. Edwin Wildman, "Mark Twain's Pets," *St. Nicholas, An Illustrated Magazine for Young Folks* XXVI, no. 3 (January 1899): 186.

27. Lanmon, *Quarry Farm*, 23.

28. Nathaniel Hawthorne, *The House of the Seven Gables* (1851; Columbus: Ohio State University Press, 1965), 86. On the importance of the garden in Hawthorne's novel, see Rita Bode, "'Within Small Compass': Hawthorne's Expansive Urban Garden," *The Brock Review* 10 (2008): 41–50.

29. Hawthorne, *House of the Seven Gables*, 145.

30. For more on the European background of gardens' association with love and sexuality, see Michael Niedermeier, "'Strolling Under Palm Trees': Gardens—Love—Sexuality," *Journal of Garden History* 17, no. 3 (1997): 186–207.

31. Downing, *Treatise*, 458.

32. "Hints and Designs for Rustic Buildings," *The Horticulturist*, II, no. 8 (February 1848): 363.

33. Samuel Sloan, "Design XIV Architectural Summer-House," in *American Houses* (Philadelphia: Henry Carey Baird, 1861), and Samuel Sloan, "Summer-Houses," in *City Homes, Country Houses, and Church Architecture, or, The American Builders' Journal* (Philadelphia: Claxton: Remsen & Haffelfinger, 1871), 499.

34. "Summer-House," *Gleason's Pictorial Drawing-Room Companion* V, no. 2 (July 9, 1853): 24–25.

35. Samuel L. Boardman, "Rustic Adornments for Gardens and Waysides," *The Gardener's Monthly* II, no. 4 (April 1860): 112.

36. John M. Smith, "Thatching and Rustic Adornments," *The Gardener's Monthly*, I:9 (September 1, 1859): 132.

37. George E. and F. W. Woodward, "Design No. 11: A Suburban Summer House," in *Woodward's Country Homes* (New York: George E. and F. W. Woodward, 1865), 64–66.

38. Samuel Sloan, "Design XXVI," *The Model Architect* 1, no. 12 (June 1852): 101–102.

39. Martha Lamb, ed., *The Homes of America* (New York: D. Appleton, 1879), 45–47.

40. Sloan, *City Homes*, 515; Alexander Jackson Davis, *Rural Residences* (1838; New York: Da Capo Press, 1980).

41. The term *gazebo* commonly in use today may come from "to gaze," although the etymology of the term may be Eastern. *Oxford English Dictionary Online*, s.v. "Gazebo, n." December 2018. Oxford University Press, accessed February 23, 2019, http://www.oed.com/view/Entry/77226?redirectedFrom=gazebo&.

42. Edward Kemp, *How to Lay Out a Garden* (New York: Wiley & Halsted, 1858), 81.

43. Sloan, "Summer-Houses," 499.

44. Frank J. Scott, *The Art of Beautifying Suburban Home Grounds of Small Extent* (New York: D. Appleton, 1870), 107.

45. Malcolm Andrews, *Landscape and Western Art* (Oxford: Oxford University Press, 1999), 108.

46. Northeastern middle-class readers were the target audience of pattern books and agricultural periodicals. For more on these publications, especially agricultural periodicals, see Sally McMurray, *Families and Farmhouses in Nineteenth-Century America: Vernacular Design and Social Change* (New York: Oxford University Press, 1988). See also Dell Upton, "Pattern Books and Professionalism: Aspects of the Transformation of Domestic Architecture in America, 1800–1860," *Winterthur Portfolio* 19, no. 2–3 (1984): 107–150.

47. "A Small and Cheap Summer-House," *New England Farmer*, VIII, no. 3 (March 1856): 132; "Plan for a Cheap Summer House," *New England Farmer*, VIII, no. 4 (April 1856): 169–170.

48. John M. Smith, "Rustic Adornments," *The Gardener's Monthly* II, no. 5 (May 1860): 131–133.

49. Daniel Harrison Jacques, *The Garden: A Pocket Manual of Practical Horticulture* (New York: Fowler and Wells, 1858), 48.

50. G. M. Kern, *Practical Landscape Gardening* (Cincinnati: Moore, Wilstach, Keys, 1855), 88.

51. "A Few Words on Rustic Arbours by an Amateur, New York," *The Horticulturist* IV, no. 7 (January 1850): 320.

52. Bronson Alcott, *The Journals of Bronson Alcott*, ed. Odell Shepard (Boston: Little, Brown, 1938), September 13, 1846, 184.

53. Nathaniel Hawthorne, "The Wayside: Introductory," in *A Wonder Book and Tanglewood Tales* (1853; Columbus: Ohio State University Press, 1972), 176.

54. *Homes of American Authors* (New York: G. P. Putnam, 1853), 305.

55. "Illustrations of Ornamental Iron Work," *The Horticulturist* 6, no. 3 (March 1856): 115.

56. Janes, Kirtland & Co., *Ornamental Ironwork* (1870; Princeton, NJ: Pyne Press, 1971), no. 4.

57. Summerhouses proliferated in warmer Southern climates. For instance, see Gwynn Cochran Prideaux, *Summerhouses in Virginia* (Richmond: Valentine Museum, 1976).

58. On Mohonk, see Harvey K. Flad, "The Parlor in the Wilderness: Domesticating an Iconic American Landscape," *The Geographical Review* 99, no. 3 (July 2009): 356–376.

59. Benjamin Matteson and Joan A. LaChance, *The Summerhouses of Mohonk* (New Paltz: Mohonk Mountain House, 1998), 10.

60. Quoted in Larry E. Burgess, *Mohonk and the Smileys: A National Historic Landmark and the Family That Created It*, New ed. (Catskill, NY: Black Dome Press, 2019), 57.

61. Frederick E. Partington, *The Story of Mohonk* (Fulton, NY: Morrill Press, 1911), 17–18.

62. G. Murch, "Ornaments for Pleasure Grounds," *Illustrated Annual Register of Rural Affairs* VIII (1878): 223. This article was originally published in the *Country Gentleman*.

63. Thomas S. Kirkbride, *Report of the Pennsylvania Hospital for the Insane for the Year 1844* (Philadelphia: James C. Haswell, 1845), 24–25.

64. *The North American Tourist* (New York: A. T. Goodrich, 1839), 249, 214.

65. "Lake Mohonk Mountain-House," (New Paltz, NY, 1876), n.p.

66. Quoted in Marilyn Fish, "In Harmony with Arts & Crafts Ideals: The Mohonk Mountain House," *Style 1900* 14, no. 3 (Summer-Fall 2001): 43.

67. Davis's illustration of *The Cataract* did not appear in Downing's original article but was the basis for an illustration in the 1849 edition of Downing's book *Landscape Gardening*. This cataract formed the boundary between Robert Donaldson's estate Blithewood to the north and Montgomery Place to the south. For more on Montgomery Place, see Jacquetta M. Haley, ed., *Pleasure Grounds: Andrew Jackson Downing and Montgomery Place* (Tarrytown, NY: Sleepy Hollow Press, 1988). On Davis and landscape architecture at Montgomery Place and other Hudson Valley estates, see Peter A. Watson, "Picturesque Transformations: A.J. Davis in the Hudson Valley and Beyond," MA thesis, Columbia University, 2012.

68. Matteson and LaChance, *Summerhouses of Mohonk*, 2.

69. "An Ulster County Nook: Life Among the Rocks at Lake Mohonk," *New York Times*, August 14, 1882, 5.

70. In 1865, *Frank Leslie's Illustrated Newspaper* described "The Leland Palace at New Rochelle," a castellated suburban house in which hotelier Simeon Leland lived. The article called him a "business prince [who] retires to enjoy the domesticity of life." The newspaper both illustrated and described in detail the house and grounds, which contained "rural nooks" and "summer houses." *Frank Leslie's Illustrated Newspaper*, October 21, XXI, no. 525 (1865): 71, 77.

71. Quoted in Susan Henderson, "Llewellyn Park, Suburban Idyll," *Journal of Garden History* 7, (July/September 1987): 225. See also Richard Guy Wilson, "Idealism and the Origin of the First American Suburb: Llewellyn Park, New Jersey," *The American Art Journal* XI, no. 4 (October 1979): 79–90.

72. G. Albert Lewis, *The Old Houses and Stores with Memorabilia Relating to Them and My Father and Grandfather* (Philadelphia: G. Albert Lewis, 1900), n.p. See also Oliver E. Allen, "The Lewis Albums," *American Heritage* (December 1962): 65–80.

73. W. P. Cutler and J. P. Cutler, *Life, Journals, and Correspondence of Rev. Manasseh Cutler, LL.D*, vol. I (Cincinnati: Robert Clarke, 1888), 274. Quoted in Harold D. Eberlein and Cortlandt van Dyke Hubbard, "The American 'Vauxhall' of the Federal Era," *Pennsylvania Magazine of History and Biography* 68, no. 2 (April 1944): 164. See also Naomi J. Stubbs, *Cultivating National Identity through Performance: American Pleasure Gardens and Entertainment* (New York: Palgrave Macmillan, 2013) and Jonathan Conlin, ed., *The Pleasure Garden: From Vauxhall to Coney Island* (Philadelphia: University of Pennsylvania Press, 2013).

74. "Gilmore's Summer Concert Garden," *Frank Leslie's Illustrated Newspaper*, XL, no. 1032 (June 10, 1875): 317, 322.

75. Quoted in Kowsky, *Country, Park, and City*, 115.

76. Kowsky, *Country, Park, and City*, 118. Vaux designed a rustic summerhouse named "Restawhile," which he perched dramatically in the Palisades above the Hudson River north of New York City in 1877. Kowsky, *Country, Park, and City*, 7–8, 254–255.

77. Downing, *Treatise*, 456.

78. Schuyler, *Apostle of Taste*, 88. Adam Sweeting writes, "At heart a pedagogue, Downing hoped that engravings and descriptions of [Hudson] Valley properties would impart a trickle-down lesson in taste, that the aesthetic elite represented by Valley landowners would show less fortunate property owners how to organize their grounds." Adam Sweeting, *Reading Houses and Building Books: Andrew Jackson Downing and the Architecture of Popular Antebellum Literature, 1835–1855* (Hanover, NH: University Press of New England, 1996), 25.

79. "The Home of the Late A. J. Downing," *The Horticulturist* 3, no. 1 (January 1, 1853): 24.

4. Towers

1. William Beiswanger, "The Temple in the Garden: Thomas Jefferson's Vision of the Monticello Landscape," *Eighteenth-Century Life* VIII, no. 2 (January 1983): 175. Beiswanger notes that the flimsy quality of the architectural plank decoration and the one decorated side (the one visible from Monticello) indicate that this tower "would have functioned as a 'sham' or eye-catcher" rather than a fully realized building.

2. Beiswanger, "Temple in the Garden," 175. See also Kerry Dean Carso, "Gothic Monticello: Thomas Jefferson's Garden Narratives," chap. 1 in *American Gothic Art and Architecture in the Age of Romantic Literature*, 9–28 (Cardiff: University of Wales Press, 2014).

3. Quoted in Kenneth Hafertepe, "An Inquiry into Thomas Jefferson's Ideas of Beauty," *Journal of the Society of Architectural Historians* 59, no. 2 (June 2000): 222.

4. Therese O'Malley defines the "belvedere," or "prospect tower" or "observatory" as a "raised structure or tower placed either on top of a building or as an independent structure in the garden." Therese O'Malley, "Belvedere / Prospect Tower / Observatory," *Keywords in American Landscape Design* (New Haven: National Gallery of Art in association with Yale University Press, 2010), 136.

5. Art historians have viewed the popular landscape paintings of the Hudson River School in similar terms. Albert Boime uses the phrase *magisterial gaze*. Boime writes "It is this gaze of command, or commanding view—as it was so often termed in the nineteenth-century literature—that I will call the magisterial gaze, the perspective of the American on the heights searching for new worlds to conquer." Albert Boime, *The Magisterial Gaze: Manifest Destiny and American Landscape Painting c. 1830–1865* (Washington, DC: Smithsonian Institution Press, 1991), 20–21.

6. Alan Wallach has published several essays on the "panoptic sublime." See Alan Wallach, "Making a Picture of the View from Mount Holyoke," in *American Iconology: New Approaches to Nineteenth-Century Art and Literature*, ed. David C. Miller (New Haven, CT: Yale University Press, 1993), 80–91; Alan Wallach, "Wadsworth's Tower: An Episode in the History of American Landscape Vision," *American Art* 10, no. 3 (Autumn, 1996): 9–27; and Alan Wallach, "Some Further Thoughts on the Panoramic Mode in Hudson River School Landscape Painting," in *Within the Landscape: Essays on Nineteenth-Century American Art and Culture*, eds. Phillip Earenfight and Nancy Siegel (Carlisle, PA: The Trout Gallery, Dickinson College, 2005), 99–128.

7. Wallach, "Making a Picture," 83. In this analysis, Wallach is borrowing two eighteenth-century terms: *panopticon* and *sublime*. In the late eighteenth-century, English philosopher Jeremy Bentham introduced the panopticon, a type of prison in

which guards at the center monitor inmates in cells laid out in a circle around the central guard tower. This form of surveillance ensures the cooperation of inmates at the periphery and makes the guard tower a locus of power. Twentieth-century philosopher Michel Foucault, in his seminal book *Discipline and Punish: The Birth of the Prison* (1975), explores how modern culture functions as a sort of panopticon, and it is his analysis that informs Wallach's interpretation of the "panoptic sublime." On surveillance and nineteenth-century American architecture, see Anna Vemer Andrzejewski, *Building Power: Architecture and Surveillance in Victorian America* (Knoxville: University of Tennessee Press, 2008). As defined by Edmund Burke in *A Philosophical Enquiry into the Origin of Our Ideas of the Sublime and Beautiful* (Oxford: Oxford University Press, 1757), the sublime is an aesthetic category encompassing awe and terror.

8. Wallach, "Wadsworth's Tower," 9.

9. Wallach, "Wadsworth Tower," 14. Decades later in Massachusetts, Joseph S. Potter opened to the public an elaborate garden called Potter's Grove, where visitors enjoyed a three-story prospect tower and other garden ornaments. Alan Emmet, *So Fine a Prospect: Historic New England Gardens* (Hanover, NH: University Press of New England, 1996), 118–129.

10. Wallach, "Wadsworth's Tower," 17. At Mohonk Mountain House (discussed in chapter 3), guests experienced something similar. Albert Smiley constructed prospect towers on both Eagle Cliff and Sky Top. Elevated high above the lake and surrounding landscape, these towers allowed visitors to indulge in the panoptic sublime. Nineteenth-century accounts of the belvedere experience support Wallach's interpretation; after visiting Sky Top Tower at Mohonk Mountain House, one visitor wrote in the *New York Independent*, "We came down from Sky-Top with enlarged ideas of power and sublimity . . ." Quoted in "Mohonk Lake Mountain House," 1888, 12.

11. "View from the Summit of Red Hill," *Ballou's Pictorial Drawing-Room Companion*, VIII, no. 20 (May 19, 1855): 312.

12. *Second Annual Report of the Commissioners of Fairmount Park* (Philadelphia: King & Baird, Printers, 1870), 55.

13. "The Pagoda," *The Casket and Philadelphia Monthly Magazine*, 11 (November 1828): 509.

14. Thomas Bender, "The 'Rural' Cemetery Movement: Urban Travail and the Appeal of Nature," in *Material Life in America, 1600–1860*, ed. Robert Blair St. George (Boston: Northeastern University Press, 1988), 505–518.

15. Blanche M. G. Linden, *Silent City on a Hill: Picturesque Landscapes of Memory and Boston's Mount Auburn Cemetery* (Amherst: University of Massachusetts Press, in association with the Library of American Landscape History, 2007), 228–230.

16. Linden, *Silent City on a Hill*, 230. For instance, see Nathaniel Dearborn, *Dearborn's Guide Through Mount Auburn*, 11th ed. (Boston: N. S. Dearborn, 1857), 2; and *Guide Through Mount Auburn, Boston: A Hand-book for Passengers over the Cambridge Railroad* (Boston: Bricher and Russell, 1860), 68. After the Civil War, attitudes changed and the belvedere function of cemetery towers was downplayed. Meanwhile, a new narrative involving the commemorative function of cemetery towers becomes paramount, as people struggle with the heavy loss of life from the war. A good example is the stone bridge and tower at Thornrose Cemetery in Staunton, Virginia. This tower, built at the turn of the century, has two plaques, one dedicated to the memory of the settlers of the Shenandoah Valley and another to the Virginia volunteers who served

in the Confederate Army. The difference in function between, for example, the Washington Tower at Mount Auburn and the tower at Thornrose, between tourist belvedere and memorial, signals a change in cemetery usage from the heyday of rural cemeteries as tourist attractions to the post-Civil War's emphasis on commemoration rather than garden pleasures.

17. "Portland," *Gleason's Pictorial Drawing-Room Companion* V, no. 13 (September 24, 1853): 200.

18. Professor Larrabee, "Vacation Rambles," *The Ladies' Repository*, 12, no. 1 (January 1852): 18–19.

19. Horatio A. Parson, *Steele's Book of Niagara Falls* (Buffalo: Oliver G. Steele, 1840), 33–34.

20. N. J. Watkins, ed., *The Pine and the Palm Greeting* (Baltimore: J. D. Ehlers & Co.'s Engraving and Printing House, 1873), 60.

21. David Clapp, Travel Diary, 1843, Accession # 63x51.4, Winterthur Library, Winterthur, Delaware.

22. "Niagara," *Harper's New Monthly Magazine* 7, no. 39 (August 1853): 299.

23. "Impressions of Niagara Falls," *The Ladies' Repository* 8, no. 5 (May 1848): 130.

24. "Two Days at Niagara," *Southern Literary Messenger* 11, no. 12 (December 1845): 730.

25. D. W. Clark, "Two Days at Niagara," *The Ladies' Repository* 16, no. 9 (September 1856): 560.

26. Archer Butler Hulbert, *History of the Niagara River* (1908; Harrison, NY: Harbor Hill Books, 1978), 37–38. For example, the editor of *The Ladies' Repository* wrote in 1874, "That beautiful landmark and lookout, Terrapin Tower, exists no longer. It became unsafe, and was blown up two years ago." "Editor's Table," *The Ladies' Repository* 14, no. 1 (July 1874): 77.

27. Quoted in Bruce Robertson, "The Picturesque Traveler in America," in *Views and Visions: American Landscape before 1830*, eds. Edward J. Nygren with Bruce Robertson (Washington, DC: The Corcoran Gallery of Art, 1986), 206.

28. Elizabeth McKinsey, *Niagara Falls: Icon of the American Sublime* (Cambridge: Cambridge University Press, 1985), 102–103.

29. Cooper wrote: "Europe itself is a Romance, while all America is a matter of fact, humdrum, common sense region." James Fenimore Cooper, *The Letters and Journals of James Fenimore Cooper*, ed. James Franklin Beard, vol. 2, (Cambridge, MA: The Belknap Press of Harvard University Press, 1960), 170.

30. "Second Illustrated Series of Views of Niagara Falls," *Gleason's Pictorial and Drawing-Room Companion*, III: no. 5 (July 31, 1852): 69.

31. John R. Stilgoe, *Common Landscape of America, 1580–1845* (New Haven, CT: Yale University Press, 1982), 111.

32. Michael W. Fazio, "Benjamin Latrobe's Designs for a Lighthouse at the Mouth of the Mississippi River," *Journal of the Society of Architectural Historians*, 48, no. 3 (September 1989): 232.

33. Robert Mills, *The American Pharos, or Light-House Guide* (Washington, DC: Thompson & Homans, 1832).

34. Anthony Trollope, *North America*, vol. 1 (Philadelphia: J. B. Lippincott, 1863), 106–107.

35. Trollope, *North America*, 107.

36. James C. Morden, *Historical Monuments and Observatories of Lundy's Lane and Queenston Heights* (Niagara Falls, Ontario: Lundy's Lane Historical Society, 1929), 12–15.

37. Quoted in Morden, *Historical Monuments*, 15–16.

38. McKinsey, *Niagara Falls*, 247.

39. Hulbert, *History of the Niagara River*, 37–38.

40. McKinsey, *Niagara Falls*, 140.

41. John F. Sears, *Sacred Places: American Tourist Attractions in the Nineteenth Century* (New York: Oxford University Press, 1989), 54.

42. Linden, *Silent City on a Hill*, 211–212. The Egyptian government presented Cleopatra's Needle, an ancient obelisk from Alexandria, to the city of New York, where it was placed near the Metropolitan Museum of Art in 1881, functioning as an eye-catcher in Central Park. See Martina D'Alton, *The New York Obelisk or How Cleopatra's Needle Came to New York and What Happened When It Got Here* (New York: Metropolitan Museum of Art, 1993). For a discussion of obelisks in American landscape design, see O'Malley, *Keywords*, 441–447.

43. Military connotations of obelisks are not always at the forefront of associations. For example, some recommended an obelisk for the memorial to Prince Albert in London, citing its associations with funerary monuments and commemoration, but not military exploits. See G. Alex Bremner, "The 'Great Obelisk' and Other Schemes: The Origins and Limits of Nationalist Sentiment in the Making of the Albert Memorial," *Nineteenth-Century Contexts* 31, no. 3 (September 2009): 229. On commemoration in American art history, see Albert Boime, *The Unveiling of the National Icons: Plea for Patriotic Iconoclasm in a Nationalist Era* (Cambridge: Cambridge University Press, 1998).

44. Thomas Jefferson, "Notes on a Tour of English Gardens," in *The Papers of Thomas Jefferson*, ed. Julian P. Boyd, vol. 9 (Princeton, NJ: Princeton University Press, 1954), 369–375, 369. Visitors to Jefferson's grave chipped away pieces as souvenirs, and in 1883, the American government erected a new obelisk at Jefferson's grave. Jefferson's grandchildren gave the original obelisk to the University of Missouri, where it still stands today. Robert H. Kean, "History of the Graveyard at Monticello," in *Collected Papers to Commemorate Fifty Years of the Monticello Association of the Descendants of Thomas Jefferson*, ed. George Green Schelford, vol. 1 (Charlottesville, VA: Monticello Association, 1965), accessed April 30, 2014, http://web.archive.org/web/20080308090223/http://www.monticello-assoc.org/articles/graveyard.html. See also William Peden, "The Jefferson Monument at the University of Missouri," *Missouri Historical Review* 72, no. 1 (October 1977): 67–77.

45. Joy M. Giguere, *Characteristically American: Memorial Architecture, National Identity, and the Egyptian Revival* (Knoxville: University of Tennessee Press, 2014), 226. Giguere quotes *The New York Times*'s description of the Washington Monument in 1885: "There is at least something characteristically American in this gigantic obelisk, towering above the altitude of the great pyramid and the highest cathedral spires designed by the devout and daring architects of the Middle Ages." Quoted in Giguere, 168.

46. Quoted in John Zukowsky, "Monumental American Obelisks: Centennial Vistas," *The Art Bulletin* 58, no. 4 (December 1976): 578.

47. Giguere, *Characteristically American*, 96.

48. Zukowsky writes that the obelisk's function as an observation tower "made it an image of continental expansion and national unity during the centennial era." Zukowsky, "Monumental American Obelisks," 581. In a letter to the editor of *The Art Bulletin*, Diane Ghirardo critiqued Zukowsky's argument, noting that the obelisks he investigates are mostly in the original thirteen states, where the view did not include the western frontier. Diane Ghirardo, "Letters to the Editor," *The Art Bulletin* 59, no. 4 (December 1977): 660–661. One might argue that these obelisks are not primarily follies in that their commemorative purpose outweighs their function as prospect towers. However, the fact that many American obelisks were hollow so as to allow visitors to enjoy a prospect, suggests that the view was an important aspect of the viewer's experience. Also, obelisks introduce Egyptian historicism into the American landscape, creating an ornamental focal point of associationism.

49. Early parks in New York City were private and "became an expression of social and political inequality." Catherine McNeur, "Parks, People, and Property Values: The Changing Role of Green Spaces in Antebellum Manhattan," *Journal of Planning History* 16, no. 2 (May 2017): 103.

50. Frederick Law Olmsted, "Walks and Talks of an American Farmer in England," in *American Garden Design: An Anthology of Ideas that Shaped Our Landscape*, ed. Diane Kostial McGuire (New York: Prentice Hall, 1994), 22.

51. Roy Rosenzweig and Elizabeth Blackmar, *The Park and the People: A History of Central Park* (Ithaca: Cornell University Press, 1992). Andrew Jackson Downing had advocated for the construction of a public park in New York City. Biographer David Schuyler calls Downing "a major figure in the democratization of culture." Downing believed that everyone, not just the leisure class, should participate in genteel activities. Hence, Downing advocated "institutions of popular refinement—parks and gardens, museums, libraries, and other repositories of 'intellectual and moral culture'—that would be attractive to and accessible by all citizens." David Schuyler, *Apostle of Taste: Andrew Jackson Downing, 1815–1852* (Baltimore: Johns Hopkins University Press, 1996), 4. There is a larger project here among the elites to assimilate recent immigrants as well. David Wall writes, "Tied closely to [Downing's] understanding of, and belief in, the redemptive powers of nature, taste, and republicanism, Downing perceived his landscapes as the physical embodiment of virtue and believed that by encouraging the internalization of a bourgeois republicanism the rising waves of urban disorder would be quelled." David Wall, "Andrew Jackson Downing and the Tyranny of Taste," *American Nineteenth Century History* 8, no. 2 (June 2007): 192. On Central Park, see also David Schuyler *The New Urban Landscape: The Redefinition of City Form in Nineteenth-Century America* (Baltimore: Johns Hopkins University Press, 1986); Morrison Heckscher, "Creating Central Park," *Metropolitan Museum of Art Bulletin* 65, no. 3 (Winter 2008): 1–74; Sara Cedar Miller, *Central Park: An American Masterpiece* (New York: Harry N. Abrams Publishers in association with the Central Park Conservancy, 2003); Frederick Law Olmsted, The *Papers of Frederick Law Olmsted, Creating Central Park, 1857–1861*. Edited by Charles E. Beveridge and David Schuyler, vol. 3 (Baltimore: Johns Hopkins University Press, 1983); and Therese O'Malley and Kathryn R. Barush, "In the Park": Lewis Miller's Chronicle of American Landscape at mid-Century," *Nineteenth-Century Art Worldwide: A Journal of Nineteenth-Century Visual Culture* 12, no. 1 (Spring 2013), accessed September 12, 2016, http://www.19thc-artworldwide.org/spring13/in-the-park-lewis-miller-chronicle-of-american-lanscape-midcentury.

52. See Francis R. Kowsky, *Country, Park, and City: The Architecture and Life of Calvert Vaux* (New York: Oxford University Press, 1998), 192–194. Vaux also designed an elaborate tower for Lookout Hill in Prospect Park, but it was never erected. See Kowsky, 220–221.

53. Quoted in George Scheper, "The Reformist Vision of Frederick Law Olmsted and the Poetics of Park Design," *The New England Quarterly* 62, no. 3 (September 1989): 372.

54. *A Century After: Picturesque Glimpses of Philadelphia and Pennsylvania* (Philadelphia: Allen, Lane and Scott and J. W. Lauderbach, Publishers, 1875), 30.

55. Karen Lystra, *Searching the Heart: Women, Men, and Romantic Love in Nineteenth-Century America* (New York: Oxford University Press, 1989). See especially chapter 3, "'Lie Still and Think of the Empire': Sexuality in Victorian Courtship and Marriage," 56–87. According to Barbara Wells Sarudy's book on early American gardens, garden buildings formed the backdrop to courtship rituals: "Shady arbors, alcoves, and summerhouses were favorite meeting spots in sunny gardens. They provided privacy and seating. . . . Young couples naturally took advantage of these garden nooks. Clever suitors chose the sensuousness of the garden as a setting for seduction. Then, as now, gardens were sometimes the site of weddings, even large ones." Barbara Wells Sarudy, *Gardens and Gardening in the Chesapeake 1700–1805* (Baltimore: Johns Hopkins University Press, 1998), 112.

56. *A Century After*, 30–31.

57. O'Malley, *Keywords*, 235.

58. Dell Upton, "White and Black Landscapes in Eighteenth-Century Virginia," in *Material Life in America, 1600–1860*, ed. Robert Blair St. George (Boston: Northeastern University Press, 1988), 357–369. Building on Upton's work, Terrence W. Epperson writes that "At Monticello, Jefferson combined literal and aesthetic appropriation to create a landscape that could be only appreciated from the top of 'his' little mountain. The enslaved human beings that actually constructed the gardens and landscapes and made the plantation economically possible were rendered invisible to the observer occupying the position of privilege." Terrence W. Epperson, "Panoptic Plantations: The Garden Sights of Thomas Jefferson and George Mason," in *Lines that Divide: Historical Archaeologies of Race, Class, and Gender*, eds. James A. Delle, et al. (Knoxville: University of Tennessee Press, 2000), 73.

5. Ruins

1. Thomas Jefferson, "Notes of a Tour through Holland and the Rhine Valley," *The Papers of Thomas Jefferson*, ed. Julian P. Boyd, vol. 13, March 7 to October 1788 (Princeton, NJ: Princeton University Press, 1956), 17, accessed September 12, 2018, https://founders.archives.gov/documents/Jefferson/01-13-02-0003. On Jefferson's interest in sham ruins, see William Beiswanger, "The Temple in the Garden: Thomas Jefferson's Vision of the Monticello Landscape," *Eighteenth-Century Life* 8, no. 2 (January 1983): 180. On the influence of German culture on Jefferson, see Sandra Rebok, "Thomas Jefferson and Germany: His Travel Experience, Scientific and Philosophical Influences," *Yearbook of German-American Studies* 48 (spring 2013): 1–23; and Madison Brown, "Thomas Jefferson and Things German: Preliminary Findings," *The Report: A Journal of German-American History* 37 (1987): 29–33.

2. Quoted in David Watkin, *The English Vision: The Picturesque in Architecture, Landscape and Garden Design* (New York: Harper & Row, 1982), 51.

3. Quoted in Watkin, *English Vision*, 51.

4. Alexis de Tocqueville, *Democracy in America*, trans. and ed. Harvey C. Mansfield and Delba Winthrop (Chicago: University of Chicago Press, 2000), 271–272.

5. Margaret Fuller, *Summer on the Lakes in 1843* (1844), facsimile with an Introduction by Madeleine B. Stern (Nieuwkoop: B. De Graaf, 1972), 171.

6. Sarah Burns, *Painting the Dark Side: Art and the Gothic Imagination in Nineteenth-Century America* (Berkeley: University of California Press, 2004); and Nick Yablon, *Untimely Ruins: An Archaeology of American Urban Modernity, 1819–1919* (Chicago: University of Chicago Press, 2009), 3–4.

7. Quoted in Maggie Lane, *Jane Austen's England* (London: Hale, 1986), 25–26.

8. William Gilpin, *Observations on Several Parts of the Counties of Cambridge, Norfolk, Suffolk, and Essex* (London: T. Cadell and W. Davies, 1809), 122; Thomas Whately, *Observations on Modern Gardening*, 4th ed. (London: T. Payne, 1770), 131–132.

9. Nicholas B. Wainwright, "Andalusia: Countryseat of the Craig Family and Nicholas Biddle and His Descendants," *The Pennsylvania Magazine of History and Biography* 101, no. 1 (1977): 3–69.

10. James Biddle, "Nicholas Biddle's Andalusia, a Nineteenth-Century County Seat Today," in *Great Houses from the Pages of the Magazine Antiques*, ed. Constance M. Greiff (New York: Weathervane Books, 1973), 288.

11. Despite its relative obscurity today, the Cruger's Island ruins have had an outsized influence on American artists. Kevin Avery argues that the ruins may have influenced Hudson River School artist Frederic Edwin Church in painting a Pre-Columbian artifact in the lower left corner of his canvas *Cayambe* (1858). Kevin J. Avery, "Maya on the Hudson: Church's *Cayambe* and Cruger's 'Folly,'" *The Hudson River Valley Review* 31, no. 1 (Autumn 2014): 50–61. Jennifer L. Roberts interprets twentieth-century earthworks artist Robert Smithson's work in Yucatán as "an inversion or undoing of Stephens's operations." Smithson would have seen the stones from Cruger's Island at his favorite museum, the American Museum of Natural History, as a boy. Jennifer L. Roberts, "Landscapes of Indifference: Robert Smithson and John Lloyd Stephens in Yucatán," *The Art Bulletin* 82, no. 3 (September 2000): 551–552.

12. Herbert J. Spinden, "The Stephens Sculptures from Yucatán," *Natural History: The Journal of the American Museum of Natural History* 20 (102): 381.

13. Spinden, "Stephens Sculptures," 381.

14. Quoted in Avery, "Maya on the Hudson," 59.

15. Quoted in Yablon, *Untimely Ruins*, 305, n. 71.

16. Stephens portrayed the Maya descendants as lazy in his books and unworthy of their own heritage. According to Roberts, "Their [the Maya descendants'] antiquarian ineptitude effectively disqualifies them from any claim to their own history—an abdication that then renders it conveniently available to the United States, whose modern, disciplined intellects become the worthy heirs of this American heritage and the rightful directors of any project designed to illuminate it." Roberts, "Landscapes of Indifference," 550. The ruins on Cruger's Island still exist today, although they are more ruinous than when originally constructed. For a recent photograph of the site's appearance, see Thomas E. Rinaldi and Robert J. Yasinsac, *Hudson Valley Ruins: Forgotten Landmarks of an American Landscape* (Hanover, NH: University Press of New England, 2006), 9.

17. Mary H. Mitchell, *Hollywood Cemetery: The History of a Southern Shrine* (Richmond: Virginia State Library, 1985), 95–96. John Notman designed the cemetery in 1847. Francis Peabody designed a cemetery gateway, similarly covered in vegetation with a ruinous effect, for Harmony Grove Cemetery in Salem, Massachusetts, in 1839 (demolished). Arthur Krim, "An Early Rustic Arch in Salem," *The Journal of the Society of Architectural Historians* 51, no. 3 (September 1992): 315–317. The Bentinck Egan Monument in Metaine Cemetery in New Orleans takes the form of a ruined chapel. Peggy McDowell and Richard E. Meyer, *The Revival Styles in American Memorial Art* (Bowling Green, OH: Bowling Green State University Popular Press, 1994), 122, 126.

18. Richard Guy Wilson, et al., "Hollywood Cemetery" [Richmond, Virginia], SAH Archipedia, eds. Gabrielle Esperdy and Karen Kingsley (Charlottesville: University of Virginia Press, 2012), accessed September 17, 2018, http://sah-archipedia .org/buildings/VA-01-RI251. According to Hollywood historian Mary H. Mitchell, "Dimmock used rectangular blocks of James River granite to add height to the Gothic tower, crenelating the top of the tower and capping it with a Buckingham slate roof." Dimmock then added an adjoining chapel to the tower. Mitchell, *Hollywood Cemetery*, 119.

19. Timothy S. Sedore, *An Illustrated Guide to Virginia's Confederate Monuments* (Carbondale: Southern Illinois University Press, 2011), 159–160. For an image of the pyramid looking ruinous, see the cover of *Register of the Confederate Dead Interred in Hollywood Cemetery, Richmond, VA* (Richmond: Gary, Clemmitt & Jones, Printers, 1869).

20. Andrew Jackson Downing, *A Treatise on the Theory and Practice of Landscape Gardening, Adapted to North America; with a View to the Improvement of Country Residences*, 4th ed. (New York: George P. Putnam, 1850), 405.

21. See Kerry Dean Carso, *American Gothic Art and Architecture in the Age of Romantic Literature* (Cardiff: University of Wales Press, 2014), 95–113.

22. Emily B. Todd, "Walter Scott and the Nineteenth-Century American Literary Marketplace: Antebellum Richmond Readers and the Collected Editions of the Waverley Novels," *The Papers of the Bibliographical Society of America* 94, no. 4 (1999): 497.

23. Washington Irving, "Abbotsford," *The Crayon Miscellany*, ed. Dahlia Kirby Terrel (Boston: Twayne, 1979), 125–168.

24. Washington Irving, "The Voyage," in *The Sketch Book of Geoffrey Crayon, Gent.* (1819–1820; New York: Penguin Books, 1981), 20–21.

25. Alice P. Kenney and Leslie J. Workman, "Ruins, Romance, and Reality: Medievalism in Anglo-American Imagination and Taste, 1750–1840," *Winterthur Portfolio* 10 (1975): 162. See also Carso, *American Gothic Art*, 77–94.

26. See Elizabeth Durfee Hengen, *Life Everlasting: The History, Art and People of Woodlawn Cemetery 1850–2000* (Everett, MA: Woodlawn Cemetery Corporation, 2001).

27. George E. Ellis, *Address Delivered at the Consecration of the Woodlawn Cemetery in Chelsea and Malden on Wednesday, July 2, 1851* (Boston: Printed by John Wilson & Son, 1851), 31.

28. Henry Weld Fuller. *The Woodlawn Cemetery in North Chelsea and Malden* (Boston: Higgins & Bradley, 1856), 44. The cemetery is located in what is now called Everett, Massachusetts.

29. David Pulsifer, *Guide to Boston and Vicinity* (Boston: A. Williams, 1868), 236.

30. The tower fell into disrepair and was removed in the early 1990s.

31. Fuller, *Woodlawn Cemetery*, 45.

32. Downing, *Treatise*, 464.

33. See Michel Ragon, *The Space of Death: A Study in Funerary Architecture, Decoration and Urbanism*, trans. Alan Sheridan (Charlottesville: University of Virginia Press, 1983), 77. Of course, English landscape gardens often had commemorative elements, such as Alexander Pope's memorial to his mother in his garden at Twickenham. Rural cemeteries conflate the picturesque beauty of English gardens with the gardens' secondary importance as sites of remembrance.

34. Fuller, *Woodlawn Cemetery*, 45.

35. *Guide to Laurel Hill Cemetery Near Philadelphia* (Philadelphia: C. Sherman, Printer, 1847), 20–21.

36. Benson J. Lossing, *Vassar College and Its Founder* (New York: C. A. Alvord Printer, 1867), 67. On Springside, see Harvey Flad, "Matthew Vassar's Springside: '. . . the hand of Art, when guided by Taste,'" in *Prophet with Honor: The Career of Andrew Jackson Downing, 1815–1852*, eds., Elizabeth B. MacDougall and George B. Tatum (Washington, DC: Dumbarton Oaks, 1989), 219–257; Robert M. Toole, *Landscape Gardens on the Hudson, A History: The Romantic Age, the Great Estates, & the Birth of American Landscape Architecture* (Hensonville, NY: Black Dome Press, 2010), 127–136; Robert M. Toole, "Springside: A. J. Downing's Only Extant Garden," *Journal of Garden History* 9, no. 1 (1989): 20–39; and Harvey Flad, "Saving Springside: Preserving Andrew Jackson Downing's Last Landscape," *The Hudson River Valley Review* 34, no. 1 (Autumn 2017): 18–44.

37. John Claudius Loudon, *An Encyclopedia of Cottage, Farm and Villa Architecture and Furniture* (London: Longman, Orme, Rees, 1835), 787.

38. Quoted in Linda S. Ferber, *William Trost Richards: American Landscape & Marine Painter 1833–1905* (New York: The Brooklyn Museum, 1973), 90.

39. John Harris Morden, "Engla-Land and the Abiding Memorials of its Antiquity" *Potter's American Monthly*, V, no. 48 (December 1875): 937–944.

40. Karl Whittington, "Casper David Friedrich's Medieval Burials," *Nineteenth Century Art Worldwide* 11, no. 1 (2012), accessed May 2016, http://www.19thc-artworldwide.org/spring12/whittington-on-caspar-david-friedrichs-medieval-burials.

41. James Fenimore Cooper, *The Deerslayer, or, The First War-Path* (Albany: State University of New York Press, 1987), 466–467.

42. Michel Makarius, *Ruins*, trans. David Radzinowicz (Paris: Éditions Flammarion, 2004), 140.

43. James Austin Holden, "'The Last of the Mohicans, Cooper's Historical Inventions, and His Cave,'" *Proceedings of the New York State Historical Association* 16 (1917): 231.

44. Quoted in Holden, "Last of the Mohicans," 235–237.

45. Quoted in Holden, "Last of the Mohicans," 239.

46. Holden, "Last of the Mohicans," 246.

47. Wayne Franklin, *James Fenimore Cooper: The Early Years* (New Haven: Yale University Press, 2007), 435.

48. Franklin, *James Fenimore Cooper*, 235.

49. Quoted in Franklin, *James Fenimore Cooper*, 435. Smith-Stanley was the future fourteenth earl of Derby and a future British prime minister.

50. James Fenimore Cooper, *The Last of the Mohicans: A Narrative of 1757* (Albany: State University of New York Press, 1983), 52.

51. Allen Grove, Introduction to *The Cavern of Death* (Chicago: Valancourt Books, 2005), 3–4.

52. Cooper, *Last of the Mohicans*, 54.

53. Donald A. Ringe, "Mode and Meaning in *The Last of the Mohicans*," in *James Fenimore Cooper: New Historical and Literary Contexts*, ed. W. M. Verhoeven (Amsterdam: Rodophi, 1993), 112.

54. Donald A. Ringe, "*The Last of the Mohicans* as a Gothic Novel," in *James Fenimore Cooper, His Country and His Art (no. 6): Papers from the 1986 Conference at State University College of New York*, ed. George A. Test (Oneonta: State University of New York College, 1987), 46, accessed October 2020, https://jfcoopersociety.org/articles/SUNY /1986SUNY-RINGE.HTML.

The Last of the Mohicans became the subject of four paintings by Thomas Cole (1801–1848), the landscape artist who is often referred to as the "founder" of the Hudson River School of painting: *Scene from "The Last of the Mohicans," Cora Kneeling at the Feet of Tamenund* (1827; Wadsworth Atheneum Museum of Art); *Landscape Scene from "The Last of the Mohicans" (Cora Kneeling at the Feet of Tamenund)* (1827; Fenimore Art Museum); *Landscape Scene from "The Last of the Mohicans"* (1827; University of Pennsylvania Art Collection); and *Landscape with Figures: A Scene from "The Last of the Mohicans"* (1826; Terra Foundation for American Art). Robert Gray Katz, "Thomas Cole: Reading the Paintings from *The Last of the Mohicans*," in *James Fenimore Cooper, His Country and His Art (no. 18): Papers from the 1986 Conference at State University College of New York*, eds. Steven Harthorn and Hugh MacDougall (Oneonta: State University of New York College, 1987), 56–63, accessed May 2016, http://external.oneonta.edu/cooper/articles /suny/2011suny-katz.html

55. J. Bard McNulty, *The Correspondence of Thomas Cole and Daniel Wadsworth: Letters in the Watkinson Library, Trinity College, Hartford, and in the New York State Library, Albany, New York* (Hartford: Connecticut Historical Society, 1983), 38.

56. Barbara Dayer Gallati, "Early Morning at Cold Spring, 1850" in *American Paradise: The World of the Hudson River School* (New York: Metropolitan Museum of Art, 1987), 111.

57. Henry T. Tuckerman, *Book of the Artists* (New York: G. P. Putnam, 1867), 518.

58. Anthony F. Janson, *Worthington Whittredge* (Cambridge: Cambridge University Press, 1989), 83.

59. William Cullen Bryant, *Poems of William Cullen Bryant* (Philadelphia: Carey and Hart, 1847), 130.

60. Kevin J. Avery, "Kauterskill Falls, 1871," in *Hudson River School Visions: The Landscapes of Sanford R. Gifford*, eds. Kevin J. Avery and Franklin Kelly (New York: Metropolitan Museum of Art, 2003), 203.

61. Barbara B. Millhouse, "The Old Hunting Grounds, 1864, Worthington Whittredge 1820–1910," in *American Originals: Selections from Reynolda House, Museum of American Art*, eds. Charles C. Eldredge and Barbara B. Millhouse (New York: Abbeville Press; American Federation of Arts, 1990), 64.

62. Matthew Sivils, "American Gothic and the Environment, 1800–Present" in *The Gothic World*, eds. Glennis Byron and Dale Townshend (London: Routledge, 2014), 124.

63. Washington Irving, "The Catskill Mountains" in *The Home Book of the Picturesque or American Scenery, Art, and Literature* (New York: G. P. Putnam, 1852), 72.

64. Quoted in David Schuyler, *Sanctified Landscape Writers, Artists, and the Hudson River Valley, 1820–1909* (Ithaca: Cornell University Press, 2012), 11.

65. Schuyler, *Sanctified Landscape*, 10.

66. Benson J. Lossing, "Dover Stone Church," *Poughkeepsie Casket: A Semi-Monthly Literary Journal* 2, no. 18 (December 15, 1838): 137.

67. Philip H. Smith, *General History of Dutchess County, From 1609 to 1876, Inclusive* (Pawling, NY: published by the author, 1877), 150.

68. Benson J. Lossing, *Dover Stone Church* (Amenia, NY: DeLacey & Walsh, 1876).

69. Roberta J. M. Olson, *Drawn by New York: Six Centuries of Watercolors and Drawings at the New-York Historical Society* (New York: New-York Historical Society, 2008), 184–187. Still in existence today, the Dover Stone Church is now owned by the village of Dover Plains and twenty-first-century tourists still make the short walk from town to see this local wonder.

70. Joyce Henri Robinson, "An American Cabinet of Curiosities: Thomas Jefferson's Indian Hall at Monticello," *Winterthur Portfolio* 30, no. 1 (spring 1995): 49.

71. Barbara Novak, *Nature and Culture: American Landscape and Painting 1825–1875* (New York: Oxford University Press, 1995), 58–59. See also Rebecca Bedell, *The Anatomy of Nature: Geology & American Landscape, 1825–1875* (Princeton, NJ: Princeton University Press, 2001).

72. Benson J. Lossing, *Pictorial Field-Book of the Revolution*, vol. 1 (New York: Harper & Brothers, 1851), 121, 127–129. In volume 2, Lossing also includes an illustration of the towered remains of a seventeenth-century Jamestown church. In ruins by the nineteenth century, the church attracted relic-hunters, until being rebuilt in 1907 as the Memorial Church after a preservation campaign by the Association for the Preservation of Virginia Antiquities. Benson J. Lossing, *Pictorial Field-Book of the Revolution*, vol. 2 (New York: Harper & Brothers, 1852), 447–448. For the full history of the Jamestown Church, see Lou Ann Meadows Ladin, Catherine Dean, and Dia Idleman, *The Jamestown Church, Jamestown, VA* (Richmond, VA: Dementi Milestone Publishing and APVA Preservation Virginia, 2007).

73. Annette Kolodny, *In Search of First Contact: The Vikings of Vinland, the Peoples of the Dawnland, and the Anglo-American Anxiety of Discovery* (Durham, NC: Duke University Press, 2012), 122, 327.

74. James Fenimore Cooper, *The Red Rover: A Tale* (New York: Stringer & Townsend, 1856), 58.

75. Roylance argues that the identification of the skeleton as a Viking, rather than a member of the Narragansett tribe, "metaphorically [minimized] the evidence and emotional power of Indians' prior ownership of the land." Patricia Jane Roylance, "Northmen and Native Americans: The Politics of Landscape in the Age of Longfellow," *The New England Quarterly* 80, no. 3 (September 2007): 444.

76. Quoted in Kolodny, *In Search of First Contact*, 155–156. Kolodny details the story behind Longfellow's poem on pages 151–167. Why were New Englanders fascinated by Vikings? Literary scholar Patricia Jane Roylance explains: "The region's economic and cultural stature was diminishing in this period, and locating the first European landfall and sustained settlement on their very doorstep flattered their [New Englanders'] bruised egos." She continues: "The Vinland craze, with its extensive and elaborate mapping of Viking sites, therefore illustrates the allure of history, especially history grounded in the landmarks of the local landscape. Fostering a sense of intimate connection between oneself and historical figures who once occupied the same physical space, such history is motivated by and feeds a personal stake in stories of the

past. It is not surprising, then, that Vinlanders would have wanted an active role in shaping that history to promote and protect their own self-interested versions of it." Roylance, "Northmen and Native Americans," 437, 440. An 1889 replica of a Norse Tower, Norumbega Tower, in Weston, Massachusetts—a true folly—celebrated this Vinland myth. Roylance, "Northmen and Native Americans," 442.

77. Henry Wadsworth Longfellow, "The Skeleton in Armour," in *American Poetry: The Nineteenth Century, Volume One, Philip Freneau to Walt Whitman*, ed. John Hollander (New York: Library of America, 1993), 381.

78. Samuel Adams Drake, *Nooks and Corners of the New England Coast* (New York: Harper & Brothers, 1875), 24.

79. Richard Guy Wilson, "Oscar Wilde, Colonialists, and Vikings: Newport and the Aesthetic Movement," *Nineteenth Century* 19, no. 1 (Spring 1999): 9–10. Among other replicas of the Newport Ruin was a facsimile made entirely of spool cotton by J. & P. Coats for the World's Industrial and Cotton Centennial Exposition at New Orleans in 1885. Half the size of the original, this version of the Old Stone Mill revolved in a glass case and featured an eagle at its apex and a quotation from Longfellow's poem in the cornice. See "The Aesthetic in Spool Cotton," *Frank Leslie's Illustrated Newspaper* 1545:LX (May 2, 1885): 180; and *Practical Common Sense Guide Book through the World's Industrial and Cotton Centennial Exposition at New Orleans* (Harrisburg, PA: Lane S. Hart Printer and Binder, 1885), 64. Thank you to Bert Arnold Shankle for alerting me to the spool cotton replica.

80. Kenneth Myers, *The Catskills: Painters, Writers, and Tourists in the Mountains 1820–1895* (Yonkers, NY: Hudson River Museum of Westchester, 1987), 41.

81. Sarah Burns, *Painting the Dark Side: Art and the Gothic Imagination in Nineteenth-century America* (Berkeley: University of California Press, 2004), 2.

82. "Academy of Design—Landscape Department," *Frank Leslie's Illustrated Newspaper* 1, no. 18 (April 12, 1856): 281–282.

83. Thomas Cole, "Essay on American Scenery," in *American Art 1700–1960. Sources and Documents*, ed. John W. McCoubrey (Englewood Cliffs, NJ: Prentice-Hall, 1965), 101.

84. "D.," "Garden Decorations," *The Gardener's Monthly* 111, no. 8 (August 1861): 236.

Conclusion

1. Robert W. Rydell, *All the World's a Fair: Visions of Empire at American International Expositions, 1876–1916* (Chicago: University of Chicago Press, 1984), 10–11.

2. James D. McCabe, *The Illustrated History of the Centennial Exhibition* (Philadelphia: National Publishing, 1876), 663.

3. McCabe, *Illustrated History*, 666–667.

4. Clay Lancaster, "The Philadelphia Centennial Towers," *Journal of the Society of Architectural Historians* 19, no. 1 (March 1960): 13. Relocated to Coney Island, the Iron Tower stood until it collapsed during the 1911 Dreamland fire. Lancaster, "Philadelphia Centennial Towers," 15.

5. *Magee's Centennial Guide of Philadelphia*, 2nd edition (Philadelphia: R. Magee & Son, 1876), 96. For an in-depth description of Georges Hill, see Charles S. Keyser, *Fairmount Park and the International Exhibition at Philadelphia* (Philadelphia: Claxton, Remsen & Haffelfiner, 1876), 72–74.

6. Bruno Giberti, *Designing the Centennial: A History of the 1876 International Exhibition in Philadelphia* (Lexington: University Press of Kentucky, 2002), 116.

7. *Magee's Centennial Guide of Philadelphia*, 96.

8. Thomas Westcott, *Centennial Portfolio: A Souvenir of the International Exhibition at Philadelphia* (Philadelphia: Thomas Hunter, publisher, 1876), 46.

9. Mona Domosh, *American Commodities in an Age of Empire* (New York: Routledge, 2006), 59.

10. McCabe, *Illustrated History*, 633–634.

11. "The Centennial Exposition," *Scientific American* 35, no. 3 (July 15, 1876): 33; and "The Centennial Exposition," *Scientific American* 35, no. 6 (August 5, 1876): 81.

12. On Edward Clark, see Nicholas Fox Weber, *The Clarks of Cooperstown, Their Singer Sewing Machine Fortune, Their Great and Influential Art Collections, Their Forty-Year Feud* (New York: Alfred A. Knopf, 2007), 11–40; and Andrew Alpern, *The Dakota: A History of the World's Best-Known Apartment Building* (New York: Princeton Architectural Press, 2015), 15–22.

13. On Hardenbergh, see Alpern, *Dakota*, 23–32.

14. Edward Clark, "Kingfisher Tower," *The Freeman's Journal*, September 7, 1876, 3. Clark published this defense of Kingfisher Tower anonymously, but he is identified in S. M. Shaw, ed., *A Centennial Offering, Being a Brief History of Cooperstown* (Cooperstown, NY: Freeman's Journal Office, 1886), 104–105. See also Ralph Birdsall, *The Story of Cooperstown* (Cooperstown, NY: Arthur H. Crist, 1917), 327; Field Horne, "Kingfisher Tower—Folly or Art?" in *Bicentennial Essays of Cooperstown and the Town of Otsego*, ed. Wendell Tripp (Cooperstown, NY: Town of Otsego Bicentennial Committee, 1976), 35–38; and Julian Cavalier, *American Castles* (South Brunswick, NJ: A. S. Barnes, 1973), 225–226.

15. The Clark family still owns Kingfisher Tower, and most people are only able to view the tower from boats on the lake. In some historic images, the tower appears to rise directly out of the water because the causeway connecting it to the shore was submerged at the time of the photograph. Today, the tower is surrounded by water on three sides but is usually reachable by the narrow causeway connecting it to the shore.

16. Clark, "Kingfisher Tower," 3.

17. Clark, "Kingfisher Tower," 3.

18. Clark, "Kingfisher Tower," 3.

19. Nancy K. Anderson, "'The Kiss of Enterprise:' The Western Landscape as Symbol and Resource," in *Reading American Art*, eds. Marianne Doezema and Elizabeth Milroy (New Haven, CT: Yale University Press, 1998), 210.

20. Birdsall, *Story of Cooperstown*, 327.

21. Clark, "Kingfisher Tower," 3.

22. Weber, *Clarks of Cooperstown*, 34–35.

23. Kerry Dean Carso, *American Gothic Art and Architecture in the Age of Romantic Literature* (Cardiff: University of Wales Press, 2014), 73.

24. Nick Yablon, *Untimely Ruins: An Archaeology of American Urban Modernity, 1819–1919* (Chicago: University of Chicago Press, 2009), 305, n. 72.

25. "A Windmill Tower and Water Tank at Narragansett Pier, R. I." *Scientific American, Architects and Builders Edition* 3, no. 3 (March 1887): 45–47; "Design for a Windmill Tower and Water Tank," *Scientific American* 59, no. 7 (August 18, 1888): 105. The illustration also appears in Judith Lynch Waldhorn, ed., *American Victoriana Floor Plans*

and *Renderings from the Gilded Age* (San Francisco: Chronicle Books, 1979), 55. See also Walter Nebiker, Robert Owen Jones, and Charlene K. Roice, *Historic and Architectural Resources of Narragansett, Rhode Island* (Providence: Rhode Island Historical Preservation Commission, 1991), 14–15, 38–39. Other historicized water towers include the Chicago Water Tower designed by William W. Boyington in 1869 and the Weehawken Water Tower designed by Frederick Withers in 1883.

26. Quoted in Jeff L. Rosenheim, *Walker Evans and the Picture Postcard* (Göttingen, Germany: Steidl, 2009), 29.

27. Christopher Derganc, "Rockford Water Tower," Historic American Engineering Record (HAER DE-16) (Washington, DC: National Park Service, 1976), 2. See also W. Barksdale Maynard, *Buildings of Delaware* (Charlottesville: University of Virginia Press, 2008), 140.

28. G. A. Parker, "Tower at Hubbard Park, Meriden, Conn.," *Park and Cemetery and Landscape Gardening* 5 (March 1900–February 1901): 223. A strikingly similar cylindrical tower, meant to resemble "the Castles on the Rhine," rises above the Mississippi River in Dubuque, Iowa. The Julien Dubuque Monument opened in 1897 to house the remains of Julien Dubuque, the city's "first white settler." The little limestone castle's loophole windows suggest that the tower might frame a view, but there are no stairs inside this funerary monument. Richard Hermann, *Julien Dubuque, His Life and Adventures* (Dubuque, IA: Times-Journal, 1922), 64.

29. *Somerville* (Boston: Edison Electric Illuminating Co, 1909), 5–6.

30. Carol Miles and John J. Galluzzo, *Beauty, Strength, Speed: Celebrating 100 Years of Thomas W. Lawson's Dreamwold* (Virginia Beach, VA: Donning, 2002), 52–63. The tower contains bells and a clock as well. See also "Lawson Tower," National Register of Historic Places Nomination Form (Washington, DC: National Park Service, Department of the Interior, September 28, 1976).

31. William B. Rhoads, *Ulster County, New York: The Architectural History and Guide* (Delmar, NY: Black Dome, 2011), 162. See also Benjamin H. Matteson and Joan A. LaChance, *The Story of Sky Top and its Towers* (New Paltz, NY: Mohonk Mountain House, 1998).

32. Frederick Eugene Partington, Albert Keith Smiley, and Daniel Smiley, *The Story of Mohonk* (Fulton, NY: Morrill, 1932), 45.

33. William B. Rhoads writes, "Although Smiley, as a Quaker, worked for peace, the image of the fortress tower was still appropriate for Smiley's memorial, sturdily defending Mohonk against the onslaught of the dissolute world beyond." Rhoads, *Ulster County*, 163.

34. Mary Elizabeth Jane Colter, *Manual for Drivers and Guides Descriptive of the Indian Watchtower at Desert View and its Relation Architecturally, to the Prehistoric Ruins of the Southwest* (1933; Grand Canyon, AZ: Grand Canyon Association, 2015), 3–4. See Arnold Berke, and Alexander Vertikoff. *Mary Colter, Architect of the Southwest* (New York: Princeton Architectural Press, 2002), 187–207.

35. Colter, *Manual for Drivers*, 15.

36. Colter, *Manual for Drivers*, 20.

37. C. Gordon Tyrell, "The History and Development of the Winterthur Gardens," *Winterthur Portfolio* 1 (1964): 131–132; Robin Karson, *A Genius for Place: American Landscapes of the Country Place Era* (Amherst: University of Massachusetts Press in

association with the Library of American Landscape History, 2007), 215; and Maggie Lidz, "Latimeria Summer House," Winterthur Garden Blog, accessed on October 6, 2018, http://gardenblog.winterthur.org/2011/04/01/latimeria-summer-house/.

38. Andrew Jackson Downing, *A Treatise on the Theory and Practice of Landscape Gardening, Adapted to North America; with a View to the Improvement of Country Residences*, 4th ed. (New York: George P. Putnam, 1850), 59.

39. Quoted in Maureen Cassidy-Geiger, *The Philip Johnson Glass House: An Architect in the Garden* (New York: Skira Rizzoli, 2016), 13.

40. Cassidy-Geiger, *Philip Johnson Glass House*, 154.

41. Quoted in Cassidy-Geiger, *Philip Johnson Glass House*, 148.

42. Quoted in Adele Tutter, "'The Path of Phocion: Disgrace and Disavowal at the Philip Johnson Glass House," *American Imago* 68, no. 3 (Fall 2011): 467.

43. Russell Thayer, *The Public Parks and Gardens of Europe: A Report to the Commissioners of Fairmount Park* (Philadelphia: Gillis & Nagle, Printers, 1880), 37.

44. Quoted in Tutter, "Path of Phocion," 467.

45. Cassidy-Geiger, *Philip Johnson Glass House*, 48. See also Tutter, "Path of Phocion," 449–488.

46. B. J. Archer and Anthony Vidler, *Follies: Architecture for the Late-Twentieth-Century Landscape* (New York: Rizzoli, 1983), 7.

47. Archer and Vidler, *Follies*, 8.

48. Archer and Vidler, *Follies*, 9.

49. Edgar Allan Poe, "The Landscape Garden," in Archer and Vidler, *Follies*, 16.

50. Archer and Vidler, *Follies*, 14.

51. Archer and Vidler, *Follies*, 42.

52. Philip Johnson and Mark Wigley, *Deconstructivist Architecture* (Boston: Little, Brown, 1988), 92.

53. John Beardsley, Cathy Byrd, and Robin B. Williams, *Functional Follies: 20 Architectural Objects of Delight* (Savannah, GA: Savannah College of Art and Design, 1999); and Barbara Toll, *Follies: Fantasy in the Landscape: May 20 Through July 22, 2001* (Southampton, NY: Parrish Art Museum, 2001).

54. The exhibition website is https://www.olana.org/exhibitions/follies-function-form-imagining-olanas-summer-house/ (accessed September 21, 2020). The cult of ruins continues to fascinate photographers, both professional and amateur, in this visual age. Some examples include Monica Randall, *Phantoms of the Hudson Valley: The Glorious Estates of a Lost Era* (Woodstock, NY: Overlook, 1995); Thomas E. Rinaldi and Rob Yasinsac, *Hudson Valley Ruins: Forgotten Landmarks of an American Landscape* (Hanover, NH: University Press of New England, 2006); Shaun O'Boyle, *Modern Ruins: Portraits of Place in the Mid-Atlantic Region* (University Park: Pennsylvania State University Press, 2010); Yves Marchand, et al., *The Ruins of Detroit* (Göttingen, Germany: Steidl, 2014); and Marisa Scheinfeld, Stefan Kanfer, and Jenna Weissman Joselit, *The Borscht Belt: Revisiting the Remains of America's Jewish Vacationland* (Ithaca, NY: Cornell University Press, 2016). "Ruin Porn" is currently having a moment in the popular realm, while "Ruins Theory" is an emergent academic field.

55. The exhibition ended in early 2020.

56. David R. Collens, Nora R. Lawrence, and Sarah Diver, with Sarina Basta, et al., *Mark Dion: Follies* (New Windsor, NY: Storm King Art Center, 2019).

57. Kathleen Quigley, "Inside Architecture's New Classicism Boom," *Architectural Digest*, August 7, 2018, accessed October 7, 2018, https://www.architecturaldigest.com/story/new-classical-architecture.

58. Quoted in John Grossman, "Ken Burns's Jeffersonian Pavilion," *Inc.*, 2002, accessed October 7, 2018, https://www.inc.com/magazine/20020101/23795.html.

59. Mark Hall, "An Interview with Ken Burns," PBS, January 21, 1997, accessed October 7, 2018, https://www.pbs.org/jefferson/making/KB_00.htm.

60. William Beiswanger, "The Temple in the Garden: Thomas Jefferson's Vision of the Monticello Landscape," *Eighteenth-Century Life* 8, no. 2 (January 1983): 94.

61. Thomas Jefferson Foundation, Inc., "The Site of the Vegetable Garden," accessed October 7, 2018, https://www.monticello.org/site/house-and-gardens/site-vegetable-garden.

62. Gary Krist, "Not for Sale: Gazebo w/Writer Fully Attached," *New York Times*, February 15, 2002, G22.

BIBLIOGRAPHY

"Academy of Design—Landscape Department." *Frank Leslie's Illustrated Newspaper* 1, no. 18 (April 12, 1856): 281–282.

"Account of the Grand Federal Procession in Philadelphia." *American Museum* (July 1788): 57–75.

Adams, John. "Notes on a Tour of English Country Seats, &c., with Thomas Jefferson, 4–10? April 1786." http://founders.archives.gov/documents/Adams /01-03-02-0005-0002-0001.

"The Aesthetic in Spool Cotton." *Frank Leslie's Illustrated Newspaper* 1545, no. LX (May 2, 1885): 180.

Alcott, Bronson. *The Journals of Bronson Alcott*, edited by Odell Shepard. Boston: Little, Brown, 1938.

Alison, Archibald. *Essays on the Nature and Principles of Taste. By Archibald Alison.* From the Edinburgh ed. of 1811. Boston: Cummings and Hilliard, 1812.

Allen, Oliver E. "The Lewis Albums." *American Heritage* (December 1962): 65–80.

Allen, Thomas M. *A Republic in Time: Temporality & Social Imagination in Nineteenth-Century America.* Chapel Hill: University of North Carolina Press, 2008.

Alpern, Andrew. *The Dakota: A History of the World's Best-Known Apartment Building.* New York: Princeton Architectural Press, 2015.

Anderson, Benedict. *Imagined Communities: Reflections on the Origin and Spread of Nationalism.* London: Verso, 1993.

Anderson, Nancy K. "'The Kiss of Enterprise:' The Western Landscape as Symbol and Resource." In *Reading American Art*, edited by Marianne Doezema and Elizabeth Milroy, 208–231. New Haven, CT: Yale University Press, 1998.

Andrews, Malcolm. *Landscape and Western Art.* Oxford: Oxford University Press, 1999.

Andrzejewski, Anna Vemer. *Building Power: Architecture and Surveillance in Victorian America.* Knoxville: University of Tennessee Press, 2008.

Appleby, Joyce. *Thomas Jefferson.* New York: Henry Holt, 2003.

Appleton, Jay. *The Experience of Landscape.* London: Wiley, 1975.

Archer, B. J., and Anthony Vidler. *Follies: Architecture for the Late-Twentieth-Century Landscape.* New York: Rizzoli, 1983.

Archer, John. "The Beginnings of Association in British Architectural Esthetics." *Eighteenth-Century Studies* 16, no. 3 (Spring 1983): 241–264.

Armstead, Myra B. Young. *Freedom's Gardener: James F. Brown, Horticulture, and the Hudson Valley in Antebellum America.* New York: New York University Press, 2012.

Austen, Jane. *Northanger Abbey*. Toronto: Bantam Books, 1985.

Avery, Kevin. "Kauterskill Falls, 1871." In *Hudson River School Visions: The Landscapes of Sanford R. Gifford*, edited by Kevin J. Avery and Franklin Kelly, 201–203. New York: Metropolitan Museum of Art, 2003.

Avery, Kevin J. "Maya on the Hudson: Church's *Cayambe* and Cruger's 'Folly.'" *The Hudson River Valley Review* 31, no. 1 (Autumn 2014): 50–61.

Axelrod, Alan. *Charles Brockden Brown: An American Tale*. Austin: University of Texas Press, 1983.

Babbidge, Sandra A. *Bremo Fountain Temple: Monument to John Hartwell Cocke and the Temperance Movement*. Charlottesville: School of Architecture, University of Virginia, 1989.

Barnard, Henry. *Armsmear: The Home, The Arm, and the Armory of Samuel Colt: A Memorial*. New York: Alvord, Printer, 1866.

Bear, James A., Jr., and Lucia C. Stanton, eds. *Jefferson's Memorandum Books: Accounts, with Legal Records and Miscellany, 1767–1826*. 2 vols. Princeton, NJ: Princeton University Press, 1997.

Beardsley, John, Cathy Byrd, and Robin B. Williams. *Functional Follies: 20 Architectural Objects of Delight*. Savannah, GA: Savannah College of Art and Design, 1999.

Bedell, Rebecca. *The Anatomy of Nature: Geology and American Landscape Painting, 1825–1875*. Princeton, NJ: Princeton University Press, 2001.

Beiswanger, William, "The Temple in the Garden: Thomas Jefferson's Vision of the Monticello Landscape." *Eighteenth-century Life*, VIII, no. 2 (January 1983): 170–188.

Bender, Thomas. "The 'Rural' Cemetery Movement: Urban Travail and the Appeal of Nature." In *Material Life in America, 1600–1860*, edited by Robert Blair St. George, 505–518. Boston: Northeastern University Press, 1988.

Berke, Arnold, and Alexander Vertikoff. *Mary Colter, Architect of the Southwest*. New York: Princeton Architectural Press, 2002.

Betts, Edwin Morris, ed. *Thomas Jefferson's Garden Book 1766–1824*. Charlottesville, VA: Thomas Jefferson Memorial Foundation, 1999.

Betts, Richard J. "The Woodlands." *Winterthur Portfolio* 14, no. 3 (Autumn 1979): 213–234.

Biddle, Edward. "Joseph Bonaparte As Recorded in the Private Journal of Nicholas Biddle." *Pennsylvania Magazine of History and Biography* 55, no. 3 (1931): 208–224.

Biddle, James. "Nicholas Biddle's Andalusia, a Nineteenth-Century County Seat Today." In *Great Houses from the Pages of the Magazine Antiques*, edited by Constance M. Greiff, 286–290. New York: Weathervane Books, 1973.

Birdsall, Ralph. *The Story of Cooperstown*. Cooperstown, NY: Arthur H. Crist, 1917.

Boardman, Samuel L. "Rustic Adornments for Gardens and Waysides." *The Gardener's Monthly* II, no. 4 (April 1860): 112.

Bode, Rita. "'Within Small Compass': Hawthorne's Expansive Urban Garden." *The Brock Review* 10 (2008): 41–50.

Boime, Albert. *The Magisterial Gaze: Manifest Destiny and American Landscape Painting c. 1830–1865*. Washington, DC: Smithsonian Institution Press, 1991.

Boime, Albert. *The Unveiling of the National Icons: Plea for Patriotic Iconoclasm in a Nationalist Era*. Cambridge: Cambridge University Press, 1998.

Bowe, Patrick. "Pückler-Muskau's Estate and Its Influence on American Landscape Architecture." *Garden History* 23, no. 2 (Winter 1995): 192–200.

Bremner, G. Alex. "The 'Great Obelisk' and Other Schemes: The Origins and Limits of Nationalist Sentiment in the Making of the Albert Memorial." *Nineteenth-Century Contexts* 31, no. 3 (September 2009): 225–249.

Brooks, Chris, *The Gothic Revival.* London: Phaidon Press, 1999.

Brown, Charles Brockden. *Wieland or the Transformation, An American Tale.* Edited by Sydney J. Krause and S. W. Reid. Kent, OH: Kent State University Press, 1988.

Brown, Madison. "Thomas Jefferson and Things German: Preliminary Findings." *The Report: A Journal of German-American History* 37 (1987): 29–33.

Bryant, William Cullen. *Poems of William Cullen Bryant.* Philadelphia: Carey and Hart, 1847.

Bullington, Judy. "Cultivating Meaning: The Chinese Manner in Early American Gardens." In *Global Trade and Visual Arts in Federal New England,* edited by Patricia Johnston and Caroline Frank, 157–179. Durham: University of New Hampshire Press, 2014.

Burgess, Larry E. *Mohonk and the Smileys: A National Historic Landmark and the Family That Created It.* New ed. Catskill, NY: Black Dome Press, 2019.

Burke, Edmund. *A Philosophical Enquiry Into the Origin of Our Ideas of the Sublime and Beautiful.* Edited by Adam Phillips. Oxford: Oxford University Press, 1990.

Burns, Sarah. *Painting the Dark Side: Art and the Gothic Imagination in Nineteenth-Century America.* Berkeley: University of California Press, 2004.

Burstein, Andrew. *America's Jubilee: How in 1826 A Generation Remembered Fifty Years of Independence.* New York: Alfred A. Knopf, 2001.

Butler, James A. *Charles Willson Peale's 'Belfield': A History of a National Historic Landmark, 1684–1984.* Philadelphia: La Salle University Art Museum, 2009.

Campbell, Gordon. *The Hermit in the Garden: From Imperial Rome to Ornamental Gnome.* Oxford: Oxford University Press, 2013.

Carso, Kerry Dean. *American Gothic Art and Architecture in the Age of Romantic Literature.* Cardiff: University of Wales Press, 2014.

Cassidy-Geiger, Maureen. *The Philip Johnson Glass House: An Architect in the Garden.* New York: Skira Rizzoli, 2016.

Cavalier, Julian. *American Castles.* South Brunswick, NJ: A. S. Barnes, 1973.

"The Centennial Exposition." *Scientific American* 35, no. 3 (July 15, 1876): 33.

"The Centennial Exposition." *Scientific American* 35, no. 6 (August 5, 1876): 81.

A Century After: Picturesque Glimpses of Philadelphia and Pennsylvania. Philadelphia: Allen, Lane and Scott and J. W. Lauderbach, 1875.

Chesney, Sarah. "The Root of the Matter: Searching for William Hamilton's Greenhouse at the Woodlands Estate, Philadelphia, Pennsylvania." In *Historical Archaeology of the Delaware Valley, 1600–1850,* edited by Richard Veit and David Orr, 273–296. Knoxville: University of Tennessee Press, 2014.

Clapp, David. "Travel Diary, 1843, Accession # 63x51.4," unpublished manuscript, Winterthur Library, Winterthur, Delaware.

Clark, D. W. "Two Days at Niagara." *The Ladies' Repository* 16, no. 9 (September 1856): 556-562.

Clark, Edward. "Kingfisher Tower." *The Freeman's Journal,* September 7, 1876, 3.

Clubbe, John. *Cincinnati Observed: Architecture and History*. Columbus: Ohio State University Press, 1992.

Cole, Thomas, "Essay on American Scenery." In *American Art 1700–1960: Sources and Documents*, edited by John McCoubrey, 98–110. Englewood Cliffs, NJ: Prentice-Hall, 1965.

Collens, David. R., Nora R. Lawrence, and Sarah Diver, with Sarina Basta, Mark Dion, Piper Faust, Nora R. Lawrence, Victoria Lichtendorf, Denise Markonish, Armelle Pradalier, Lauren Ross, Dana Sherwood, John P. Stern, Dana Turkovic, *Mark Dion: Follies*, New Windsor, NY: Storm King Art Center, 2019.

Colter, Mary Elizabeth Jane. *Manual for Drivers and Guides Descriptive of the Indian Watchtower at Desert View and its Relation Architecturally, to the Prehistoric Ruins of the Southwest*. Grand Canyon, AZ: Grand Canyon Association, 2015.

Conlin, Jonathan, ed. *The Pleasure Garden: From Vauxhall to Coney Island*. Philadelphia: University of Pennsylvania Press, 2013.

Cooper, James Fenimore. *The Deerslayer; or, The First War-Path*. Albany: State University of New York Press, 1987.

Cooper, James Fenimore. *The Last of the Mohicans: A Narrative of 1757*. Albany: State University of New York Press, 1983.

Cooper, James Fenimore, *The Letters and Journals of James Fenimore Cooper*. Edited by James Franklin Beard, vol. 2. Cambridge, MA: The Belknap Press of Harvard University Press, 1960.

Cooper, James Fenimore. *The Red Rover: A Tale*. New York: Stringer & Townsend, 1856.

Cooperman, Emily T. "Belfield, Springland and Early American Picturesque: The Artist's Garden in the American Early Republic." *Studies in the History of Gardens and Designed Landscapes* 26, no. 2 (2006): 118–131.

Cox, Oliver. "A Mistaken Iconography? Eighteenth-Century Visitor Accounts of Stourhead." *Garden History* 40:1 (Summer 2012): 98–116.

Cromley, Elizabeth. "A Room with a View." In *Resorts of the Catskills*, 5–30. New York: St. Martin's Press, 1979.

Crowley, John E. *The Invention of Comfort: Sensibilities and Design in Early Modern Britain and Early America*. Baltimore: Johns Hopkins University Press, 2001.

Cutler, W. P., and J. P. Cutler. *Life, Journals, and Correspondence of Rev. Manasseh Cutler, LL.D*, vol. I. Cincinnati: Robert Clarke, 1888.

"D." "Garden Decorations." *The Gardener's Monthly* 111, no. 8 (August 1861): 235–236.

D'Alton, Martina. *The New York Obelisk or How Cleopatra's Needle Came to New York and What Happened When It Got Here*. New York: Metropolitan Museum of Art, 1993.

Dams, Bernd H., and Andrew Zega. *Pleasure Pavilions and Follies in the Gardens of the Ancien Régime*. Paris: Flammarion, 1995.

Davis, Alexander Jackson. *Rural Residences*. New York: Da Capo Press, 1980.

Dearborn, Nathaniel. *Dearborn's Guide Through Mount Auburn*. 11th ed. Boston: N. S. Dearborn, 1857.

De Caro, Frank, and Rosan Augusta Jordan, eds. *Louisiana Sojourns: Travelers' Tales and Literary Journeys*. Baton Rouge: Louisiana State University Press, 1998.

DeLorme, Eleanor P. *Garden Pavilions and the 18th Century French Court.* Woodbridge, Suffolk: Antique Collectors' Club, 1996.

DeLue, Rachael Ziady. *George Inness and the Science of Landscape.* Chicago: University of Chicago Press, 2004.

Derganc, Christopher. "Rockford Water Tower." Historic American Engineering Record (HAER DE-16). Washington, DC: National Park Service, 1976.

"Design for a Windmill Tower and Water Tank." *Scientific American* 59, no. 7 (August 18, 1888): 105.

Dodenhoff, Donna C. "The View from Montpelier: James Madison's Configuration of the Ideal Republican Landscape." *Journal of the New England Garden History Society* 9 (Fall 2001): 1–10.

Doell, M. Christine Klim. *Gardens of the Gilded Age: Nineteenth-Century Gardens and Homegrounds of New York State.* Syracuse: Syracuse University Press, 1986.

Domosh, Mona. *American Commodities in an Age of Empire.* New York: Routledge, 2006.

Downing, Andrew Jackson. *The Architecture of Country Houses.* New York: Da Capo Press, 1968.

Downing, Andrew Jackson. *A Treatise on the Theory and Practice of Landscape Gardening, Adapted to North America; with a View to the Improvement of Country Residences.* 4th ed. New York: George P. Putnam, 1850.

Drake, Samuel Adams. *Nooks and Corners of the New England Coast.* New York: Harper & Brothers, 1875.

Ducamp, Pierre Arizzoli-Clémentel Emmanuel. *Views and Plans of the Petit Trianon at Versailles.* Paris: A. de Gourcuff, 1998.

Eberlein, Harold D., and Cortlandt van Dyke Hubbard. "The American 'Vauxhall' of the Federal Era." *Pennsylvania Magazine of History and Biography* 68, no. 2 (April 1944): 150–174.

"Editor's Table." *The Ladies' Repository* 14, no. 1 (July 1874): 75–80.

Eldredge, Charles C., and Barbara B. Millhouse, eds. *American Originals: Selections from Reynolda House, Museum of American Art.* New York: Abbeville Press; American Federation of Arts, 1990.

Ellis, George E. *Address Delivered at the Consecration of the Woodlawn Cemetery in Chelsea and Malden on Wednesday, July 2, 1851.* Boston: Printed by John Wilson & Son, 1851.

Emmet, Alan. *So Fine a Prospect: Historic New England Gardens.* Hanover, NH: University Press of New England, 1996

Eno, Arthur L. Jr., and Thomas A. Smith, eds., *The Middlesex Canal: Prints by Louis Linscott.* Billerica, MA: Middlesex Canal Association, 1978.

Epperson, Terrence W. "Panoptic Plantations: The Garden Sights of Thomas Jefferson and George Mason." In *Lines that Divide: Historical Archaeologies of Race, Class, and Gender,* edited by James A. Delle, Stephen A. Mrozowski, and Robert Paynter, 58–77. Knoxville: University of Tennessee Press, 2000.

Favretti, Rudy J. "Thomas Jefferson's 'Ferme Ornée' at Monticello." *Proceedings of the American Antiquarian Society* 103, no. 1 (1993): 17–29.

Fazio, Michael W. "Benjamin Latrobe's Designs for a Lighthouse at the Mouth of the Mississippi River." *Journal of the Society of Architectural Historians* 48, no. 3 (September 1989): 232–247.

Ferber, Linda S. *William Trost Richards: American Landscape & Marine Painter 1833–1905*. New York: Brooklyn Museum, 1973.

"A Few Words on Rustic Arbours by an Amateur, New York." *The Horticulturist* IV, no. 7 (January 1850): 320–321.

Finkel, Kenneth, and Susan Oyama. *Philadelphia, Then and Now: 60 Matching Photographic Views from 1859–1952 and from 1986–1988*. New York: Dover Publications in cooperation with the Library Company of Philadelphia, 1988.

Finney, Barbara. "Washington Irving's Cockloft Summerhouse: Literature Transformed into Architecture." *Nineteenth Century* 26, no. 1 (Spring 2006): 23–28.

The First Jubilee of American Independence: and Tribute of Gratitude to the Illustrious Adams and Jefferson. Newark, NJ: M. Lyon, 1826.

Fish, Marilyn. "In Harmony with Arts & Crafts Ideals: The Mohonk Mountain House." *Style 1900* 14, no. 3 (Summer-Fall 2001): 40–46.

Flad, Harvey. "Matthew Vassar's Springside: '. . . the hand of Art, when guided by Taste." In *Prophet with Honor: The Career of Andrew Jackson Downing, 1815–1852*, edited by Elizabeth B. MacDougall and George B. Tatum, 219–257. Washington, DC: Dumbarton Oaks, 1989.

Flad, Harvey K. "The Parlor in the Wilderness: Domesticating an Iconic American Landscape." *The Geographical Review* 99, no. 3 (July 2009): 356–376.

Flad, Harvey. "Saving Springside: Preserving Andrew Jackson Downing's Last Landscape." *The Hudson River Valley Review* 34, no. 1 (Autumn 2017): 18–44.

Fleming, John, Hugh Honour, and Nikolaus Pevsner. *The Penguin Dictionary of Architecture and Landscape Architecture*. 5th ed. London: Penguin Books, 1998.

Foucault, Michel. *Discipline and Punish: The Birth of the Prison*. Translated by Alan Sheridan. New York: Vintage Books, 1995.

Fowler, Orson S. and Madeleine B. Stern. *The Octagon House: a Home for All*. New York: Dover Publications, Inc., 1973.

Franklin, Wayne. *James Fenimore Cooper: The Early Years*. New Haven, CT: Yale University Press, 2007.

Fry, Joel T. "America's 'Ancient Garden': The Bartram Botanic Garden, 1728–1850." In *Knowing Nature: Art and Science in Philadelphia, 1740–1840*, edited by Amy R. W. Meyers, 60–95. New Haven, CT: Yale University Press, 2011.

Fry, Joel T. "John Bartram and His Garden: Would John Bartram Recognize His Garden Today?" In *America's Curious Botanist: A Tercentennial Reappraisal of John Bartram, 1699–1777*, edited by Nancy E. Hoffmann and John C. Van Horne, 155–183. Philadelphia: The American Philosophical Society, 2004.

Fuller, Henry Weld. *The Woodlawn Cemetery in North Chelsea and Malden*. Boston: Higgins & Bradley, 1856.

Fuller, Margaret. *Summer on the Lakes in 1843*, facsimile with an Introduction by Madeleine B. Stern. Nieuwkoop: B. De Graaf, 1972.

Gallati, Barbara Dayer. "Early Morning at Cold Spring, 1850." In *American Paradise: The World of the Hudson River School*, 111. New York: Metropolitan Museum of Art, 1987.

Ghirardo, Diane. "Letters to the Editor." *The Art Bulletin* 59, no. 4 (December 1977): 660–661.

Giannetto, Raffaella Fabiani, ed. *Foreign Trends in American Gardens: A History of Exchange, Adaptation, and Reception.* Charlottesville: University of Virginia Press, 2016.

Giberti, Bruno. *Designing the Centennial: A History of the 1876 International Exhibition in Philadelphia.* Lexington: University Press of Kentucky, 2002.

Gibson, Jane Mork, and Robert Wolterstorff, "The Fairmount Waterworks." *Philadelphia Museum of Art Bulletin* 84, no. 360/361 (Summer 1988): 1–46.

Giguere, Joy M. *Characteristically American: Memorial Architecture, National Identity, and the Egyptian Revival.* Knoxville: University of Tennessee Press, 2014.

"Gilmore's Summer Concert Garden." *Frank Leslie's Illustrated Newspaper* XL, no. 1032 (June 10, 1875): 317, 322.

Gilpin, William. *Observations on Several Parts of the Counties of Cambridge, Norfolk, Suffolk, and Essex.* London: T. Cadell and W. Davies, 1809.

Giordano, Ralph G. *The Architectural Ideology of Thomas Jefferson.* Jefferson, NC: McFarland, 2012.

Greiff, Constance M. *Lost America: From the Mississippi to the Pacific.* Princeton, NJ: Pyne Press, 1971.

Gröning, Gert. "Parks and International Exchange." *SiteLINES: A Journal of Place* 1, no. 2 (Spring 2006): 11–13.

Grossman, John. "Ken Burns's Jeffersonian Pavilion." *Inc.*, 2002. https://www.inc .com/magazine/20020101/23795.html.

Grove, Allen. Introduction to *The Cavern of Death.* Chicago: Valancourt Books, 2005, 1–9.

Grove, Carol. "Aesthetics, Horticulture, and the Gardenesque: Victorian Sensibilities at Tower Grove Park." *Journal of the New England Garden History Society* 6 (Fall 1998): 32–41.

Grove, Carol. *Henry Shaw's Victorian Landscapes: The Missouri Botanical Garden and Tower Grove Park.* Amherst: University of Massachusetts Press in Association with Library of American Landscape History, 2005.

Guide through Mount Auburn, Boston: A Hand-book for Passengers over the Cambridge Railroad. Boston: Bricher and Russell, 1860.

Guide to Laurel Hill Cemetery Near Philadelphia. Philadelphia: C. Sherman, Printer, 1847.

Hafertepe, Kenneth. "An Inquiry into Thomas Jefferson's Ideas of Beauty." *Journal of the Society of Architectural Historians* 59, no. 2 (June 2000): 216–231.

Haley, Jacquetta M. ed. *Pleasure Grounds: Andrew Jackson Downing and Montgomery Place.* Tarrytown, NY: Sleepy Hollow Press, 1988.

Hall, Mark. "An Interview with Ken Burns." PBS, January 21, 1997. https://www.pbs .org/jefferson/making/KB_00.htm.

Halsey, Francis Whiting ed., *Authors of our Day in their Homes, Personal Descriptions and Interviews.* New York: James Pott, 1902.

Hamilton, Thomas. *Men and Manners in America*, vol. 1. Edinburgh: William Blackwood, 1833.

Harris, Jennifer. "At One with the Land: The Domestic Remove—Charles Brockden Brown's *Wieland* and Matters of National Belonging." *Canadian Review of American Studies/Revue canadienne d'études américaines* 33, no. 3 (2003): 189–210.

Harwood, William S. "Luxurious Hermits: Asceticism, Luxury and Retirement in the Eighteenth-Century Garden." *Studies in the History of Gardens and Designed Landscapes* 20, no. 4 (2000): 265–196.

Hawthorne, Nathaniel. *The House of the Seven Gables*. Columbus: Ohio State University Press, 1965.

Hawthorne, Nathaniel. *A Wonder Book and Tanglewood Tales*. Columbus: Ohio State University Press, 1972.

Hays, David. "Carmontelle's Design for the Jadin de Monceau: A Freemasonic Garden in Late-Eighteenth-Century France." *Eighteenth-Century Studies* 32, no. 4 (Summer 1999): 447–462.

Hays, David L. "'This is Not a *Jardin Anglais*': Carmontelle, The Jardin de Monceau, and Irregular Garden Design in Late-Eighteenth-Century France." In *Villas and Gardens in Early Modern Italy and France*, edited by Mirka Beneš and Dianne Harris, 294–326. Cambridge: Cambridge University Press, 2001.

Headley, Gwyn. *Architectural Follies in America*. New York: Wiley, 1996.

Heckscher, Morrison. "Creating Central Park." *Metropolitan Museum of Art Bulletin* 65, no. 3 (Winter 2008): 1–74.

Henderson, Susan. "Llewellyn Park, Suburban Idyll." *Journal of Garden History* 7, (July/September 1987): 221–243.

Hengen, Elizabeth Durfee. *Life Everlasting: The History, Art and People of Woodlawn Cemetery 1850–2000*. Everett, MA: Woodlawn Cemetery Corporation, 2001.

Henry, James. *Sketches of Moravian Life and Character*. Philadelphia: J. B. Lippincott, 1859.

Hermann, Richard. *Julien Dubuque, His Life and Adventures*. Dubuque, IA: Times-Journal, 1922.

Hibberd, Shirley. *Rustic Adornments for Homes of Taste*. London: Groombridge & Sons, 1870.

Hill, May Brawley. *Furnishing the Old-Fashioned Garden: Three Centuries of American Summerhouses, Dovecotes, Pergolas, Privies, Fences & Birdhouses*. New York: Harry N. Abrams, 1998.

"Hints and Designs for Rustic Buildings." *The Horticulturist* II, no. 8 (February 1848): 363–365.

Hobsbawm, Eric J., and Terence O. Ranger, eds. *The Invention of Tradition*. Cambridge: Cambridge University Press, 1983.

Holden, James Austin. "The Last of the Mohicans, Cooper's Historical Inventions, and His Cave." *Proceedings of the New York State Historical Association* 16 (1917): 212–255.

"The Home of the Late A. J. Downing." *The Horticulturist* 3, no. 1 (January 1, 1853): 20–27.

Homes of American Authors. New York: G. P. Putnam, 1853.

Horne, Field. "Kingfisher Tower—Folly or Art?" In *Bicentennial Essays of Cooperstown and the Town of Otsego*, edited by Wendell Tripp, 35–38. Cooperstown, NY: Town of Otsego Bicentennial Committee, 1976.

Hosley, William. *Colt: The Making of an American Legend*. Amherst: University of Massachusetts Press in Association with the Wadsworth Atheneum, Hartford, 1996.

Hotchkin, Rev. S. F. *The Bristol Pike*. Philadelphia: George W. Jacobs, 1893.

Hulbert, Archer Butler. *History of the Niagara River*. Harrison, NY: Harbor Hill Books, 1978.

Hunt, John Dixon, and Peter Willis, eds. *The Genius of the Place: The English Landscape Garden 1620–1820*. Cambridge, MA: MIT Press, 1988.

"Illustrations of Ornamental Iron Work." *The Horticulturist* 6, no. 3 (March 1856): 115.

"Impressions of Niagara Falls." *The Ladies' Repository* 8, no. 5 (May 1848): 130–131.

Irving, Washington. "Abbotsford." In *The Crayon Miscellany*, edited by Dahlia Kirby Terrel, 125–168. Boston: Twayne, 1979.

Irving, Washington. "The Catskill Mountains." In *The Home Book of the Picturesque or American Scenery, Art, and Literature*, 71–78. New York: G. P. Putnam, 1852.

Irving, Washington. *The Sketch Book of Geoffrey Crayon, Gent*. New York: Penguin Books, 1981.

Jacobs, James A. "Addendum to The Woodlands." HABS No. PA-1125, Historic American Building Survey (HABS). Washington, DC: National Park Service, US Department of the Interior.

Jacques, Daniel Harrison. *The Garden: A Pocket Manual of Practical Horticulture*. New York: Fowler and Wells, 1858.

Janes, Kirtland & Co. *Ornamental Ironwork*. Princeton, NJ: Pyne Press, 1971.

Janson, Anthony F. *Worthington Whittredge*. Cambridge: Cambridge University Press, 1989.

Jefferson, Thomas. "Jefferson's Hints to Americans Travelling in Europe, 19 June 1788." https://founders.archives.gov/documents/Jefferson/01-13-02-0173.

Jefferson, Thomas. Thomas Jefferson to Maria Cosway, 12 October 1786. https://founders.archives.gov/documents/Jefferson/01-10-02-0309.

Jefferson, Thomas. Thomas Jefferson to William Carmichael, 26 December 1786. https://founders.archives.gov/documents/Jefferson/01-10-02-0489.

Jefferson, Thomas. *The Papers of Thomas Jefferson*. Edited by Julian P. Boyd. Princeton, NJ: Princeton University Press, 1950.

Jellicoe, Sir Geoffrey, Susan Jellicoe, Patrick Goode, and Michael Lancaster, eds. *The Oxford Companion to Gardens*. Oxford: Oxford University Press, 1986.

Johnson, Philip, and Mark Wigley. *Deconstructivist Architecture*. Boston: Little, Brown, 1988.

Johnston, Phillip M. "Dialogues between Designer and Client: Furnishings Proposed by Leon Marcotte to Samuel Colt in the 1850s." *Winterthur Portfolio* 19, no. 4 (Winter 1984): 257–275.

Kafer, Peter, *Charles Brockden Brown's Revolution and the Birth of American Gothic*. Philadelphia: University of Pennsylvania Press, 2004.

Karson, Robin. *A Genius for Place: American Landscapes of the Country Place Era*. Amherst: University of Massachusetts Press in association with the Library of American Landscape History, 2007.

Katz, Robert Gray. "'Thomas Cole: Reading the Paintings from *The Last of the Mohicans*." In *James Fenimore Cooper, His Country and His Art (no. 18): Papers from the 1986 Conference at State University College of New York*. Edited by Steven Harthorn and Hugh MacDougall, 56–63. Oneonta: State University of New York College, 1987.

Kelly, Catherine E. *Republic of Taste: Art, Politics, and Everyday Life in Early America.* Philadelphia: University of Pennsylvania Press, 2016.

Kelly, James C., and William M. S. Rasmussen. *The Virginia Landscape: A Cultural History.* Charlottesville, VA: Howell Press, 2000.

Kean, Robert H. "History of the Graveyard at Monticello." In *Collected Papers to Commemorate Fifty Years of the Monticello Association of the Descendants of Thomas Jefferson,* edited by George Green Schelford., Vol. 1. Charlottesville, VA: Monticello Association, 1965.

Kemp, Edward. *How to Lay Out a Garden.* New York: Wiley & Halsted, 1858.

Kenney, Alice P., and Leslie J. Workman. "Ruins, Romance, and Reality: Medievalism in Anglo-American Imagination and Taste, 1750–1840." *Winterthur Portfolio* 10 (1975): 131–163.

Kern, G. M. *Practical Landscape Gardening.* Cincinnati: Moore, Wilstach, Keys, 1855.

Ketcham, Diana. *Le Désert de Retz: A Late Eighteenth-Century French Folly Garden. The Artful Landscape of Monsieur de Monville.* Cambridge, MA: MIT Press, 1994.

Keyser, Charles S. *Fairmount Park and the International Exhibition at Philadelphia.* Philadelphia: Claxton, Remsen & Haffelfinger, 1876.

Kimball, Marie. *Jefferson and the Scene of Europe 1784 to 1789.* New York: Coward-McCann, 1950.

Kirkbride, Thomas S. *Report of the Pennsylvania Hospital for the Insane for the Year 1844.* Philadelphia: James C. Haswell, 1845.

Kolodny, Annette. *In Search of First Contact: The Vikings of Vinland, the Peoples of the Dawnland, and the Anglo-American Anxiety of Discovery.* Durham, NC: Duke University Press, 2012.

Kostof, Spiro. *A History of Architecture: Settings and Rituals.* New York: Oxford University Press, 1985.

Kowsky, Francis R. *Country, Park, and City: The Architecture and Life of Calvert Vaux.* New York: Oxford University Press, 1998.

Krim, Arthur. "An Early Rustic Arch in Salem." *The Journal of the Society of Architectural Historians* 51, no. 3 (September 1992): 315–317.

Krist, Gary. "Not for Sale: Gazebo w/Writer Fully Attached." *New York Times,* February 15, 2002, G22.

Kutchen, Larry. "'The 'Vulgar Thread of the Canvas': Revolution and the Picturesque in Ann Eliza Bleecker, Crèvecoeur, and Charles Brockden Brown." *Early American Literature* 36, no. 3 (2001): 395–425.

Ladin, Lou Ann Meadows, Catherine Dean, and Dia Idleman. *The Jamestown Church, Jamestown, VA.* Richmond, VA: Dementi Milestone Publishing and APVA Preservation Virginia, 2007.

"Lake Mohonk Mountain-House." New Paltz, NY, 1876.

Lamb, Martha J., ed. *The Homes of America.* New York: D. Appleton, 1879.

Lancaster, Clay. *Architectural Follies in America; or Hammer, Sawtooth and Nail.* Rutland, VT: C. E. Tuttle, 1960.

Lancaster, Clay. "The Philadelphia Centennial Towers." *Journal of the Society of Architectural Historians* 19, no. 1 (March 1960): 11–15.

Lane, Maggie. *Jane Austen's England.* London: Hale, 1986.

Lanmon, Lorraine Welling. *Quarry Farm: A Study of the "Picturesque."* Elmira, NY: Elmira College Center for Mark Twain Studies at Quarry Farm, 1991.

"The Largest Hotel in the World." *Scientific American* 3, no. 26 (December 22, 1860): 403.

Larrabee, Professor. "Vacation Rambles." *The Ladies' Repository*, 12, no. 1 (January 1852): 16–19.

Lawson-Peebles, Robert. *Landscape and Written Expression in Revolutionary America.* Cambridge: Cambridge University Press, 1988.

"Lawson Tower." National Register of Historic Places Nomination Form. Washington, DC: National Park Service, Department of the Interior: September 28, 1976.

"The Leland Palace at New Rochelle," *Frank Leslie's Illustrated Newspaper*, October 21, XXI, no. 525 (1865): 71, 77.

Lewis, G. Albert. *The Old Houses and Stores with Memorabilia Relating to Them and My Father and Grandfather.* Philadelphia: G. Albert Lewis, 1900.

Lewis, Michael J. *The Gothic Revival.* London: Thames and Hudson, 2002.

Lidz, Maggie. "Latimeria Summer House." Winterthur Garden Blog, http://gardenblog.winterthur.org/2011/04/01/latimeria-summer-house/.

Linden, Blanche M. G. "Nineteenth-Century German-American Landscape Designers." *SiteLINES: A Journal of Place* 1, no. 2 (Spring 2006): 9–11.

Linden, Blanche M. G., *Silent City on a Hill: Picturesque Landscapes of Memory and Boston's Mount Auburn Cemetery.* Amherst: University of Massachusetts Press, in association with the Library of American Landscape History, 2007.

Long, Timothy Preston. "The Woodlands: A Matchless Place." MA thesis, University of Pennsylvania, 1991.

Longfellow, Henry Wadsworth. "The Skeleton in Armour." In *American Poetry: The Nineteenth Century, Volume One, Philip Freneau to Walt Whitman*, edited by John Hollander, 377–381. New York: Library of America, 1993.

Lossing, Benson J. *Dover Stone Church.* Amenia, NY: DeLacey & Walsh, 1876.

Lossing, Benson J. "Dover Stone Church." *Poughkeepsie Casket: A Semi-Monthly Literary Journal* 2, no. 18 (December 15, 1838): 137.

Lossing, Benson, J. *Mary and Martha: The Mother and the Wife of George Washington.* New York: Harper and Brothers, 1886.

Lossing, Benson J. *Pictorial Field-Book of the Revolution.* 2 vols. New York: Harper & Brothers, 1851–1852.

Lossing, Benson J. *Vassar College and Its Founder.* New York: C. A. Alvord, Printer, 1867.

Loth, Calder, and Julius Trousdale Sadler Jr. *The Only Proper Style: Gothic Architecture in America.* Boston: New York Graphic Society, 1975.

Loudon, John Claudius. *An Encyclopedia of Cottage, Farm and Villa Architecture and Furniture.* London: Longman, Orme, Rees, 1835.

Lowe, Hilary Iris. "Commemorating Writers' Workplaces: The Case of Mark Twain's Study and Quarry Farm." In *From Page to Place: American Literary Tourism and the Afterlives of Authors*, edited by Jennifer Harris and Hilary Iris Lowe, 125–145. Amherst: University of Massachusetts Press, 2017.

Lyon-Jenness, Cheryl. *For Shade and for Comfort: Democratizing Horticulture in the Nineteenth- Century Midwest.* West Lafayette, IN: Purdue University Press, 2004.

Lystra, Karen. *Searching the Heart: Women, Men, and Romantic Love in Nineteenth-Century America.* New York: Oxford University Press, 1989.

Mack, Angela D., and Stephen G. Hoffius, eds., *Landscape of Slavery: The Plantation in American Art*. Columbia, SC: University of South Carolina Press, 2008.

Magee's Centennial Guide of Philadelphia. 2nd ed. Philadelphia: R. Magee & Son, 1876.

Makarius, Michel. *Ruins*. Translated by David Radzinowicz. Paris: Éditions Flammarion, 2004.

Malins, Edward. *English Landscaping and Literature, 1660–1840*. London: Oxford University Press, 1966.

Manca, Joseph. "Cicero in America: Civic Duty and Private Happiness in Charles Willson Peale's Portrait of 'William Paca'." *American Art* 17, no. 1 (Spring 2003): 68–89.

Manthorne, Katherine, and John W. Coffey. *The Landscapes of Louis Rémy Mignot: A Southern Painter Abroad*. Washington, DC: Smithsonian Institution Press for the North Carolina Museum of Art, 1996.

Marchand, Yves, Romain Meffre, Robert Polidori, and Thomas J. Sugrue. *The Ruins of Detroit*. Göttingen, Germany: Steidl, 2014.

Marks, Arthur S. "Joining the Past to the Present: William Rush's Emblematic Statuary at Fairmount." *Proceedings of the American Philosophical Society* 157, no. 2 (June 2013): 176–228.

Martin, Peter, *The Pleasure Gardens of Virginia from Jamestown to Jefferson*. Princeton, NJ: Princeton University Press, 1991.

Martineau, Harriet. *Retrospect of Western Travel*, vol. 2. London: Saunders and Otley, 1838.

A Massachusetts Subscriber. "Trees and Pleasure Grounds in Pennsylvania." *The Horticulturist* 5, no. 6 (December 1850): 253–254.

Matrana, Marc R. *Lost Plantations of the South*. Jackson: University Press of Mississippi, 2009.

Matteson, Benjamin H., and Joan A. LaChance. *The Story of Sky Top and its Towers*. New Paltz, NY: Mohonk Mountain House, 1998.

Matteson, Benjamin, and Joan A. LaChance. *The Summerhouses of Mohonk*. New Paltz: Mohonk Mountain House, 1998.

Maynard, W. Barksdale. *Architecture in the United States 1800–1850*. New Haven, CT: Yale University Press, 2002.

Maynard, W. Barksdale. *Buildings of Delaware*. Charlottesville: University of Virginia Press, 2008.

Maynard, W. Barksdale. "Thoreau's House at Walden." *The Art Bulletin*, 81:2 (June 1999): 303–325.

McCabe, James D. *The Illustrated History of the Centennial Exhibition*. Philadelphia: National Publishing, 1876.

McCarthy, Jack. "Persistent History." July 4, 2012. Accessed August 11, 2016, http://hiddencityphila.org/2012/07/letter-from-the-northeast/.

McDowell, Peggy, and Richard E. Meyer. *The Revival Styles in American Memorial Art*. Bowling Green, OH: Bowling Green State University Popular Press, 1994.

McGreevy, Patrick. *Imagining Niagara: The Meaning and Making of Niagara Falls*. Amherst: University of Massachusetts, 1994.

McGuire, Diane Kostial, ed. *American Garden Design: An Anthology of Ideas that Shaped Our Landscape*. New York: Prentice Hall, 1994.

McInnis, Maurie D. *The Politics of Taste in Antebellum Charleston*. Chapel Hill: University of North Carolina Press, 2005.

McKinsey, Elizabeth. *Niagara Falls: Icon of the American Sublime*. Cambridge: Cambridge University Press, 1985.

McMurray, Sally. *Families and Farmhouses in Nineteenth-Century America: Vernacular Design and Social Change*. New York: Oxford University Press, 1988.

McNeur, Catherine. "Parks, People, and Property Values: The Changing Role of Green Spaces in Antebellum Manhattan." *Journal of Planning History* 16, no. 2 (May 2017): 98–111.

McNulty, Bard. *The Correspondence of Thomas Cole and Daniel Wadsworth: Letters in the Watkinson Library, Trinity College, Hartford, and in the New York State Library, Albany, New York*. Hartford: Connecticut Historical Society, 1983.

Meehan, Thomas. *The American Handbook of Ornamental Trees*. Philadelphia: Lippincott, Grambo, 1853.

M. E. W. S. "The Homes of America, VII—Armsmear." In *The Art Journal for 1876*, vol. 2. New York: D. Appleton, 1875, 321–325.

Miles, Carol, and John J. Galluzzo, *Beauty, Strength, Speed: Celebrating 100 Years of Thomas W. Lawson's Dreamwold*. Virginia Beach, VA: Donning, 2002.

Miller, Angela, *The Empire of the Eye: Landscape Representation and American Cultural Politics, 1825–1875*. Ithaca, NY: Cornell University Press, 1993.

Miller, Naomi. *Heavenly Caves: Reflections on the Garden Grotto*. New York: George Braziller, 1982.

Miller, Ralph N. "Thomas Cole and Alison's Essays on Taste." *New York History* 37, no. 3 (July 1956): 281–299.

Miller, Sara Cedar. *Central Park: An American Masterpiece*. New York: Harry N. Abrams in association with the Central Park Conservancy, 2003.

Mills, Robert. *The American Pharos, or Light-House Guide*. Washington, DC: Thompson & Homans, 1832.

Milroy, Elizabeth. *The Grid and the River: Philadelphia's Green Places, 1682–1876*. University Park: Pennsylvania State University Press, 2016.

Mitchell, Mary H. *Hollywood Cemetery: The History of a Southern Shrine*. Richmond: Virginia State Library, 1985.

Mitnick, Barbara J., ed. *George Washington: American Symbol*. New York: Hudson Hills, 1999.

Mohonk Lake Mountain House. New Paltz, NY: Mohonk Mountain House, 1888.

Morden, James C. *Historical Monuments and Observatories of Lundy's Lane and Queenston Heights*. Niagara Falls, Ontario, Canada: Lundy's Lane Historical Society, 1929.

Morden, John Harris. "Engla-Land and the Abiding Memorials of its Antiquity." *Potter's American Monthly* V, no. 48 (December 1875): 937–944.

Moser, Monique. "Paradox in the Garden: A Brief Account of *Fabriques*." In *The Architecture of Western Gardens: A Design History from the Renaissance to the Present Day*, edited by Monique Moser and Georges Teyssot, 263–280. Cambridge, MA: MIT Press, 1990.

Mowl, Timothy. *Gentlemen and Players: Gardeners of the English Landscape*. Stroud: Sutton Publishing, 2004.

Murat, Princess Caroline. *My Memoirs*. London: Eveleigh Nash, 1910.

Murch, G. "Ornaments for Pleasure Grounds." *Illustrated Annual Register of Rural Affairs* VIII (1878): 222–224.

Myers, Kenneth. *The Catskills: Painters, Writers, and Tourists in the Mountains 1820–1895*. Yonkers, NY: Hudson River Museum of Westchester, 1987.

Nebiker, Walter, Robert Owen Jones, and Charlene K. Roice. *Historic and Architectural Resources of Narragansett, Rhode Island*. Providence: Rhode Island Historical Preservation Commission, 1991.

Nevius, Blake. *Cooper's Landscapes: An Essay on the Picturesque Vision*. Berkeley: University of California Press, 1976.

Newbury, Diane. "'But That Garden Now Became His Hobby-Horse': Charles Willson Peale and His Garden at Belfield." *Journal of the New England Garden History Society*, 4 (Spring 1996): 38–47.

Newell, Robert and Sons. *Old Landmarks and Relics of Philadelphia*. 6 vols. Philadelphia: Newell, 1876.

"Niagara." *Harper's New Monthly Magazine* 7, no. 39 (August 1853): 289–305.

Nichols, Frederick Doveton. *Thomas Jefferson's Architectural Drawings, Compiled and with a Commentary and a Check List*. Boston: Massachusetts Historical Society, 1961.

Nichols, Frederick Doveton, and Ralph E. Griswold. *Thomas Jefferson: Landscape Architect*. Charlottesville: University Press of Virginia, 1978.

Niedermeier, Michael. "'Strolling Under Palm Trees': Gardens—Love—Sexuality." *Journal of Garden History* 17, no. 3 (1997): 186–207.

The North American Tourist. New York: A. T. Goodrich, 1839.

Novak, Barbara. *Nature and Culture: American Landscape and Painting 1825–1875*. New York: Oxford University Press, 1995.

O'Boyle, Shaun. *Modern Ruins: Portraits of Place in the Mid-Atlantic Region*. University Park: Pennsylvania State University Press, 2010.

Olmert, Michael. *Kitchens, Smokehouses, and Privies: Outbuildings and the Architecture of Daily Life in the Eighteenth-Century Mid-Atlantic*. Ithaca, NY: Cornell University Press, 2009.

Olmsted, Frederick Law. *The Papers of Frederick Law Olmsted: Creating Central Park, 1857–1861*. Edited by Charles E. Beveridge and David Schuyler, vol. 3. Baltimore: Johns Hopkins University Press, 1983.

Olson, Roberta J. M. *Drawn by New York: Six Centuries of Watercolors and Drawings at the New-York Historical Society*. New York: New-York Historical Society, 2008.

O'Malley, Therese. "Charles Willson Peale's Belfield: Its Place in American Garden History." In *New Perspectives on Charles Willson Peale: A 250th Anniversary Celebration*, edited by Lillian B. Miller and David C. Ward, 267–282. Pittsburgh: University of Pittsburgh Press, 1991.

O'Malley, Therese. *Keywords in American Landscape Design*. New Haven, CT: National Gallery of Art in association with Yale University Press, 2010.

O'Malley, Therese, and Kathryn R. Barush. "'In the Park': Lewis Miller's Chronicle of American Landscape at mid-Century." *Nineteenth-Century Art Worldwide: A Journal of Nineteenth-Century Visual Culture* 12, no. 1 (Spring 2013). http://www.19thc-artworldwide.org/spring13/in-the-park-lewis-miller-chronicle-of-american-lanscape-midcentury.

"The Pagoda." *The Casket and Philadelphia Monthly Magazine* 11 (November 1828): 509.

Parker, G. A. "Tower at Hubbard Park, Meriden, Conn." *Park and Cemetery and Landscape Gardening* X (March 1900–February 1901): 223.

Parson, Horatio A. *Steele's Book of Niagara Falls*. Buffalo: Oliver G. Steele, 1840.

Partington, Frederick E. *The Story of Mohonk*. Fulton, NY: Morrill Press, 1911.

Partington, Frederick Eugene, Albert Keith Smiley, and Daniel Smiley. *The Story of Mohonk*. Fulton, NY: Morrill, 1932.

Peale, Charles Willson. *The Selected Papers of Charles Willson Peale and His Family*. Edited by Lillian B. Miller, vol. 1. New Haven, CT: Yale University Press, 1983.

Peale, Charles Willson. *The Selected Papers of Charles Willson Peale and His Family*. Edited by Lillian B. Miller, vol. 3. New Haven, CT: Yale University Press, 1991.

Peale, Charles Willson. *The Selected Papers of Charles Willson Peale and His Family*. Edited by Lillian B. Miller and Sidney Hart, vol. 5. New Haven, CT: Yale University Press, 2000.

Peden, William. "The Jefferson Monument at the University of Missouri." *Missouri Historical Review* 72, no. 1 (October 1977): 67–77.

Peterson, Merrill D., ed. *Visitors to Monticello*. Charlottesville: University Press of Virginia, 2006.

"Philadelphia Water Works." *Gleason's Pictorial Drawing-Room Companion* IV, no. 13 (March 26, 1853): 201.

"Plan for a Cheap Summer House." *New England Farmer* VIII, no. 4 (April 1856): 169–170.

Poesch, Jessie J. "Mr. Peale's 'Farm Persevere': Some Documentary Views." *Proceedings of the American Philosophical Society* 100, no. 6 (December 17, 1956): 545-556.

"Portland." *Gleason's Pictorial Drawing-Room Companion* V, no. 13 (September 24, 1853): 200.

Powell, Earl A., III. "Thomas Cole and the American Landscape Tradition: Associationism." *Arts Magazine* 52, no. 4 (April 1978): 113–117.

Practical Common Sense Guide Book through the World's Industrial and Cotton Centennial Exposition at New Orleans. Harrisburg, PA: Lane S. Hart Printer and Binder, 1885.

Prideaux, Gwynn Cochran. *Summerhouses in Virginia*. Richmond: Valentine Museum, 1976.

Pulsifer, David. *Guide to Boston and Vicinity*. Boston: A. Williams, 1868.

Quigley, Kathleen. "Inside Architecture's New Classicism Boom." *Architectural Digest*, August 7, 2018, https://www.architecturaldigest.com/story/new-classical-architecture.

Ragon, Michel. *The Space of Death: A Study in Funerary Architecture, Decoration and Urbanism*. Translated by Alan Sheridan. Charlottesville: University of Virginia Press, 1983.

Randall, Monica. *Phantoms of the Hudson Valley: The Glorious Estates of a Lost Era*. Woodstock, NY: Overlook, 1995.

Rebok, Sandra. "Thomas Jefferson and Germany: His Travel Experience, Scientific and Philosophical Influences." *Yearbook of German-American Studies* 48 (spring 2013): 1–23.

Register of the Confederate Dead Interred in Hollywood Cemetery, Richmond, VA. Richmond: Gary, Clemmitt & Jones, Printers, 1869.

Reinberger, Mark E., and Elizabeth McLean. *The Philadelphia Country House: Architecture and Landscape in Colonial America.* Baltimore: Johns Hopkins University Press, 2015.

Rhoads, William B. *Ulster County, New York: The Architectural History and Guide.* Delmar, NY: Black Dome, 2011.

Rigal, Laura. "'Raising the Roof': Authors, Spectators and Artisans in the Grand Federal Procession of 1788." *Theatre Journal* 48, no. 3 (1996): 253–277.

Rinaldi, Thomas E., and Robert J. Yasinsac. *Hudson Valley Ruins: Forgotten Landmarks of an American Landscape.* Hanover, NH: University Press of New England, 2006.

Ringe, Donald A. "*The Last of the Mohicans* as a Gothic Novel." In *James Fenimore Cooper, His Country and His Art (no. 6): Papers from the 1986 Conference at State University College of New York.* Edited by George A. Test, 41–53. Oneonta: State University of New York College, 1987.

Ringe, Donald A. "Mode and Meaning in *The Last of the Mohicans.*" In *James Fenimore Cooper: New Historical and Literary Context.* Edited by W. M. Verhoeven, 109–125. Amsterdam: Rodophi, 1993.

Ripley, Eliza. *Social Life in Old New Orleans: Being Recollections of my Girlhood.* New York: D. Appleton, 1912.

Risk, Kevin. *Valcour Aime Plantation Garden: 'Le Petit Versailles,' Cultural Landscape Report.* Baton Rouge, LA: Louisiana State Dept. of Culture, Recreation, and Tourism, Office of Cultural Development, Division of Historic Preservation, 2002.

Roberts, Jennifer L. "Landscapes of Indifference: Robert Smithson and John Lloyd Stephens in Yucatán." *The Art Bulletin* 82, no. 3 (September 2000): 554–567.

Robertson, Bruce. "The Picturesque Traveler in America." In *Views and Visions: American Landscape before 1830,* edited by Edward J. Nygren with Bruce Robertson, 189–211. Washington, DC: The Corcoran Gallery of Art, 1986.

Robinson, John Martin. *Temples of Delight: Stowe Landscape Garden.* London: National Trust, 1990.

Robinson, Joyce Henri. "An American Cabinet of Curiosities: Thomas Jefferson's Indian Hall at Monticello." *Winterthur Portfolio* 30, no. 1 (spring 1995): 41–58.

Rogers, Elizabeth Barlow. *Landscape Design: A Cultural and Architectural History.* New York: Harry N. Abrams, 2001.

Rogers, Elizabeth Barlow, Elizabeth S. Eustis, and John Bidwell. *Romantic Gardens: Nature, Art, and Landscape Design.* New York: Morgan Library & Museum, 2010.

Rosenheim, Jeff L. *Walker Evans and the Picture Postcard.* Göttingen, Germany: Steidl, 2009.

Rosenzweig, Roy, and Elizabeth Blackmar. *The Park and the People: A History of Central Park.* Ithaca, NY: Cornell University Press, 1992.

Rossiter, Thomas Prichard. *Description of the Picture of the Home of Washington After the War Painted by T. P. Rossiter and L. R. Mignot.* New York: D. Appleton, 1859.

Roylance, Patricia Jane. "Northmen and Native Americans: The Politics of Landscape in the Age of Longfellow." *The New England Quarterly* 80, no. 3 (September 2007): 435–458.

"Rustic Adornments." *The Gardener's Monthly* II, no. 11 (November 1860): 338.

Rydell, Robert W. *All the World's a Fair: Visions of Empire at American International Expositions, 1876–1916*. Chicago: University of Chicago Press, 1984.

Sanford, Charles B. *Thomas Jefferson and His Library: A Study of His Literary Interests and the Religious Attitudes Revealed by Relevant Titles in his Library*. Hamden, CT: Archon Books, 1977.

Sarudy, Barbara Wells. *Gardens and Gardening in the Chesapeake 1700–1805*. Baltimore: Johns Hopkins University Press, 1998.

Saltar, Fanny. "Fanny Saltar's Reminiscences of Colonial Days in Philadelphia, Contributed by Mrs. E. B. Hoskins." *The Pennsylvania Magazine of History and Biography* XL (1916): 187–198.

Scheinfeld, Marisa, Stefan Kanfer, and Jenna Weissman Joselit, *The Borscht Belt: Revisiting the Remains of America's Jewish Vacationland*. Ithaca, NY: Cornell University Press, 2016.

Scheper, George. "The Reformist Vision of Frederick Law Olmsted and the Poetics of Park Design." *The New England Quarterly* 62, no. 3 (September 1989): 369–402.

Schloss, Dietmar. "The Nation as Spectacle: The Grand Federal Procession in Philadelphia, 1788." In *Celebrating Ethnicity and Nation: American Festive Culture from the Revolution to the Early 20th Century* edited by Jürgen Heidekin, Geneviève Fabre, and Kai Dreisbach, 44–62. New York: Berghahn Books, 2001.

Schuyler, David, *Apostle of Taste: Andrew Jackson Downing, 1815–1852*. Baltimore: Johns Hopkins University Press, 1996.

Schuyler, David. *The New Urban Landscape: The Redefinition of City Form in Nineteenth-Century America*. Baltimore: Johns Hopkins University Press, 1986.

Schuyler, David. *Sanctified Landscape: Writers, Artists, and the Hudson River Valley, 1820–1909*. Ithaca: Cornell University Press, 2012.

Scott, Frank J. *The Art of Beautifying Suburban Home Grounds of Small Extent*. New York: D. Appleton, 1870.

Sears, John F. *Sacred Places: American Tourist Attractions in the Nineteenth Century*. New York: Oxford University Press, 1989.

Second Annual Report of the Commissioners of Fairmount Park. Philadelphia: King & Baird, Printers, 1870.

"Second Illustrated Series of Views of Niagara Falls." *Gleason's Pictorial and Drawing-Room Companion* III, no. 5 (July 31, 1852): 68–69.

Sedore, Timothy S. *An Illustrated Guide to Virginia's Confederate Monuments*. Carbondale: Southern Illinois University Press, 2011.

Sellers, Charles Coleman. *Mr. Peale's Museum: Charles Willson Peale and the First Popular Museum of Natural Science and Art*. New York: W. W. Norton, 1980.

Sellers, Charles Coleman. "William Rush at Fairmount." In *Sculpture of a City: Philadelphia's Treasures in Bronze and Stone*, edited by Nicholas B. Wainwright, 8–15. New York: Walker Publishing, 1974.

Shackelford, George Green. *Thomas Jefferson's Travels in Europe, 1784–1789*. Baltimore: Johns Hopkins University Press, 1995.

Shaw, S. M., ed. *A Centennial Offering, Being a Brief History of Cooperstown*. Cooperstown, NY: Freeman's Journal Office, 1886.

Sheldon, John P. "A Description of Philadelphia in 1825." *Pennsylvania Magazine of History and Biography* LX, no. 1 (January 1936): 74–76.

Sienkewicz, Julia. "Citizenship by Design: Art and Identity in the Early Republic." PhD dissertation, University of Illinois at Urbana-Champaign, 2009.

Sivils, Matthew. "American Gothic and the Environment, 1800–Present." In *The Gothic World*, edited by Glennis Byron and Dale Townshend, 121–131. London: Routledge, 2014.

Sloan, Samuel. *American Houses*. Philadelphia: Henry Carey Baird, 1861.

Sloan, Samuel. *City Homes, Country Houses, and Church Architecture, or, The American Builders' Journal*. Philadelphia: Claxton, Remsen & Haffelfinger, 1871.

Sloan, Samuel. "Design XXVI." *The Model Architect* 1, no. 12 (June 1852): 101–102.

"A Small and Cheap Summer-House." *New England Farmer* VIII, no. 3 (March 1856): 132.

Smith, David. "The Gothic Temple: Epistemology and Revolution in Charles Brockden Brown's *Wieland*." *Gothic Studies* 18, no. 2 (November 2016): 1–17.

Smith, John M. "Rustic Adornments." *The Gardener's Monthly* II, no. 5 (May 1860): 131–133.

Smith, John M. "Thatching and Rustic Adornments." *The Gardener's Monthly* I, no. 9 (September 1, 1859): 131–132.

Smith, Philip H. *General History of Dutchess County, From 1609 to 1876, Inclusive*. Pawling, NY: published by the author, 1877.

Smith-Rosenberg, Carroll. *This Violent Empire: The Birth of an American National Identity*. Chapel Hill: University of North Carolina Press for the Omohundro Institute of Early American History and Culture, 2010.

Soltis, Carl Eaton. *The Art of the Peales in the Philadelphia Museum of Art: Adaptations and Innovations*. Philadelphia: Philadelphia Museum of Art in Association with Yale University Press, 2017.

Somerville. Boston: Edison Electric Illuminating Co, 1909.

Spasskey, Natalie, et. al. *American Paintings in the Metropolitan Museum of Art*. Vol. II, edited by Kathleen Luhrs. New York: Metropolitan Museum of Art, 1985.

Spinden, Herbert J. "The Stephens Sculptures from Yucatán." *Natural History: The Journal of the American Museum of Natural History* 20 (1920): 378–389.

Staiti, Paul. *Of Arms and Artists: The American Revolution through Painters' Eyes*. New York: Bloomsbury, 2016.

Stevick, Philip. *Imagining Philadelphia: Travelers' Views of the City from 1800 to the Present*. Philadelphia: University of Pennsylvania Press, 1996.

Stilgoe, John R. *Common Landscape of America, 1580–1845*. New Haven, CT: Yale University Press, 1982.

Stroud, Dorothy. *Capability Brown*. London: Faber and Faber, 1975.

Stroud, Patricia Tyson. *The Emperor of Nature: Charles-Lucien Bonaparte and His World*. Philadelphia: University of Pennsylvania Press, 2000.

Stroud, Patricia Tyson. *The Man Who Had Been King: The American Exile of Napoleon's Brother Joseph*. Philadelphia: University of Pennsylvania Press, 2005.

Stubbs, Naomi J. *Cultivating National Identity through Performance: American Pleasure Gardens and Entertainment*. New York: Palgrave Macmillan, 2013.

"Summer-House." *Gleason's Pictorial Drawing-Room Companion* V, no. 2 (July 9, 1853): 24–25.

Sweeting, Adam. *Reading Houses and Building Books: Andrew Jackson Downing and the Architecture of Popular Antebellum Literature, 1835–1855*. Hanover, NH: University Press of New England, 1996.

Symes, Michael. "The Concept of the 'Fabrique.'" *Garden History* 42, no. 1 (Summer 2014): 120–127.

Tamir, Yael. "The Engima of Nationalism." *World Politics* 47, no. 3 (April 1995): 418–440.

Thacker, Christopher. *The History of Gardens*. Berkeley: University of California Press, 1979.

Thayer, Russell. *The Public Parks and Gardens of Europe: A Report to the Commissioners of Fairmount Park*. Philadelphia: Gillis & Nagle, Printers, 1880.

Thomas Jefferson Foundation, Inc. "The Site of the Vegetable Garden." https://www.monticello.org/site/house-and-gardens/site-vegetable-garden.

Thornton, Tamara Plakins. *Cultivating Gentlemen: The Meaning of Country Life Among the Boston Elite, 1785–1860*. New Haven, CT: Yale University Press, 1989.

Todd, Emily B. "Walter Scott and the Nineteenth-Century American Literary Marketplace: Antebellum Richmond Readers and the Collected Editions of the Waverley Novels." *The Papers of the Bibliographical Society of America* 94, no. 4 (1999): 495–513.

Tocqueville, Alexis de. *Democracy in America*, translated and edited by Harvey C. Mansfield and Delba Winthrop. Chicago: University of Chicago Press, 2000.

Toledano, Roulhac B. "Louisiana's Golden Age: Valcour Aime in St. James Parish." *Louisiana History: The Journal of the Louisiana Historical Association* 10, no. 3 (Summer 1969): 211–224.

Toll, Barbara. *Follies: Fantasy in the Landscape: May 20 through July 22, 2001*. Southampton, N.Y.: Parrish Art Museum, 2001.

Toole, Robert M. *Landscape Gardens on the Hudson, A History: The Romantic Age, the Great Estates, & the Birth of American Landscape Architecture*. Hensonville, NY: Black Dome Press, 2010.

Toole, Robert M. "Springside: A. J. Downing's Only Extant Garden." *Journal of Garden History* 9, no. 1 (1989): 20–39.

Tompkins, Jane. *Sensational Designs: The Cultural Work of American Fiction 1790–1860*. Oxford: Oxford University Press, 1985.

Townshend, Dale. *Gothic Antiquity: History, Romance, and the Architectural Imagination*. Oxford: Oxford University Press, 2019.

Trollope, Anthony. *North America*. vol. 1. Philadelphia: J. B. Lippincott, 1863.

Tuckerman, Henry T. *Book of the Artists*. New York: G. P. Putnam, 1867.

Tutter, Adele. "The Path of Phocion: Disgrace and Disavowal at the Philip Johnson Glass House." *American Imago* 68, no. 3 (Fall 2011): 449–488.

"Two Days at Niagara." *Southern Literary Messenger* 11, no. 12 (December 1845): 728–733.

Tyrell, C. Gordon. "The History and Development of the Winterthur Gardens." *Winterthur Portfolio* 1 (1964): 122–138.

Tyrrell, Ian R. "Drink and Temperance in the Antebellum South: An Overview and Interpretation." *The Journal of Southern History* 48, no. 4 (November 1982): 485–510.

"An Ulster County Nook: Life Among the Rocks at Lake Mohonk." *New York Times*, August 14, 1882, 5.

Upton, Dell. "Pattern Books and Professionalism: Aspects of the Transformation of Domestic Architecture in America, 1800–1860." *Winterthur Portfolio* 10, no. 2–3 (1984): 107–150.

Upton, Dell. "White and Black Landscapes in Eighteenth-Century Virginia." In *Material Life in America, 1600–1860*, edited by Robert Blair St. George, 357–369. Boston: Northeastern University Press, 1988.

Vernon, Noël Dorsey. "Adolph Strauch: Cincinnati and the Legacy of Spring Grove Cemetery." In *Midwestern Landscape Architecture*, edited by William H. Tishler, 5–24. Urbana: University of Illinois Press in association with the Library of American Landscape History, 2000.

Vernon, Noël Dorsey. "Strauch, Adolph." In *Pioneers of American Landscape Design*, edited by Charles A. Birnbaum, 384–388. New York: McGraw-Hill, 2000.

Viator. "Philadelphia Surroundings." *The Pennsylvania Farm Journal* 12, no. 9 (December 1852): 269–70.

"View from the Summit of Red Hill." *Ballou's Pictorial Drawing-Room Companion* VIII, no. 20 (May 19, 1855): 312.

"Visit of Manasseh Cutler to William Hamilton at the Woodlands." *Pennsylvania Magazine of History and Biography* 8 (1884): 109–111.

Wainwright, Nicholas B. "Andalusia: Countryseat of the Craig Family and Nicholas Biddle and His Descendants." *The Pennsylvania Magazine of History and Biography* 101, no. 1 (1977): 3–69.

Waldhorn, Judith Lynch, ed. *American Victoriana Floor Plans and Renderings from the Gilded Age*. San Francisco: Chronicle Books, 1979.

Wall, David. "Andrew Jackson Downing and the Tyranny of Taste." *American Nineteenth Century History* 8, no. 2 (June 2007): 187–203.

Wallach, Alan, "Making a Picture of the View from Mount Holyoke." In *American Iconology: New Approaches to Nineteenth-Century Art and Literature*, edited by David C. Miller, 80–91. New Haven, CT: Yale University Press, 1993.

Wallach, Alan, "Some Further Thoughts on the Panoramic Mode in Hudson River School Landscape Painting." In *Within the Landscape: Essays on Nineteenth-Century American Art and Culture*, edited by Phillip Earenfight and Nancy Siegel, 99–128. Carlisle, PA: The Trout Gallery, Dickinson College, 2005.

Wallach, Alan. "Wadsworth's Tower: An Episode in the History of American Landscape Vision." *American Art* 10, no. 3 (Fall 1996): 8–27.

Ward, David C. "Charles Willson Peale's Farm Belfield: Enlightened Agriculture in the Early Republic." In *New Perspectives on Charles Willson Peale: A 250th Anniversary Celebration*, edited by Lillian B. Miller and David C. Ward, 282–301. Pittsburgh: University of Pittsburgh Press, 1991.

Watkin, David. *The English Vision: The Picturesque in Architecture, Landscape and Garden Design*. New York: Harper & Row, 1982.

Watkins, N. J., ed. *The Pine and the Palm Greeting*. Baltimore: J. D. Ehlers & Co.'s Engraving and Printing House, 1873.

Watson, Peter A. "Picturesque Transformations: A.J. Davis in the Hudson Valley and Beyond." MA thesis, Columbia University, 2012.

Watson, Ross. "Thomas Jefferson's Visit to England, 1786." *History Today* 27, no. 1 (January 1977): 3–13.

Weber, Bruce. *Every Kind of a Painter: The Art of Thomas Prichard Rossiter (1818–1871).* Garrison, NY: Boscobel House and Gardens, 2015.

Weber, Nicholas Fox. *The Clarks of Cooperstown, Their Singer Sewing Machine Fortune, Their Great and Influential Art Collections, Their Forty-Year Feud.* New York: Alfred A. Knopf, 2007.

Webster, Constance A. "Bonaparte's Park: A French Picturesque Garden in America." *Journal of Garden History* 6, no. 4 (1986): 330 347.

Webster, Constance A. "Recreating an American Landscape: Artistic and Literary Images of Joseph Bonaparte's Park at Point Breeze, New Jersey." *Journal of the New England Garden History Society* 4 (Spring 1996): 13–21.

Weinstock, Jeffrey Andrew. *Charles Brockden Brown.* Cardiff: University of Wales Press, 2011.

Westcott, Thomas. *Centennial Portfolio: A Souvenir of the International Exhibition at Philadelphia.* Philadelphia: Thomas Hunter, publisher, 1876.

Westmacott, Richard. *African-American Gardens and Yards in the Rural South.* Knoxville: University of Tennessee Press, 1992.

Whately, Thomas. *Observations on Modern Gardening.* 4th ed. London: T. Payne, 1770.

Whiting, K. Brooke. *Gen. J. H. Cocke's Vanishing Legacy: The Gardens and Landscape of Bremo.* Richmond: The Garden Club of Virginia, 2000.

Whittington, Karl. "Casper David Friedrich's Medieval Burials." *Nineteenth Century Art Worldwide* 11, no. 1 (2012).

Wibenson, Dora. *The Picturesque Garden in France.* Princeton, NJ: Princeton University Press, 1978.

Wildman, Edwin. "Mark Twain's Pets." *St. Nicholas, An Illustrated Magazine for Young Folks* XXVI, no. 3 (January 1899): 185–188.

Williamson, Tom. *Polite Landscapes: Gardens and Society in Eighteenth-Century England.* Baltimore: Johns Hopkins University Press, 1995.

Wilson, Richard Guy. "Idealism and the Origin of the First American Suburb: Llewellyn Park, New Jersey." *The American Art Journal* XI, no. 4 (October 1979): 79–90.

Wilson, Richard Guy. "Jefferson and England." In *Thomas Jefferson Architect: Palladian Models, Democratic Principles, and the Conflict of Ideas,* edited by Lloyd DeWitt and Corey Piper, 42–50. Norfolk, VA: Chrysler Museum of Art, 2019.

Wilson, Richard Guy. "Oscar Wilde, Colonialists, and Vikings: Newport and the Aesthetic Movement." *Nineteenth Century* 19, no. 1 (Spring 1999): 4–11.

Wilson, Richard Guy, et al. "Hollywood Cemetery" [Richmond, Virginia]. In SAH Archipedia, edited by Gabrielle Esperdy and Karen Kingsley. Charlottesville: University of Virginia Press, 2012. http://sah-archipedia.org/buildings/VA-01 -RI251.

"A Windmill Tower and Water Tank at Narragansett Pier, R. I." *Scientific American, Architects and Builders Edition* 3, no. 3 (March 1887): 45–47.

Woodbridge, Kenneth. *Landscape and Antiquity: Aspects of English Culture at Stourhead 1718–1838.* Oxford: Clarendon, 1970.

Woodward, E. M. *Bonaparte's Park and The Murats.* Trenton, NJ: MacCrellish & Quigley, 1879.

Woodward, George E., and F. W. Woodward. *Woodward's Country Homes*. New York: George E. and F. W. Woodward, 1865.

Wulf, Andrea. *Founding Gardeners: The Revolutionary Generation, Nature, and the Shaping of the American Nation*. New York: Alfred A. Knopf, 2011.

Wunsch, Aaron V. "Woodlands Cemetery." Historic American Landscape Survey (HALS) No. PA-5. Washington, DC: National Park Service, US Department of the Interior, 2003–2004.

Yablon, Nick. *Untimely Ruins: An Archaeology of American Urban Modernity, 1819–1919*. Chicago: University of Chicago Press, 2009.

Zukowsky, John. "Monumental American Obelisks: Centennial Vistas." *The Art Bulletin* 58, no. 4 (December 1976): 571–584.

INDEX

Italicized page numbers indicate illustrations.